The Great Loop
EXPERIENCE

From Concept to Completion

A Practical Guide for Planning, Preparing, and Executing Your Great Loop Adventure

By Captain George and Patricia Hospodar

THE GREAT LOOP EXPERIENCE – FROM CONCEPT TO COMPLETION: A PRACTICAL GUIDE FOR PLANNING, PREPARING, AND EXECUTING YOUR GREAT LOOP ADVENTURE

Copyright © 2015 Atlantic Publishing Group, Inc.
1405 SW 6th Avenue • Ocala, Florida 34471 • Phone: 800-814-1132 • Fax: 352-622-1875
Website: www.atlantic-pub.com • Email: sales@atlantic-pub.com
SAN Number: 268-1250

Library of Congress Cataloging-in-Publication Data

Hospodar, George, 1946-

The Great Loop experience--from concept to completion : a practical guide for planning, preparing, and executing your Great Loop adventure / by Captain George Hospodar and Patricia Hospodar.

   pages cm

Includes bibliographical references and index.

ISBN 978-1-60138-940-4 (alkaline paper) -- ISBN 1-60138-940-X (alkaline paper) 1. Boats and boating--East (U.S.)--Guidebooks. 2. Boats and boating--Canada, Eastern--Guidebooks. 3. Waterways--East (U.S.)--Guidebooks. 4. Waterways--Canada, Eastern--Guidebooks. 5. East (U.S.)--Guidebooks. 6. Canada, Eastern--Guidebooks. I. Hospodar, Patricia, 1946- II. Title.

GV776.E48H67 2014

797.10973--dc23

                          2014035824

INTERIOR LAYOUT, INSERT & COVER DESIGNS: Jackie Miller • millerjackiej@gmail.com

Disclaimer

This book is designed to provide information about cruising America's Great Loop, and is intended to act as a supplement to, and not a replacement for, complete marine travel guidebooks. Although every effort has been made to provide accurate information, the authors do not take any responsibility for errors, incorrect information, or omissions. Conditions at marinas, anchorages, and on waterways are constantly changing, so it is the captain's responsibility to verify all information found in this book to ensure accuracy. The authors and publisher have neither liability nor responsibility to any person or entity with respect to any loss or damage caused, or alleged to be caused, directly or indirectly by the information contained in this book. The purpose of this book, which is based on the authors' own experiences on America's Great Loop, is to give the reader some thoughtful guidance in making his own personal boating decisions.

None of the charts or maps in this book are to be used for navigation.

Authors' Dedication

To the wonderful readers of our previous book, "Reflection on America's Great Loop"
– the story of our own personal boating adventure, to our enthusiastic seminar audi-
ences who requested us to write a book of this type, and to all America's Great Loop
dreamers everywhere: We hope that the information in this guide will inspire, assist,
and give you the confidence to cast off your boat's lines and begin your own tale.
This one is for you!!!

Acknowledgments

Our first word of thanks goes out to our publisher, Doug Brown, and his fine staff at Atlantic Publishing Company, especially Office Manager Crystal Edwards, Linda Hambright in Fulfillment, Editor Letreze Jordan, and Jackie Miller, our fabulous Graphic Artist. You have all been most kind and gracious to us, and have made our entrance into the literary world an easy one!

We are also most grateful for our terrific friend, advisor, and agent, Raymond Barton, who continues to work on our behalf in pursuing new areas of media development for us.

Next, we would like to express our appreciation to "Passage Maker" magazine for affording us the opportunities to speak at the Miami, Palm Beach, and Fort Lauderdale boat shows over the past few years, and for inviting us to give seminars at Trawler Fests in Baltimore and Lake Park, Florida, and to teach our full-day course at Trawler Fest University. The "Passage Maker" staff is amazing, and works tirelessly to make these shows run smoothly and efficiently. Their events have provided us the chance to meet many of our readers, and it is at the urging of these enthusiastic audiences that we have written this book. We would also like to recognize some of our fellow speakers: Curtis Stokes of Curtis Stokes and Associates Inc., Captains Chris and Alyce Caldwell of Captain Chris Yacht Services, and Keith Ruse of Deltaville Boatyard. You are all experts in your areas of specialty, and are excellent and interesting presenters as well.

We want to particularly acknowledge some of the important contributors to the writing of this book: Ken MacDonald of Bay Port Yachting Centre in Midland, Ontario, who was not only kind enough to be a guest speaker as part of our Great Loop course at Trawler Fest University, but who also continues to furnish us with a wealth of information on conditions in Georgian Bay and the North Channel in Canada; our friends and marina neighbors in Marathon, Florida: Nancy Murphy, for her additional suggestions as to what we should include on our medical kit list, and Sharon Starling, whose photos of us grace our book covers; our Great Loop "Boat Buddy", Andrew Newton, for the use of some of his photos from our journey together; new "Gold Looper", Tom Goodman, who gave us up-to-date information on the Champlain route that he chose to take as part of the Great Loop adventure that he and his wife, Melesia, recently completed; and additional marina neighbors, Susan Hunter Blake, who asked important questions about the practicalities of having her fabulous dog, Crew, on board on the long and somewhat remote Mississippi River run on this trip, as well Karen Holtze, who is a Canadian citizen, and suggested the appropriate Canadian Border Services Agency website regarding bringing "Ship's Stores" into Canada.

We continue to be blessed with fantastic friends! Our "home support" crew watches our home, takes care of our mail, has fantastic "Welcome Home" meals for us when we return, and makes our lives so much fun when we are there. Thank you, Lou and Judy Ianniello, Tony and Evelyn Christiano, and Ernie and Kay Giordano! We are also a family of neighbors who weathered the damaging effects of "Superstorm Sandy" together, and today we can be proud to say that we continue to be "Stronger than the Storm".

We also want to recognize our "marina support" crew at Banana Bay Marina in beautiful Marathon, Florida, which for a number of months each year is our second home. (Yes, we do lead a charmed life!) Thank you, Jim and Betty Howe and Bob and Sue Grote, not only for assistance with boat repairs, appliance installations, and your great "Pizza on the Grill" parties, but also for your enthusiastic support of our writing endeavors, your knocks on our door to make sure that we were "okay" after we were hunkered down in our salon for long periods of time aboard *Reflection* while we were in the process of writing this book, and for the tons of laughs at the end of each day.

Each evening at Banana Bay Marina, many boaters gather at picnic tables on the beach to watch the sunset over Florida Bay, hoping to catch a glimpse of the special "Green Flash" phenomena. At a number of these gatherings, we loved listening to Skip and Karan Hamilton's intriguing stories about their early sailing adventures while traveling down the Midwest Rivers before anyone ever heard about the Great Loop journey. Thank you for sharing them with us! We also want to acknowledge both George Murphy and Donnie McDaniel (our marina's outstanding guitarist and singer) for using their diving skills to keep the bottom of our boat free of grass and barnacle growth, and Dave Boblitt for keeping *Reflection* looking clean and pretty! Banana Bay Marina is privileged as well to have a great Dockmaster, who is also a great Chef! Thanks, Larry Wade, for your outstanding pork barbecues and for keeping a watchful eye on our beloved "girl" in our absence.

During the past few years, we had several occasions when Pat's mother's declining health before her death had caused Pat to either have to remain at home when the boat was in the process of moving north or south on the AICW between New Jersey and Florida, or otherwise have the ability to return home quickly in case of an emergency. We were fortunate, however, during those stressful periods to be able to call on three special people to come to our assistance as crew members. George Telschow, whom we met some 40 years ago when we were members together of The Bristol Sailing Club in Bay Head, New Jersey, and Ray Houle and his wife, Caryl Moulder, whom we met as fellow boaters on America's Great Loop, all unselfishly sacrificed significant amounts of their own schedules and personal lives to help us in our times of need. We so appreciate all of you, and we will always be immensely grateful for your generosity and for the gift of your friendship.

Perhaps one of the most important things we have learned in life is that there are no coincidences (Yes, Les Levy, we will always consider you to be one of our "angels"!), so having all these special people in our lives is not an accident! We are honored to have these friends, and we look forward to the future and discovering others who we haven't even met yet!

Table of Contents

Part III: Underway on the Loop 91

Foreword

LCDR, Ray Houle, USN, Ret.

"All hands, lay to the starboard rail to take in all lines and get underway again with Cap'n George and 'Admiral' Pat Hospodar aboard the motor vessel, *Reflection!*"

If you've read their first book, "*Reflection* on America's Great Loop", then you already know that this Baby Boomer couple has figured out how to have fun on and off the water and that they make this year-long adventure seem like an easy cruise across Barnegat Bay, their homeport and local cruising area. The anecdotes are laced with humor, love, laughter, and keen insight into human nature, which makes this book one of the hallmarks of their success in pleasure boating and in life.

Now we get to see the serious side of the Hospodars in their second book, "The Great Loop Experience from Concept to Completion". The cover says it all, and as you turn the pages, you will understand that all their fun and excitement in the Great Loop adventure is underpinned with some serious planning, detailed preparation, and expert underway skills backed by over forty years of boating experiences on several sailboats, and aboard their beautifully maintained *Reflection,* a 48' Symbol cockpit motor yacht with fly bridge and sundeck.

My wife, Caryl, and I met George and Pat during our own Great Loop adventure in 2009. We docked nearby or alongside them at several of the Great Stops on the Great Loop listed in Part III of this book. We also had the pleasure of traveling with them for 35 days aboard their boat on their annual fall homeport relocation from Brick, New Jersey, to Banana Bay Marina in Marathon, Florida. During that time, we got to see, up close, how this couple goes about their daily travels, starting with a methodical early morning study of the weather forecasts by "Admiral" Pat, and the Captain's engine checks of his two "girls," their well- behaved Cat 3208 diesels. Next comes a review of the charts and guidebooks by both of them, followed by the engines' startup, equipment power-up, gear stowage, safety equipment check, and ultimately, an anchor hoist or lines cast off from the dock. Underway, the routine is also very professional with a steady hand on the helm, an ear to the VHF radio, and a watchful eye on the instruments and course with regular looks abeam and astern to observe other boat traffic or obstacles. Each travel day ends with an "all secure" of the dock lines or anchor snubbing lines before the sundeck chairs are positioned and the "docktails" are ordered up. We got to enjoy several of the fine anchorages listed in this book, and that is where we took our nightly "humblings" by "Admiral" Pat as we learned to play "Mexican Train Dominos" on the aft deck table. We were on the hook with no way to escape! Thankfully, the crew rum ration was sufficient to dull the pain of losing so badly to this "Master of the Ivories"!

In Part I of this new book, you will discover what you need to know to begin to plan your route on the Great Loop adventure, including the financial and other considerations that are of importance, as well as the outfitting of your vessel with such necessities as electronics, charts, and safety gear. Part II includes suggestions on preparing yourself as well as your boat for moving on-board, including stowage and provisioning tips, and provides many good informational resources for the journey. In Part III, George and Pat share chart excerpts, photos, and coordinates for some of their favorite anchorages. Also, in this section, entitled, "Underway," they help take the apprehension out of locking, docking, and anchoring along the Great Loop route. Their techniques are solid and proven by experience. Take good notes about fenders and setting up locking lines, and don't forget the disposable gloves! Their list, "Many of the Great Stops on the Great Loop," is impressive. There also are many more, and you will find those that enrich your experience as we did.

While reading this book, I could barely resist the urge to break out my charts and guidebooks and start noting in the margins and on the lat/lon lines the spots favored by our authors. I encourage you to do just that, and to also carry this book to the nightly "docktail" parties to discuss the next day's cruise with your mates and other "Loopers" on the Great Loop. Add a pencil and lanyard to the cover of this book to ensure that you will always be able to jot down an answer to the thought-provoking questions that this book inspires. Finally, after you read this book, re-read "Reflection on America's Great Loop". You will then understand where and why all the fun and excitement occurs as you undertake your own Great Loop adventure. Enjoy both books with our regards and respect! If you still didn't get enough info, go meet and visit with George and Pat personally at one of the many seminars they conduct during the year. You will make two new friends, I guarantee. Safe travels, always. "All hands…CAST - OFF!"

— Ray Houle

Lieutenant Commander, Civil Engineer Corps, United States Navy, Retired

Ray Houle enlisted in the U.S. Navy in 1977, and he has served in a number of locations around the world, performing shore facility construction and maintenance as a Navy Seabee. While enlisted, he was promoted to Chief Petty Officer and was later commissioned as a Civil Engineer Corps Officer on Diego Garcia in the Indian Ocean in 1987. His naval career has included assignments in Norfolk, Portsmouth, and Little Creek, Virginia, Antigua in the West Indies, Guam,

Midway Island, Nea Makri in Greece, Port Hueneme and the Reagan Presidential Ranch in California, Roosevelt Roads in Puerto Rico, Rota in Spain, Sigonella in Sicily, and also Gulfport, Mississippi. He retired with the rank of Lieutenant Commander in 2000 after 23 years of service, and he is now a licensed residential builder and remodeler in the state of Mississippi.

As a boater for over 35 years, Ray's on-the-water experience is broad and diverse, as he has sailed not only on the Atlantic, Pacific and Indian Oceans, but also on the Gulf of Mexico, Chesapeake Bay, the Great Lakes, and the Inland Rivers. As an active racing sailor for 25 years, he participated in a dozen Key West Race weeks, two Antigua Race weeks, the race to Isla Mujeres in Mexico, and in numerous off-shore races and club regattas on the Chesapeake Bay and the Gulf Coast. Ray has owned a half a dozen boats, has lived aboard his 36' Catalina and 42' Whitby sailboats and his Nova trawler for a combined time period of 11 years, and has captained and delivered sailboats to and from Key West, Florida, as well as on return trips from Isla in Mexico.

Ray and his wife, Caryl, completed their own America's Great Loop journey in 2009 aboard their 40' sundeck trawler, *Houlegan,* and they currently make their home in Gulfport, Mississippi. Their next adventure is to retrace the Lewis and Clark Expedition of Discovery from St. Louis, Missouri to Cape Disappointment on the Pacific Ocean in their C-class motor-home.

Preface

Traveling America's Great Loop is an adventure that many, who have completed it, describe as the "journey of a lifetime." This may sound like an exaggeration; however, we assure you it is not! Along this marvelous expedition, you will travel on some of the most historic waterways in North America. Various routes include passages on the Erie Canal, the Champlain Canal, the Rideau Waterway, the Trent-Severn Waterway, and the Gulf and the Atlantic Intracoastal Waterways. You may also cross Lake Ontario, pass through the rugged beauty of Georgian Bay and the North Channel in Canada, and wander down Lake Michigan. Your journey will also include many of the rivers traveled by early pioneers, including the Illinois, Mississippi, Ohio, Cumberland, and Tennessee Rivers.

Your Loop odyssey will also take you to a number of historic cities and towns in the United States and Canada, including: in Canada: Trenton, Campbellford, Peterborough, Orillia, Penetanguishene, Little Current, and many more. In the United States your stops can include: New York City, Mackinac Island, Chicago, Mobile, Tampa, Key West, Miami, Saint Augustine, Savannah, Charleston, Norfolk, Baltimore, and Atlantic City, just to name a few. You can even take side trips along the route to the capitals of both countries: Ottawa in Canada, and Washington, D.C. in the U.S.

However, what you will probably remember most from this trip are the wonderful people you will meet along the way, from your fellow Loopers to the locals in the cities, towns, and villages you will visit. We still keep in touch with people we met on the Loop from Ontario, Virginia, Mississippi, Alabama, Tennessee, North Carolina, and Texas, whom we now consider to be treasured friends.

Our hope is that this book will assist you in the planning, preparation, and the execution of your own adventure. When you "cross your wake," a term used by "Loopers" to describe the completion of their circular journey, you will now become a part of a unique group of boaters. Though there are over 15,000,000 boats registered in the U. S. and Canada, less than 1,500 of those boats have fully completed America's Great Loop. When you "cross your wake," you will be in the .01 percentile of all boaters, a very select group!

Part 1

PLANNING YOUR ADVENTURE

Chapter 1

The Boat and Its Equipment

Our Boat, "Reflection", at anchor in Lake Kentucky

Boat Basics

While selecting a boat for your Great Loop journey, there are four major factors to keep in mind: the boat's length, beam, draft, and most importantly, air clearance. Each of these factors can have a direct effect on the cost of your boat and trip, besides influencing your comfort aboard as you travel. A wrong boat may even eliminate your ability to make this trip at all!

Length and Beam

If your boat is longer than 84 feet in length (We should all be so lucky!) or has a beam greater than 22 feet, then you will not be able to pass through the Trent-Severn Waterway because your vessel will exceed the limitations of the Port Severn Lock. Our boat, *Reflection,* is 48 feet long, and although we were never turned away from a marina, we spent several nights at fuel docks because some of the marinas did not have a slip big enough to accommodate her. The largest vessel we met on our journey was 54 feet in length, since very few larger vessels have the appropriate draft and height requirements to make this passage.

Draft

Next, you will want to look at the draft of the boat. Less is better. The shallower the draft, the less chance you will have of going aground; that is just common sense. Some basic guidelines are helpful. It is very desirable to have a draft of 4 feet or less, because if you will be traveling through the Trent-Severn Waterway (which is one of the most beautiful waterways on the Loop), there are areas where the depth is only 6 feet. If, on your trip, you will be traveling through the Rideau Canal, on the inland route between Naples and Marco Island, Florida, or on the New Jersey Intracoastal Waterway, depths can run as little as 5 feet in some places, so a draft of 4 feet or less is what you would really want, if you are going to travel in those areas. We will discuss how these very shallow waterways can be avoided later during route planning.

Air Clearance

The last and most important factor in selecting your boat for this trip is air clearance. Located at Mile* 300.6 on the Chicago Sanitary and Ship Canal is the ATS railroad bridge which was once an operational swing bridge. However, it is no longer in operation and now has a maximum height of 19.7 feet. If you are going to travel the Great Loop, you must be able to clear this bridge. There is just no way around it!

To summarize, the dimensions of the ideal boat for traveling the Great Loop are as follows:

All distances in this book are in statute miles.

- A boat of a length you can confidently handle

- A draft of less than 5 feet, and 4 feet or less is even better

- A beam of less than 22 feet

- An air clearance of 19-½ feet or less.

Boat Size Considerations

On our Loop adventure, we met a number of other boaters along the way. A few were on sailboats with masts laid down on their decks, but most were on various styles of power vessels ranging from 25' pocket trawlers up to 50+' yachts. We also know that there are those who have done this trip in kayaks, canoes, and even personal watercraft! The size of the boat you select has a lot to do with economics and life-style. Today there are a number of minimalists who are proponents of the idea that you should buy the smallest boat possible for the trip, chosen strictly on an economic basis. Yes, it is true that the smaller the boat's size, the less it might initially cost, and the more you might save on dockage and fuel; however, we suggest that it might also be wise to think about the quality of life that you will want to have aboard as well. Perhaps, in fact, your choice should be to find the largest boat within the Great Loop size parameters that you can competently operate, that does not break your budget, but that also has the features that will allow both the "captain" and the "admiral" (see "Glossary – Terms Often Used on the Great Loop" on page 325) to safely, confidently, and comfortably enjoy this spectacular adventure. Besides new boats, there are many great used boats available at reasonable prices. It is all a matter of your own personal preference.

When making a decision on the right-sized vessel for you, consider the following practicalities when looking at its interior:

- Will you be at ease in confined quarters? Remember that this vessel will be your home for months at a time.

- Will your sleeping cabin have enough room for you and storage for your clothes and other personal belongings? Is the bunk comfortable, and can you and your spouse/partner both enter and exit easily? Do you each have enough personal space?

- Is there an emergency exit such as a hatch or a window?

- Will the boat have adequate accommodations as well as storage for guests should they come aboard? Are their bunks easily accessed?

- What kind of head and shower arrangements are on the boat? Is one sufficient? Are they separated or combined? If guests need to use these as well, how are they accessed? Is there sufficient privacy?

- Do you want a washer/dryer?

- Will the galley accommodate your cooking style?

  » How many burners on your stove do you find adequate for food preparation, and do you want an oven and broiler? Will you also have an outdoor barbecue?

  » How large of a refrigerator/freezer will work for you? Do you want a separate icemaker?

  » Do you want a microwave oven? Will you also be using a coffee maker as well as other small appliances: blender, toaster, crock pot, pressure cooker, etc.? Where will you keep them?

  » Is there enough room for dishes, cups, glasses, silverware, pots and pans, utensils, a waste basket, etc.?

  » Will there be enough storage space for canned goods and other food staple items?

  » Do you have enough counter space?

- Will your dining and other seating areas be comfortable enough for you as well as possible guests on a long journey? Where will you entertain, watch TV, use computers, read, do desk work, etc.?

- Is your overall general storage space adequate? Do you have large enough areas to house liquor and other bottled items, extra bedding and towels, clothing for all seasons and weather, paper goods, cleaning supplies, stationery, important papers, manuals, books, charts, tools, spare parts, etc?

We have been on some beautiful boats that at first seemed ideal for a Great Loop trip until we looked closely at their storage areas and found them to be grossly lacking. Unfortunately, some boat designers do not really design for the practicalities of daily living. What you will want to decide is how much "roughing it" you will really want to do based on your own life-style and comfort level.

Other Important Boat Choice Considerations

Besides the items mentioned above, there are some additional factors to also consider when choosing a boat for the Great Loop journey. They are:

Deck Walkways/Rails/Steps/Staircases

- You must be able to move quickly and easily from the bow to the stern for tying up and line handling.

- Ideally, outside walkways should be of sufficient width with high and strong enough safety rails alongside them. Rails should not be mere decorations!

- You should be able to climb both up and down safely on any exterior and interior steps and/or staircases, especially in bad weather.

The first two items are of special importance when traveling through locks. On the New York State Canal System and on the Parks Canada Waterways, whoever is securing the boat to the lock will have to be able to get from the bow to the stern with relative ease. On the river systems, whoever is securing the boat to the lock must be able to easily access the mid-ship's cleat. You will find more details on this in the "Locking" chapter on page 101.

Engine Room Space

Engine room space is of vital importance in choosing your boat. Is there enough room for you to make repairs, and will it be easy to change the motor oil and all the filters? Along the Loop, repairs are inevitable and your engine(s) will probably require multiple oil changes. Having sufficient space to move around your engine room and all other areas of your boat where equipment will need servicing will make these tasks easier, and being able to do them yourself will definitely help your budget. Accessibility to all your systems is of key importance, and will save you time and money in the long run!

Water Tank, Holding Tank, and Fuel Tank Capacities

The next thing you will want to consider are water-tank, holding-tank, and fuel-tank capacities. There is a section on the Great Loop between Hoppie's Marine Services in Kimmswick, Illinois, on the Mississippi River and Green Turtle Bay Marina in Grand Rivers, Kentucky, on Lake Barkley where there are no services of any kind for 249 miles. We traveled an average of 50 miles a day, and it took us five days to complete this section in good weather. It is important that your boat has enough fresh water storage, a large holding tank, and the fuel capacity for a trip of this length with the understanding that your journey could be delayed a day or two due to foul weather.

Batteries/Generator/Inverter

Taking into consideration the previously mentioned section of the Great Loop, does the boat have sufficient battery/generator power for an extended stay away from the dock? You definitely don't want to be caught 100 miles down the Mississippi River with no power hookup for days to come, your batteries running down, and your refrigerator/freezer going into unintentional defrost! Also, does the boat have an inverter to convert 12 volt DC battery power to 120 volt AC power? Having one will allow you to operate AC appliances such as refrigerators, icemakers, etc. without having to run your generator constantly.

Foul Weather Operation

No matter how well you plan, there will be days when you will be operating your boat in foul weather. Be sure that you are comfortable running your boat in the rain. If the boat has an upper fair weather as well as a lower foul weather operating station, are the navigational instruments adequate in both stations? Is the visibility sufficient, and are the windshield wipers operational in the lower station?

If the boat is only operated from an enclosed fly-bridge, can you easily see through the clear vinyl? You may also want to check the canvas for leaks, as you may not want to take an unintentional shower while under way.

If you are considering a boat with a pilothouse, be sure that you have good operational visibility in all directions, including the stern.

One or Two Engines

We are constantly hearing arguments over which is the better power choice for a Great Loop cruising boat: one engine with a bow thruster, or two engines with or without a bow thruster. Both have their advantages and disadvantages. A boat with two engines will probably initially cost more, and since there are two engines, there is twice the maintenance. One advantage of having two engines, however, is that if one goes down, the other will allow you to keep going. Plus, twin-engine boats generally have a much higher cruising speed, so if you want to get somewhere fast, you can. Yet, this extra speed comes with a cost. Twin-engine boats generally burn more fuel per mile than their single engine counterparts even at the same speed. Which is better, one or two engines? Again, it is your choice. There are plenty of arguments on both sides about the virtues of each configuration.

Condition of the Boat

Take a critical look at the boat you are considering for this 5,500+ mile trip.

- In general, is it in good seaworthy condition?
- Will you and your crew feel safe and secure on long open-water crossings?
- Is (are) the engine(s) reliable?
- If new, what will you have to add to its current list of electronics, as well as other necessary equipment and amenities?
- If used, does the boat appear to have been well-maintained? What items might you have to update, replace, or add for an extended journey? If you are unsure about the overall condition of the boat, get a marine surveyor to examine it. If you are concerned about the engine(s), also get an engine surveyor to look it over. We had surveys done by both and were glad that we did.
- Are the boat's mechanical, electrical, and sanitation systems accessible for repairs? Just like in the engine room, having space for you or a mechanic to work, as well as for tools to fit in these areas, are also of vital importance, and can help you avoid stress, save time, and possibly save you money in the long run. Again, a number of boat designers could use help in planning the true practicality of working in these spaces.

No one gets everything he or she wants in a boat unless there is an unlimited budget. The purpose of the items we have listed is to get you thinking about what is of importance to you in choosing a boat that you will be living on for many months and to give you some insight into what will be expected of the boat.

Navigation Equipment

We have been boating for over 40 years. Our first boat was a 26' sailboat that we traveled on from our home, down the New Jersey Coast, up Delaware Bay and River, through the Chesapeake and Delaware Canal, and throughout Chesapeake Bay with only paper charts and guidebooks for the areas, a compass, and a VHF radio. Even on our next 30' sailboat, we again sailed that way for a number of years before all the electronic wizardry that exists today. The reality is that if you are good at piloting through channels, have a complete set of charts and guidebooks for your Great Loop journey, a compass, and a VHF radio, you already have all the basic navigational equipment you actually need to complete your trip!

There has been much discussion in boating circles recently about the need for paper charts, in view of all the modern electronics found on vessels today. We still recommend having a complete set of paper charts and guidebooks for all areas of the Great Loop! Once you leave the familiarity of your home waters, each day will be a journey into the unknown. Many "Loopers" like to view their paper charts each morning before heading out to get an overall look at the day's journey and to make notations on the charts, highlighting possible areas of concern. We believe paper charts are an excellent backup, if your electronics fail!

A story was relayed to us about a boat traveling offshore along Long Island, New York. The captain called in a "May Day" to the Coast Guard. The Coast Guard, in asking what the nature of the distress was, found out that the boat was not in distress, but that its electronics had failed. The captain was advised to plot a course on his paper chart and to use his compass to find his way home. The captain replied that he had no paper charts onboard, and that he did not know how to use a compass! A towing service had to be sent out to find the boat and had to guide the captain home. In our opinion, both high- and low-tech navigation equipment has its place on a boat.

In fact, we were recently given a bridge tour on a cruise ship. This huge vessel was equipped with all of the most modern state-of-the-art navigational equipment and their backups, but, alongside these instruments, we also observed their paper charts with penciled-in markings and a course line! If cruise ships, which carry thousands of passengers and crew and have incredible instrumentation aboard, still use paper charts, we believe that it is still wise for us to do the same. Redundancy on your vessel can be a good idea!

For free NOAA and U. S. Army Corps of Engineers chart downloads, see: "Websites and Apps – Chart Downloads" on page 81.

We find that paper guidebooks also still have their place. All the information about a particular cruising area will be contained in a single book, and it is available to you all the time. Many boaters today like to rely on the Internet for all their information. That is fine until the computer goes down, or you cannot get Internet connection. Despite what you may have heard, there are places out there with no Internet and no phone service unless you have a satellite connection.

Let us now look at some of the electronic gadgets that can increase the safety and comfort of your Great Loop adventure.

Depth Sounder

One of the elementary electronic devices aboard most boats today is a depth sounder. It is very useful for telling you how deep the water is under your boat, yet it has its limitations. It cannot tell you how deep the water is in front or along side of your boat. Relying on it too heavily to keep you from going aground can give you a false sense of security. It is very important that you observe where you are traveling. Are you in the channel? Is the wind or current pushing you sideways out of the channel? Although when looking forward it may appear that you are in the center of the channel, also take a look behind your boat at the last set of markers to see if you have slipped to the side.

GPS

A color GPS chart plotter is one of our favorite electronic marvels. The information provided is amazing because it not only shows your position on an electronic chart, but it also provides information on your boat speed, time to your destination, tide and current information, sun and moon rise and set, information about marinas, and much more. Although extremely useful, a GPS is only a guide and should not be relied on exclusively to keep you out of trouble. There are errors in the GPS transmissions, and there can also be errors in the layout of the electronic charts you are viewing. Additionally, there can be errors in the positioning of markers and navigational lines on the charts. For example, on the Atlantic Intracoastal Waterway if you were to strictly follow the "Magenta Line", we guarantee that you would go aground numerous times. A GPS chart plotter is just a "best guess" device, as there is no substitution for your observation of the waterway around you. Sandbars build up, buoys are moved, and channels shift, so you might say that the situation is very fluid!

AIS

An Automatic Identification System (AIS) is another electronic device that is nice to have onboard for your Great Loop journey. It allows you to receive information such as the name, type, location, and speed of vessels near you. This information is displayed along with an icon of the vessels' location on your GPS chart plotter. When we traveled the Great Loop, we did not have an AIS receiver onboard at the time. However, we learned of its value while traveling down the Tombigbee Waterway. We were following a boat that had just installed an AIS receiver, and as we approached a narrow "S" curve in the Waterway, the captain of that boat ahead called to tell us to hold our position, since he had spotted a towboat on his chart plotter entering the "S" curve. He contacted the captain of the towboat and found out that he was pushing a long line of barges, which would mean that our trying to pass in this area would be extremely dangerous. We held back, and about twenty minutes later around the curve came the line of barges that then passed us safely in a straight wide part of the Waterway. Soon after this incident, we installed an AIS receiver on our own boat.

An AIS can also have its drawbacks. While traveling in the Palm Beach area of Florida, our AIS "Dangerous Target" alarm kept going off. It turned out that our AIS had detected sixty dangerous targets, each of which caused our alarm to sound and to be responded to individually. These all were pleasure craft at docks and were not even underway! Our solution to these annoying alarms was to turn off the alarm feature on our system, essentially rendering it useless. Unfortunately, when alerting of a "Dangerous Target", AIS does not distinguish between a boat sitting at a dock or one underway, nor does it distinguish between a 30' sailboat and a 600' ship.

Radar

Like the electronic wonders already mentioned, radar can be a useful tool to have onboard, and like all the others, it has its limits. When traveling on narrow inland waterways, it is nearly useless, especially if the waterway is lined with trees. Its greatest value is on open water in limited visibility. For example, it was of great value when we crossed the "Big Bend of Florida" (a 175 statute mile trip across the Gulf of Mexico from Carrabelle to Clearwater, Florida). We were making a night crossing and traveling with another boat; both of us had radar. The night was jet-black, with no moon and no stars, and we could not see the horizon. However, with our radar we could easily see the boat behind us, even without visual contact. We were able to monitor our buddy boat's progress, and if we saw that it might be going off course on the radar screen, we would give a call on the VHF radio to be sure the helmsman was still awake.

Autopilot

Although technically not a piece of navigational equipment, you may want to consider an autopilot for your boat. It is not essential for a Great Loop trip; however, we wouldn't own a boat without one! When traveling on open waterways, our autopilot steers the boat. It is like having another person onboard who does not care how long he is at the helm, does not complain or need "potty breaks", does not eat or drink, yet can steer the boat straighter than any human we know. On our "Big Bend" crossing, the autopilot steered our boat from inlet to inlet with only a few minor course corrections. Having one can definitely take the fatigue factor out of a long trip.

From our own experience, and in speaking with others who have made this journey, here is our list of navigational equipment that you will want onboard:

- A complete set of paper charts and guidebooks
- A VHF radio (two are better)
- A compass

- A depth sounder
- A GPS chart plotter

We traveled with many "Loopers" whose navigational equipment list ended here. So, it is up to you to decide for yourself what additional electronic equipment you may want on your boat to provide you with your own personal level of safety and comfort.

"Falkor" and "Freedom" – two boats we traveled with while on the Loop

Chapter 2

Selecting Your Route

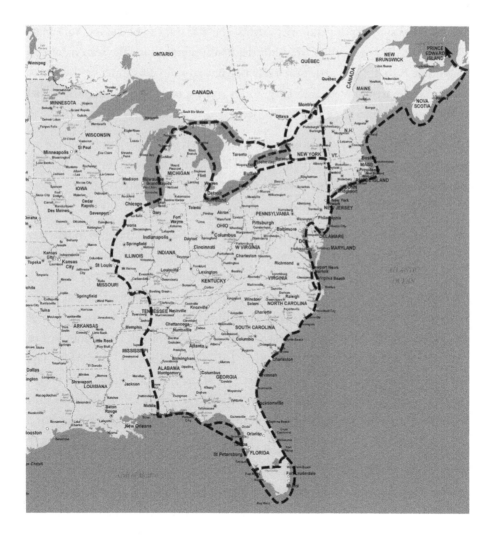

Which Way Should We Go?

There are many different routes that can be taken on your Great Loop adventure, and we will describe the most traveled ones. Since the complete journey is indeed a loop, it can be started and ended anywhere along the way. However, for this overview, we have arbitrarily chosen to start the discussion of routes in New York Harbor, and we will continue to discuss each sequential section by moving around the Loop map in a counter-clockwise direction, until we finally "cross our wake" or "tie up our 'Loop' ends" again in New York. The reason for traveling counter-clockwise is so that you will be able to take advantage of the river currents, especially in the Midwest and South.

As a rule of thumb, if you are planning to travel between New York City and Chicago during a single spring/summer season, you will want to be in New York Harbor between the last week of May and the first week of June. The reason for this time frame is that if you arrive too early in May, you can encounter cold weather as you travel north of New York City, and if you are taking one of the Erie Canal routes, you may find the Canal still closed.

The Erie Canal officially opens on May 1st each year, but heavy spring rains often keep the Canal closed due to flooding until later in the month. During 2013, the Canal was mostly closed well into July. This length of closure is rare; however, some closures in May are common.

On the other hand, you may also not want to leave New York Harbor much later than the first week of June. The reason for this is that it is a good idea to be heading south of Chicago by Labor Day to avoid any early cold weather, and leaving New York Harbor during the first week of June gives you about thirteen weeks to reach Chicago. This allows you plenty of time to enjoy the northern section of the Loop, even if you encounter delays along the way. You will really not want to be in Canada or northern Michigan after Labor Day. We have heard of boaters who lingered too long in the northern section of the Loop and then had to leave their boats up north because the weather turned so severe that they could not find many open marinas, nor could they continue their trip south without hardship.

Finally, it is wise to cross the "Big Bend" of Florida by the last week in November before chilly temperatures and winter wind and wave conditions make good open water passage days few and far between.

From New York Harbor to the Straits of Mackinac

There are five possible routes between New York Harbor and the Straits of Mackinac.

The Erie Canal and Oswego Canal Route

Route #1 (The Erie Canal and Oswego Canal Route)

The first route we will review is The Erie Canal and Oswego Canal Route. It is the one we chose, and it is also the one taken by most "Loopers." For planning purposes, we will call it Route #1. It begins in New York Harbor and proceeds north along the Hudson River to the entrance of the Erie Canal at Waterford, New York.

The Hudson River is deep, and the lowest bridge you will encounter is the 112th Street fixed bridge above the Troy Lock at Troy, New York, which has an air clearance of 25+ feet at normal pool. There is no tidal effect on this section of the Hudson River; however, rainfall or the lack of rainfall will effect what is known as "normal" pool. Subsequently, water depths as well as bridge clearances are affected by whether the pool is above or below "normal".

You will then proceed 160 miles west through the Erie Canal to Three Rivers, New York, where you will enter the 23 mile long Oswego Canal. According to the New York State Canal website, the depth in the channel of this section of the Erie Canal is 14 feet at "normal" pool and the minimum bridge clearance is 21 feet. We can tell you from personal experience that this is incorrect! The minimum bridge clearance is 20 feet! (For more information see the Erie Canal in the "Negotiating the Variety of Waterways" chapter on Page 186.)

Leaving Oswego, New York, the route crosses Lake Ontario for about 48 miles where you will then enter Adolphus Reach; turn westerly to the Bay of Quinte, and then continue on to Trenton, Ontario, the start of the Trent-Severn Waterway, which is a distance of about another 55 miles. There should be no issues with either depths or bridges on this section of the route.

Once at Trenton, you will enter the 241 mile Trent-Severn Waterway that will end at Port Severn, Ontario. The overall navigational depth of the Waterway is 6 feet, and the minimum bridge clearance is 20 feet, according to TrentSevern. com. There will be more information about this Waterway in the "Negotiating the Variety of Waterways" chapter on page 125.

After leaving Port Severn, the route takes you through Georgian Bay, the North Channel, and onto the Straits of Mackinac. There are no fixed bridge issues on this part of the route. For the most part, depths are not a problem, but watch your chart plotter and depth sounder closely, and be vigilant by honoring all buoys and staying in the channel.

The Champlain Canal Route

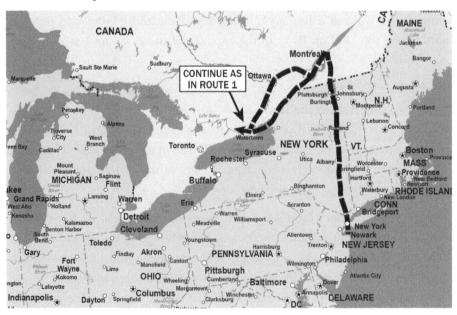

Route #2 (The Champlain Canal Route)

The next most popular route from New York Harbor is The Champlain Canal Route, which once again follows the Hudson River past Waterford, New York, but then heads north into the 60 mile long Champlain Canal to Lake Champlain and the Richelieu River/Chambly Canal. The control depth in the Champlain Canal is 12 feet; however, the Chambly Canal has a control depth of only 6-1/2 feet, and the minimum bridge clearance along this route is 17 feet at "normal" pool. From here you will enter the St. Lawrence River above Montreal and head southwest.

Below Montreal, this route splits. You can continue down the St. Lawrence River, eventually coming to Adolphus Reach, then proceed on to the Bay of Quinte, and finally to the Trent-Severn Waterway and beyond as in the previous route. Another alternate route past Montreal is to enter the Ottawa River and follow it to Ottawa. From there take the Rideau Waterway back to the St. Lawrence River, rejoin it near Kingston, Ontario, then go on to Adolphus Reach, and continue to the Straits of Mackinac as in Route #1 .

The Down East Route

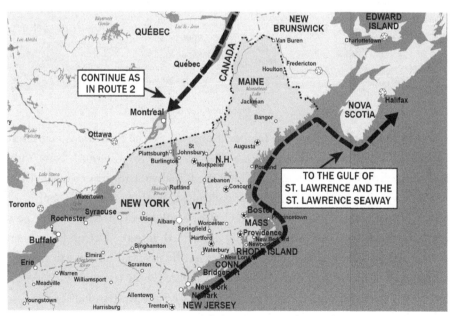

Route #3 (The Down East Route)

The next route, known as The Down East Route, begins in New York Harbor and travels northeast along the Atlantic coast past Nova Scotia into the Gulf of St. Lawrence. It then continues down the St. Lawrence River past the city of Quebec, and eventually connects with Route #2 near Montreal. Route #3 will add well over 1,000 miles to your journey, and is generally traveled by those who have already completed one of the other routes previously mentioned. Depths and bridge heights are not a concern on this route.

The Full Erie Canal/Great Lakes Route

Route #4 (The Full Erie Canal/Great Lakes Route)

The next route out of New York Harbor, Route #4, is The Full Erie Canal/Great Lakes Route which again heads up the Hudson River to Waterford, New York, and to the Erie Canal. This route follows the Canal west for its entire length of 338 miles to Lake Erie. Although the controlled depth at "normal" pool is 12 feet, bridge clearances past the Oswego Canal are as low as 15 feet. The route now heads southwest on Lake Erie, eventually turns north into the Detroit River, then on to Lake St. Clair, to the St. Clair River, and finally continues north to Lake Huron and on to the Straits of Mackinac. This route is only traveled by a very few boats for several reasons: the low bridge heights on the western half of the Erie Canal, it does not go through Canada (which has some of the best scenery and most beautiful waterways on the trip), and it requires a great deal of open water travel on the Great Lakes.

The Half Erie/Great Lakes Route

Route #5 (The Half Erie Canal/Great Lakes Route)

The last route out of New York Harbor, Route #5, is The Half Erie Canal/Great Lakes Route which, again, heads up the Hudson River to Waterford, New York, then to the Erie Canal. As in Route #1, this path again proceeds 160 miles west through the Erie Canal to Three Rivers, New York, where you will enter the 23 mile long Oswego Canal. Upon entering Lake Ontario, turn west southwest and head to the Welland Canal near the Niagara River. After passing through the Welland Canal, the route enters Lake Erie and continues as in Route #4. This route has an advantage over the previous Great Lakes route because it eliminates the low bridges found on the western end of the Erie Canal.

From the Straits of Mackinac to Mobile Bay

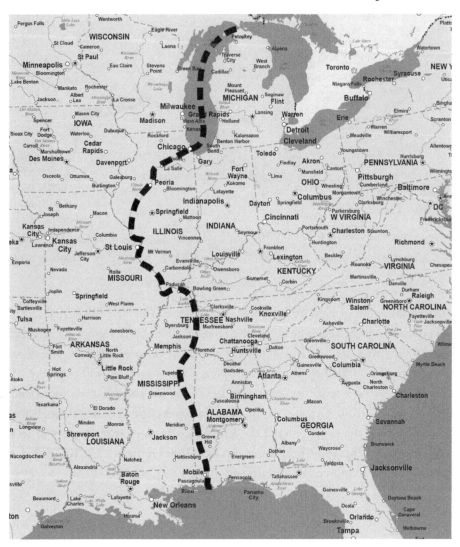

After passing through the Straits of Mackinac and entering Lake Michigan, there are two ways to go. Follow either the Michigan side or the Wisconsin side of the lake south. Both ways will eventually lead to the Chicago area where there is a choice of routes to get you to the Chicago Sanitary and Ship Canal, a waterway through which all "Loopers" must pass. The first route passes through the city of Chicago on the Chicago River with a minimum bridge height of 17 feet. The second route begins at Calumet Harbor about 12 miles south of Chicago on Lake

Michigan. Both routes eventually meet at the Chicago Sanitary and Ship Canal, where at waterway Mile Mark 300.6 is the ATS railroad bridge with a minimum height of 19.7 feet. Being able to pass under this bridge is a **must** in order to continue south on your Great Loop journey! From this point on, there are no more low-fixed bridges.

From here, the waterway follows the Des Plaines River to the Illinois River, ending at Mile Marker 0.0 on the Mississippi River. The route then follows the Mississippi River to the Ohio River.

It is not recommended that you travel south of the Ohio River on the Mississippi River. The river is very commercial past this point, and is not really friendly for pleasure craft. There are almost no services and no anchorages until you reach the New Orleans area which is a distance of over 550 miles.

Follow the Ohio River to the Cumberland River to Lake Barkley, and then go through the Barkley Canal to Lake Kentucky, which is just a wide part of the Tennessee River. There is also a second route to Lake Kentucky from the Ohio River. This route goes from the Ohio River directly to the Tennessee River, bypassing the Cumberland River, Lake Barkley and the Barkley Canal. It is shorter by distance, but it can take much longer in time since the route goes through the Kentucky Lock at Mile Marker 22 on the Tennessee River. This is one of the busiest locks on the River, and it literally could take you all day to pass through it. This alternative is not recommended.

The route now heads south along the Tennessee River, passing through Pickwick Lock and entering Pickwick Lake. From here, it is possible to take a side trip by continuing to follow the Tennessee River to Chattanooga, Tennessee, and beyond or to continue to follow the Great Loop route by entering the Tennessee–Tombigbee (Tenn-Tom) Waterway at Counce, Tennessee. The Waterway heads south and eventually becomes the Black Warrior–Tombigbee Waterway and then joins the Mobile River which empties into Mobile Bay.

From Mobile Bay to Stuart, Florida

From Mobile, if your Loop journey includes a side trip to New Orleans, turn west at the mouth of Mobile Bay into the Gulf Intracoastal Waterway (ICW); otherwise, turn east through Bon Secour Bay and into the Gulf ICW, and follow it to Dog Island, near Carrabelle, Florida. Here the Gulf ICW in the Florida Panhandle ends. The route now enters the Gulf of Mexico with two possible route choices.

The first route runs from Dog Island to the Steinhatchee River with a control depth of 5-½ feet then to Crystal River with a control depth of 4-½ feet. From here the route goes to Tarpon Springs where the Gulf ICW begins again. This route covers about 220 miles.

An alternate and preferred route is to leave Dog Island and to go straight across the Gulf of Mexico to Tarpon Springs, Florida, which is a distance of about 170 miles. This is a shorter route by about 50 miles, plus it requires only one day of good weather on the Gulf as opposed to needing three good days on the previously-mentioned route.

Most boats make this crossing sometime in mid-November to early December. However, this is a time of the year when there are usually only a few days a month with light winds and slight seas on the Gulf. Having to wait for only one good weather day to make this crossing, instead of several, gives this route a big advantage, plus this is the time of the year when you are most likely to have the company of other "Loopers" ready to go with you. (For more information see "Crossing Open Water" on page 247.)

From Tarpon Springs, follow the Gulf ICW to Fort Myers, Florida. Here the route splits once more, and you have the choice of either entering the Okeechobee Waterway, which crosses Florida to Stuart on the Atlantic Intracoastal Waterway (AICW), or of following the Gulf south to Naples and then onto the Florida Keys.

From the Keys, you will take the AICW north. However, the Waterway depths on the Florida Bay side of the Keys between Marathon and Key Largo can run as little as 5-1/2' at low water. If this is a concern, take Hawk Channel on the Atlantic side to Miami, and reenter the Waterway there. Then head north to Stuart, Florida, where the Okeechobee Waterway meets the AICW.

From Stuart, Florida to New York Harbor

The route now follows the AICW north to North Carolina, where the Alligator River meets Albemarle Sound. Here the route divides once more. The main Intracoastal Waterway route heads north through what is called the Virginia Cut Route, while the alternate route travels through the Dismal Swamp. Both have sufficient depths for most cruising boats.

The two routes come together just south of Norfolk, Virginia, where the route now heads north through Chesapeake Bay, the Chesapeake and Delaware Canal, Delaware River and Bay, and through the Cape May Canal into Cape May Harbor, New Jersey, at the southern end of the New Jersey Intracoastal Waterway (NJICW).

The NJICW runs from Cape May to Manasquan, New Jersey, where you **must** take the Atlantic Ocean route back to New York Harbor, the start of our Loop Route Planner. The inside route on the NJICW is narrow and winding in spots with MLW depths less than 5 feet in places. Also, the passage between Cape May and Atlantic City has several low drawbridges that are on opening schedules.

The preferred choice for many is to take the outside ocean route in steps: from Cape May to Atlantic City, a distance of about 38 miles from sea buoy to sea buoy; from Atlantic City to Manasquan, about 60 miles from sea buoy to sea buoy; and then on to New York Harbor, a distance of another 44 miles.

No matter which of the many route options you chose, be sure to check the latest control depths and bridge heights along the way. Conditions are constantly changing, and it is your responsibility to get the latest information to ensure a safe passage.

Chapter 3

Financial Considerations

One of the primary questions asked by most boaters who are thinking about undertaking this journey is, "How much is this trip going to cost?" In reality, there is not a definitive answer because many variables apply, but we can supply some rough estimations that will help you make an educated guess for yourself. There are some expenses that may not change very much from your life at home, such as food for daily meals. Whether you are at home or on your boat, you are still going to eat, so in this section we will concentrate on those expenses that relate specifically to your Great Loop adventure.

Fuel Costs

To calculate this number, remember that your trip will usually be at least 5,500+ miles (and possibly more), depending on the route and/or side trips you decide to take. Remember that how you operate your vessel, as well as a variety of other boating issues can also affect your mileage per gallon positively or negatively. Here are some examples of what you might encounter:

- You usually run at a slow speed for fuel efficiency, but by doing that you realize that you will not get to your desired destination before dark, so you increase speed to arrive in daylight, resulting in less fuel efficiency

- You are trying to get to a safe location ahead of bad weather, or you want to make a scheduled bridge or a lock opening, so you push the boat harder, using more fuel than you normally would

- You encounter long waits at a number of bridges and locks which force you to run the boat at idle speed for large amounts of time, thus causing you to waste fuel

- You find yourself either traveling with or going against wind, waves, or current, each of which can act as a help or a hindrance to your fuel costs.

All these types of situations have an effect on your fuel efficiency. Discovering your own boat's usual mileage per gallon is an important number to know before estimating the amount of fuel you will use, but realize that **this is only an estimate**. Another thing to remember is that fuel prices vary in different areas of the U.S., and are somewhat higher in Canada. Check the latest prices before making your calculation. One source for fuel prices is at: www.waterwayguide.com/, click on "Fuel Pricing" in the left column.

There is a simple formula to calculate the optimum fuel efficient speed for a displacement or semi-displacement boat. First, you will want to know the waterline length of the boat (LWL). You should be able to find your boat's waterline length by referring to its owner's manual, or by measuring the craft's waterline length in feet yourself. Take the square root of the LWL and multiply it by 1.34. This will give you your hull speed in knots. Take that number and multiply it by .75. The result will be your most efficient operation speed in knots. The whole formula looks like this: $\sqrt{LWL} \times 1.34 \times .75 = S$, with S being the most efficient speed for **your boat** in knots. Our boat's LWL is 45 feet. In applying the preceding formula, we come up with an optimum efficient speed of 6.7 knots, which we then round up to 7 knots.

Dockage Fees

These are some of the average rates per area:

- The U.S. East Coast and Florida's West Coast – $2.00 to $3.00+ per foot + electric

- Canada and the U.S. Midwest and South – $1.00 to $1.50 per foot + electric

- In all large cities – marina rates can often be higher + electric!

Always ask about group discounts – such as America's Great Loop Cruisers Association (AGLCA), Marine Trawler Owners Association (MTOA), and Boat Owners Association of the United States (BOAT US) discounts, as well as multiple-day discounts offered by many marinas and marina groups.

If you are a member of a yacht club listed in the Register of American Yacht Clubs, you may also be entitled to some reciprocity with courtesy dockage at other clubs on your route, and if you are a member of a yacht club in Florida which is a member of the Florida Council of Yacht Clubs, you may be entitled to full reciprocity at all their beautiful facilities.

If you check your guidebooks, you will see that a number of municipalities and parks may offer free dockage or dockage at a minimal fee to encourage local tourism, and, of course, you will also find a wealth of wonderful anchoring opportunities along the way. Keep in mind that utilizing these options will positively impact the price of your journey, when calculating your cost.

Boat Maintenance and Repairs

Boating experts estimate that the total cost of operating, docking, storing, maintaining, and repairing a boat on a yearly basis is approximately 10 percent of a boat's value, whether you are making this trip or not. You are wise to learn to do much of the maintenance work yourself, but be aware that even with the best of care, unexpected repair surprises can and will occur. These need to be factored into your costs.

Entertainment

- **Dining out** – If you dine out often at home, then you will most likely continue that lifestyle decision on this trip. Likewise, if you prefer your own cooking, then you may want to eat aboard most often. However, remember that this journey will also offer you the chance to travel through many new locales with eateries and watering holes that offer their own particular ambiances and types of cuisine. Do you want to miss taking part in these often unique opportunities?

- **Entertaining Aboard** – "Docktails" and "Happy Hours" with fellow boaters are very common at marinas on the route, as is "Rafting Up" with other boats while at anchor. This is purely a matter of choice and sociability. If you are a participant at a dock party or a guest on another's boat, in most cases it is common to bring along your own beverage of choice, and possibly an appetizer to share. If you are a person who enjoys meeting new people and likes to cook and entertain while at home, you will also be likely to do the same on your boat. Besides, it is fun! As usual, your life-style will determine your costs.

- **Sightseeing** – Like we mentioned above, you will be traveling to places that offer you the chance to visit many historical sites, museums, art galleries, and other points of interest. They may also offer special shopping districts, farmers' markets, and recreational areas. Some you may wish to visit for a day and some you may want to visit for much longer. Either touring or not is definitely your choice, but you certainly may not want to miss the opportunity of seeing certain places. After all, how often will you have the chance to do so again?

- **Transportation** – If at anchor, what transportation will you use to get to shore? A dinghy with an engine is most commonly used, but we have also seen people using a kayak or canoe as well. What is the most comfortable choice for you, and where will you carry it aboard while underway? How will you launch it from your vessel and bring it back onboard again? Do you want to carry bicycles onboard, and if so, what type do you find comfortable and how and where do you plan to keep them on the boat to avoid rusting?

  If docked, a number of marinas on the route offer "courtesy cars", which can vary from pick-up trucks and vans to even some (rare) luxury vehicles which you are allowed to use for a specified amount of time to go grocery shopping, etc. You may even find some grocery stores that will pick you up and return you to your boat. However, in many places you will be walking to visit local sites, restaurants, etc. In larger cities and towns, however, you will have the opportunity to use taxis, tour buses, and/or local buses to get around, as well have the availability of car rentals. If you have to return home for business or in the event of an emergency, the prices of airline flights, train trips, or car rentals may also have to factor into your costs.

- **Charts/Guides/Books** – A full set can run between $500 and $1000+ on average, depending on how up-to-date they are as well as whether they are new or used. Partial or full sets are often available for sale from past "Loopers" on the AGLCA web-site.

- **Canal/Lock Fees** – Costs can vary from year to year. (Some will even give you a price break, if you purchase your passes before March 31.)

Here are the websites which will give you the latest up-to-date rates for your trip:

» The New York State Canal System (Erie, Champlain, and Oswego Canals) – www.canals.ny.gov/boating/tolls.html

» Parks Canada (Chambly Canal) – www.pc.gc.ca/lhn-nhs/qc/chambly/visit/tarifs_fees_e.asp?park=106

» Parks Canada (Rideau Canal) – www.pc.gc.ca/lhn-nhs/on/rideau/visit/tarifs_fees_e.asp?park=101

» Parks Canada (Trent-Severn Waterway) - www.pc.gc.ca/lhn-nhs/on/trentsevern/visit/tarifs_fees_e.asp?park=102

» Great Lakes St. Lawrence Seaway System (St. Lawrence Seaway) – www.greatlakes-seaway.com/en/recreational/craft_tolls.html

• **Auto Insurance** – You may want to keep your automobile insurance in place even if you will not be using your vehicle(s) during your time away from home. If you have no automobile liability or collision insurance in force, you will need to purchase coverage at great expense should you rent a car. Check with your auto insurance company about collision and liability coverage when renting cars. Another reason for continuing your auto coverage is that we have heard of cases where some "Loopers", who had decided to completely drop their car insurance while away, had their former insurance companies refuse to issue new policies to them upon their return.

• **Boat Insurance** – This cost will definitely be an individual matter, depending on the age, size, and condition of your boat. However, having adequate insurance is a definite necessity! Be sure to check that you have coverage in Canada as well as throughout the U.S., and check if your plan has any travel restrictions on how far south you can be during hurricane season. Check also that you have adequate insurance coverage for the salvage value of your vessel in the unfortunate event that you have to be rescued because your boat is sinking, in immediate peril or stranded, or if you are in danger of damaging a protected marine area. For a detailed explanation, as well as for a possible salvage form to carry with you, see the Boat US website at: www.boatus.com.

- **Towing Insurance** – This again is an extremely wise investment, even if you (hopefully) don't have to use it. Check with Boat US and Sea Tow for coverage areas (including Canada) and pricing. Unlimited towing is best.

Know the difference between towing and salvage! Towing insurance covers breakdowns and light groundings when you are in no immediate danger.

- **Personal Health Insurances** – Check with your insurance companies to make sure that you will have medical and prescription coverage if you are out of the country, and how and if this may affect your premium(s). Do the same for any dental or eyeglass plans you may have.

- **Trip Time Frame/Long Term Boat Storage/Winter Marina Fees** – The length of time you plan on taking to complete your trip also affects your costs. Some boaters do it in months and others in segments over a number of years! However, if you are a non-Canadian and you choose to store your boat over the winter in Canada, be mindful that the **tax** on storage costs there is either **13 or 20 percent of the boat's value,** depending if the boat was built in North America (13) or somewhere else (20)! There is currently pressure on the Canadian Government to remove this tax, so before leaving a boat in Canada, be sure to check with the storage yard about this situation.

Most "Loopers" will end up spending the winter months somewhere in Florida, and it is often wise to make docking arrangements ahead of time to take advantage of long-term stay prices, since many marinas in popular areas fill up quickly, and waiting lists are frequent. These arrangements, too, can affect your cost estimate.

Chapter 4

Security

A true story, as related by Captain George:

While visiting Chicago aboard *Reflection,* we were unable to get dockage at any of the major marinas and found ourselves tying-up at a seawall in Monroe Harbor at Grant Park. The harbormaster, who assigned us the spot, explained that although the area was not secure, the Chicago police patrolled along here during the night.

We had crossed Lake Michigan from Holland, Michigan that day in less than ideal conditions and were tired from the journey, so after dinner we turned in early. At about 1 a.m., I woke up to the sound of footsteps on the deck above our cabin. "Somebody is on the boat!", I shouted to Pat. Then I jumped out of bed and ran out of the cabin wearing nothing but my skivvies. Flinging the door open to the aft deck, I started yelling, startling the two men on the deck. They quickly jumped overboard and ran down the path alongside the dock, but unfortunately, in my hurry to confront the intruders, I had left my eyeglasses on my night table, so there was no way that I could really see their faces. We then called the Chicago police to report the incident, but to my dismay, they did not want to be bothered with what I perceived to be an attempted robbery, because nothing was taken and I could not identify the culprits. We also found out later that the two boats docked behind us *were* robbed. So much for a great police presence!

Many of our boating friends had previously suggested that we carry a hand gun onboard for protection for this kind of a situation. However, we had decided not to do so for a couple of reasons. Bizarre laws in various areas of the United States often favor the rights of a criminal over those of a victim, so there was always the chance that if I shot an intruder, *I* might be the one to get arrested, possibly sued by the culprit, and could wind up in prison with him owning our boat! Another reason for our decision is that Canadian customs does not allow us to bring weapons into Canada!

Before this event, we had no reason to regret our decision, but now we decided that we had to develop a deterrent plan to prevent a repeat performance of that night's boarding. Thieves generally do not want a confrontation, and are usually looking for easy prey. Suspecting that we were targeted because the boat was dark and perhaps looked unoccupied, we decided to change that perception.

On the trip across Lake Michigan earlier that day, we had previously rolled up the screens that go around our aft deck and had stacked and tied up the deck furniture for the crossing. So now we brought the screens down, arranged the furniture, and turned on our aft deck spotlights, which highly illuminated both the boat and the nearby area. We also left on some lights in our main cabin that showed a glow outside. The final part of the plan was that if uninvited guests ever boarded again, instead of confronting the intruders, I would continually blast *Reflection*'s air horn from our lower steering station. Believe us; it makes a sound that could raise the dead and would definitely attract attention! Since then we have also added a battery-powered motion sensor spotlight that lights up the side of the boat. The plan seems to work because we were not bothered again in Chicago, nor have we ever been since then while either anchored out or at an unsecured dock.

Keep safe and vigilant, and develop your own security plan.

Here is a final word about carrying weapons onboard. Be sure that any weapon onboard your boat is registered in *your* name. We recently heard a story about a boater who was carrying a hand gun onboard his boat which had been given to him by a friend to hold until the friend returned from a trip. During that time, the boat was boarded by the marine police for a safety inspection in New York. When the captain was asked if he had any weapons onboard, he said that he was holding a hand gun for a friend. Because it was not *his* gun, he was quickly arrested, put in jail, and fined thousands of dollars for having a gun onboard that was not his own.

If you are ever stopped for an inspection, be sure to declare any weapons you have onboard, and make sure that you have all the proper paperwork for each weapon. If a weapon is found that you did not declare, you will be in big trouble! Also, many jurisdictions consider signal flare guns to be weapons. Under that circumstance, using New York again as an example, if you are stopped for a marine inspection and asked if you have any weapons onboard, respond to the officer, "I have a flare gun, which I am required by the U. S. Coast Guard to carry onboard." You do not need a permit to carry a flare gun onboard a vessel, but if you do not declare that you are carrying the flare gun and it is discovered by the officer, you can be in serious trouble for not having declared that you had a "weapon" onboard.

"Reflection" tied up along an unsecured wall in Monroe Harbor, Chicago

Top: Heflin Lock – Tenn-Tombigbee Waterway
Bottom: Hudson River – considered a fjord

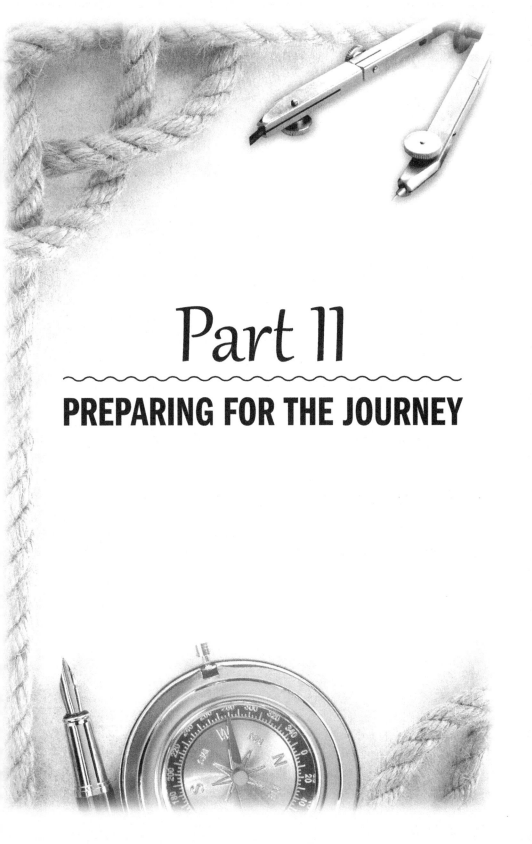

Part 11

PREPARING FOR THE JOURNEY

These are some of the charts and guidebooks that we carry aboard "Reflection"

Chapter 5

Getting the Boat Ready

The Engine(s)

You are about to depart on a 5,500+ mile expedition of the eastern third of North America. On this journey, you will be relying on your boat for transportation, and it will be your home for many months. Before heading out, it is advisable to have a trusted mechanic go over your engine(s) thoroughly, because any problem that can be dealt with at the dock before you start can save you considerable time and money when you are traveling.

We did that before our Great Loop trip. While onboard, our mechanic spotted some hoses that required replacing; he also dismantled our engines' water pumps and found some worn parts. He rebuilt and re-installed the pumps and gave us a list of parts to carry in case of emergency. They included:

- Certain critical hoses and hose clamps
- Spare water pump impellers
- A complete water pump
- A complete set of v-belts
- Extra air filters
- Enough motor oil for one complete oil change
- Enough motor oil filters and fuel filters for the entire trip.

Your mechanic may include other critical parts that are unique to your engine.

Here is our suggestion on how you can leave with the engine(s) in trip-ready condition:

- Replace any hoses that are showing wear-and-tear before you leave and keep the old ones as spares.
- Change your water pump impeller(s), v-belts, and air filters, replacing the existing ones with new parts and keeping the old ones as spares.

Unless you are taking a break during your Loop trip and returning home where you can get re-supplied with filters, we suggest that you carry enough filters for all the oil changes you will perform on the trip. Though finding motor oil along the Great Loop route is not very difficult, finding your **specific oil filter** may be a challenge.

Although motor oil can usually be found within a few days journey of your location on the Loop, we highly recommend carrying enough onboard for both daily maintenance and for the ability to do a complete oil change. The reason is that, unless you are meticulous about keeping close track when you will need your next oil change, it might come up as a surprise to you when it needs to be changed immediately, and if you don't have it onboard, you have a problem.

Something else you may want to consider is that if you are getting close to needing an oil change, do it before starting out. This can save you down time on the Loop by possibility eliminating one of the oil changes during your travels.

To calculate how many oil changes you will require, use the following formula:

Number of miles of your Great Loop journey/How many miles on average you will travel per hour/Recommended number of hours between oil changes = Number of oil changes you will perform on the Loop (leave off any fraction).

For example: If your Great Loop Journey is going to be 5,500 statute miles (that was the length of our journey), you travel at 9 statute miles per hour, and your engine requires an oil change every 200 hours, your formula would look like this:

5,500/9/200 = 3.055556 or 3 oil changes while on the Loop, assuming you changed the oil before you began the trip.

Remember that the same care and service applies to your generator. All of our suggestions for getting your main engine(s) ready for this journey also apply to your generator. You do not want to be days away from shore power when your generator goes down because of the failure of simple part that you are fully capable of replacing yourself.

Adapters and Power Cords

Some other things to consider when getting your boat ready for the trip are power cords and adapters; 50-amp power connections become scarce on inland sections of the Loop. If your boat uses 50-amp power service, we suggest that you carry a double 30 amp to single 50 amp "Y" adapter. You may also want to consider carrying a single 30-amp to 50-amp adapter for places where only a single 30-amp plug is available. We also carried a 15/20-amp standard plug to a 30-amp receptacle adapter in case we really got into a tough situation.

Also, whether you use 30- or 50-amp service, be sure that you have sufficient cord length to reach the power post. For example, on our boat we only have a power connection in the stern and we frequently dock bow-in. Our boat uses 50-amp service, so in our power cord inventory we have: a 50-foot, 50-amp cord, a 25-foot, 50-amp extension cord, and two 25-foot, 30-amp power cords to extend our reach for 30-amp service. This may sound like overkill, and you may be right; however, on our Loop trip, except for the 15/20-amp to 30-amp adapter mentioned above, we used all the cords and adapters at one time or another. You will want to analyze your situation and see what adapters and cords are appropriate for your boat.

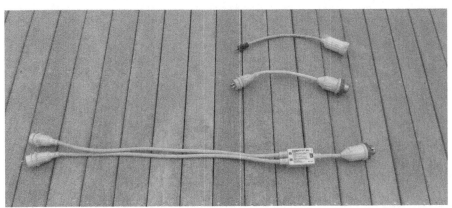

These are the adapters we carry aboard "Reflection", from top to bottom:
A standard 15/20-amp to a 30-amp adapter
A single 30-amp to a 50-amp adapter
A double 30-amp to a 50-amp adapter

Water Hose and Nozzle

Be sure to carry a water hose or hoses of sufficient length so that you will be able to wash your vessel and/or reach your boat's water fill-up. There may be some marinas or public docks where water outlets are not easily accessed, and you don't want to be caught short! Be sure to bring a good-quality nozzle to go along with it.

Additional Dock Lines

Having these should just be a "given", since you never know when they may come in handy for tying up or down in weather or other emergencies.

Fenders

You will want to carry enough fenders that are a sufficient size (The Great Loop is no place to get "chintzy" on fender size.) to protect both sides of your boat. When we travel through locks, we have three fenders deployed on both sides of the boat: one of an appropriate size in the bow, another in the stern, and an oversized one forward of the amidships cleat. It is not the number of fenders you deploy that is important, but it is their placement in key locations alongside your boat that makes the difference!

(Photo courtesy of Andrew Newton)

Upon entering some locks during our Loop trip, we saw some boats that were covered with fenders on both sides. If covering the sides of your boat with fenders gives you a sense of safety and security, then by all means go for it.

Multiple Anchors

You will want to carry at least two anchors on your Great Loop adventure, not just so that you have a spare in case you should lose one, but also because there will be places along the route where you will be anchoring in both your bow and stern. For example, on the Mississippi River you will probably anchor in Little Diversion Channel, the only safe anchorage within 69 miles. Since there is no swinging room, the only safe way to anchor in the channel is with a bow and stern anchor to keep you from moving. This is also not the only location on the Loop where you will be anchoring with two anchors.

Anchor Chain and Line

Be sure to have sufficient anchor chain and line especially for your main anchor: at least 100 feet of chain (the more the better) and another 100 to 200 feet of line. There are stunning locations on the trip like the Benjamin Islands in Canada where we anchored in a beautiful spot in over 40 feet of water. Aboard *Reflection*, we carry 110 feet of chain and 200 feet of line. That day we put out the entire 110 feet of chain plus another 50 feet of anchor line and held the bottom securely overnight.

On our secondary anchor, we only carry about 20 feet of chain and about 100 feet of line, and we have found this to be sufficient for our use. However, the more chain and line you can carry, the better off you will be.

Trip Line

There are areas on the Great Loop where the use of an anchor "trip line" and float is recommended. For example, on the Tennessee-Tombigbee Waterway it is a good idea to use a "trip line" in many of the anchorages. The reason for this is that it is a manmade waterway and when it was constructed the trees were cut down in the areas that eventually went underwater; however, the stumps were never removed. There is still a possibility today that you can foul your anchor on one of these stumps and not be able to retrieve it.

This is where a "trip line" comes into play. Many "Loopers" will connect one end of a line to the "crown" of their anchor and the other end to a float. When they deploy their anchor, the "trip line" and float are also deployed. The "trip line" will sit over the approximate location of the anchor. When raising the anchor, if it becomes fouled, recover the "trip line" and pull on it to free the anchor. Less than 50 feet of line should be sufficient for a "trip line".

Boat Hooks and a "Landing Loop"

A "Landing Loop" is a useful piece of equipment to have onboard

We suggest that you carry at least two boathooks. Here is why. When passing through certain locks, your boat will be secured only at the amidship's cleat, so to keep the boat steady while locking, one person will be in the bow and one in the stern area of the boat, guiding it up or down the lock's wall with the boathooks.

Having two boathooks has a secondary advantage. While we were entering a lock on one occasion, a guest crew member reached out too far with a boathook to grab a cable and dropped the boathook in the water. Fortunately, our boathooks float, so we used the remaining boathook to recover the one that went overboard, not to mention a number of other items that have "gone swimming" since then. It is always good to have backup!

Another item that we have found to be very handy is a "Landing Loop". This product can greatly assist the line handler in getting a line over a bollard, as well as over a piling or cleat when docking. No, we don't work for the company; we just think it is great! For more info on this item, see: www.landingloop.com.

Rust Remover

While transiting the Erie Canal, we developed large rust stains near our forward and aft cleats. The cause of this stain was the steel weights that the New York Canal system uses to keep the lines that they provide to secure boats to the locks from floating. The use of these lines will be explained further in the discussion of locks. For now, just take our word for it, you will want to have rust remover onboard.

Work Gloves

Carry several pairs of cheap, throw-away work gloves for use when locking. The lock walls, lines, cables, and pipes and just about everything else in the locks are covered with slime. No matter how careful you are, you will touch them. Wearing gloves will protect your hands and keep the crud off of you, but eventually the gloves will get to a point where they are so filthy that you will not even want to wash them, so throw them out and put on a new pair. Each of us went through about four pairs of gloves on our trip.

Spare Propeller(s)

It is a very good idea to have a spare propeller/propellers (if you have two engines) as the chance of bending a propeller on a 5,500-plus mile trip is very high. You can usually find a diver or a boatyard within a reasonable amount of time and distance to change a propeller; however, getting the damaged one straightened can be more of a challenge.

Having spare propellers can save you both time and money. For example, if you do not have a spare propeller and you bend it, a diver will have to make two trips to the boat: one to remove the propeller, and one to replace it. In addition, you will have to find a propeller shop, which might be some distance from where you are, and then have to send the propeller out to be straightened. This could take several days. If you have spare propellers, the diver would only need to make one trip to the boat, and you could then have the bent propeller straightened when you are near a shop.

Pump Parts

Besides what we have already mentioned, there are some other spare parts you may want to consider carrying onboard your boat, such as pump parts. It is a good idea to carry a spare fresh water pump or a pump rebuild kit with you. You do not want to be 100 miles from the nearest marina when your fresh water system goes down, and having a spare pump or rebuild kit can bail you out of a very unpleasant situation. It is also advisable to carry a spare bilge pump or rebuild kit. On our boat we have four bilge and two sump pumps. They are all the same type of pump, so by carrying one spare we can cover six pumps. There is also one more critical pump onboard. If you have only one head onboard and it is electric, you may want to carry a spare pump or rebuild kit for it as well. Nothing will make the crew unhappier than if they can't use the head!

Be sure to look around your boat and see what other critical spare parts you will want to take along.

Underwater Epoxy Putty

If you should spring a leak, underwater epoxy putty can save the day. While it cannot stop a major leak, it can do an excellent job of stopping a minor one. We recently sprang a leak in our lazarette where the trim tab fitting went through the hull, but by using epoxy putty we were able to stop the flow of water until we could reach a boatyard to get hauled out for a proper repair.

Sacrificial Anodes

Carry a sufficient supply of sacrificial anodes onboard for both your engine(s) and running gear. If your boat is normally in fresh water, the anodes (zincs) in your engine(s) and on the running gear of your boat can last for years; however, once your boat is in salt water they will start to deteriorate. That rate of deterioration varies from boat to boat. It is advisable for you to know where all your engine(s) anodes are located before starting out. You may want to paint the outside of the anode plug red or some other bright color so that they can easily be found later. Be sure to have at least one full set of anodes for both your engine(s) and running gear.

Proper Tools

It does not matter how vast the inventory of spare parts is on your boat, if you do not have the proper tools to make the repair. One day while we were heading up the AICW, George did a routine check of our engines and found that the water pump on the starboard engine was leaking from its shaft bearing. We carry a complete spare pump for such an emergency. That afternoon after docking the boat, he attempted to change the pump, but found that he was missing a critical wrench. There was no way that the pump was going to be replaced that day. Fortunately, the leak was not serious, and we were able to get the boat home where he could make the repair. If you have the parts, be sure that you also have the correct tools!

Screens

You will definitely be traveling through areas where flying insects are prevalent, so having screens on your cabin windows are a necessity. They are also recommended for your fly-bridge and/or your aft deck, if you like to sit outside enjoying "nature", especially in the early evenings! Despite even these efforts, some noseeums will still have a way of making themselves known, so bring plenty of bug spray.

Binoculars

These are essential to have near your helm station, and some boaters carry more than one set.

Hand-Held Spotlight

This item should also be kept near your helm station, and it is invaluable for pointing out markers, buoys, other vessels, and obstructions while moving your vessel in the dark.

Folding Cart

This is very useful for transporting groceries and other items from stores and markets, as well as laundry if you are using a laundromat.

Personal Flotation Devices (PFD)

Be sure that you have the correct type of PFDs onboard for the size of your boat, and carry enough of them not only for yourselves but also for possible guests.

We hope that the above list of suggested items to carry onboard your boat for your Great Loop journey will start you thinking about what other spare parts and equipment you will want to take along.

Courtesy Boat Inspection

As the time approaches for you to begin your journey, it is a good idea, if you are from the U. S., to contact your local U.S. Coast Guard Auxiliary or U.S Power Squadron, or if you are from Canada to contact the Canadian Power and Sail Squadrons, for a vessel safety check. This is your chance to make sure that you are compliant in all areas on your boat. Each entity can issue you a decal for a successful inspection.

When out on the water, if you are called by the Coast Guard or any other marine authority and asked when you last had your vessel inspected, you can tell them that you were recently inspected by one of these organizations. Although this is not a "free pass" when it comes to some government agencies, most will not bother to board you for another inspection.

Shakedown Cruise

Now that your boat is ready to go, before you set out on your adventure, it is advisable that you take a shakedown cruise to ensure that everything on the boat is truly working properly. This cruise can be just an overnight at anchor at a nearby cove. During this time be sure to run every system on your vessel; you will want to simulate the cruising experience as much as possible. Also, it is a good idea to go on this shakedown a few weeks before you leave on your Great Loop journey. The reason is, that if anything major comes up, you will have time to have it repaired without putting off your departure date.

We did a shakedown before our Great Loop trip and found some minor problems that we were able to take care of within a couple of days. However, after our winter layover in the Florida Keys, because we were living on the boat at that time, we did not do a shakedown before heading north in the spring. We started the generator which ran fine, checked the operation of the windlass, electronics, etc., but did not go on an actual shakedown after sitting at the dock for several months. When we finally got underway and anchored out on the first night of our trip north, we found to our dismay that although the generator started right up, it produced no power. This forced us to travel from marina to marina on our way home from Florida to New Jersey before it could be repaired, instead of anchoring for the night in lovely places as we often prefer to do. Learn by our mistake; take a shakedown cruise.

Additional Safety Equipment Required by Transport Canada

Boat safety equipment varies somewhat between the U. S. and Canada. Transport Canada, the agency that sets the rules for marine safety equipment in Canada, has a website that describes these rules and regulations. It can be found at: http://www.tc.gc.ca/media/documents/marinesafety/TP-511e.pdf. In the website table of contents find "Safety Equipment Requirements". Depending on the size of the boat, it may be necessary to carry additional flares, buckets, an axe, etc.

Sample Pre-Start Check List

Below is a list of the things that we check on our boat and the operations that we perform each morning before starting out:

1. Check engine oil.

2. Check engine coolant.

3. Check transmission oil.

4. Secure all loose items in cabins.

5. If at a dock, fill the water tank, switch from dockside AC power to the Inverter, bring the stairs, TV cable, water hose, and power cords aboard

6. If at anchor, turn on the windlass and the seawater wash-down pump.

7. If it is on, turn off the generator.

8. Power up the GPS, AIS, Radar, VHF Radio, and Depth Sounder.

9. Secure the outside deck furniture, and roll-up screens or vinyl curtains.

10. Secure all hatches, windows, and blinds.

11. Lower any antennas, lights, the radar arch, or the dinghy davit, if necessary, to clear any bridges for the day.

12. Turn off both battery chargers.

13. Turn off the hot-water heater.

14. Start the engine(s).

15. Secure all exterior hand-rail openings.

16. Secure all doors.

17. Switch refrigeration from AC power to DC power.

The above list is merely a guide and is specific to our own boat, *Reflection*. You may want to design one especially for your vessel.

Roberts Bayou Anchorage in Alabama

Chapter 6

Organizing Your Onboard Life

Operator License

Many U.S. states, and Canada, require boat operators to be licensed. The license can be in the form of a commercial captain's license or a recreational boating license issued by a government agency. If you do not have either of these because the area where you boat does not require licensing, a certificate of completion of a safe-boating course, such as the ones given by the U.S. Coast Guard Auxiliary, the U.S Power Squadron, or any other safe boating course certified by National Association of State Boating Law Administrators (NASBLA) will usually suffice.

VHF Radio Operators Certificate

U.S. Regulations:

U.S. citizens do not need a license to operate a marine VHF radio, radar, or EPIRBs aboard voluntary ships operating domestically that are less than 65 feet (20 meters). The term "voluntary ships" refers to ships that are not required by law to carry a radio. Generally, this term applies to recreation or pleasure craft.

Canadian and other foreign vessels traveling through the United States do not need a VHF operator's license if the vessel is less than 65 feet (20 meters).

For more information on the above, go to the Federal Communications Commission website at: wireless.fcc.gov/services/index.htm?job=licensing&id=ship_stations for more information on licensing.

Canadian Regulations:

U. S. and other foreign vessels traveling through Canada are not required to have a VHF operator's or station license for the first 45 days while traveling in Canada. Once a vessel leaves Canada and returns, the 45 days start over again from the beginning. If a foreign vessel stays in Canada over 45 days, it must comply with all Canadian requirements. The above information was provided by Transport Canada, the agency that issues marine VHF licenses. For additional information see the Transport Canada website at: https://www.tc.gc.ca/eng/marinesafety/oep -navigation-radiocomms-faqs-1489.htm.

Although the U. S. does not require a VHF station licenses for vessels in U. S. waters, it does require that U. S. vessels sailing in foreign waters obtain a VHF station license. However, the U. S. Coast Guard does not enter Canadian waters, so they cannot enforce this regulation and the Canadian Coast Guard does not enforce U. S. laws.

Therefore, if you are entering Canada with a U.S. registered vessel and you want to stay strictly within the law, obtain an operator's certificate. Go to the Federal Communications Commission website at: wireless.fcc. gov/services/index .htm?job=licensing&id=ship_stations for information on how to apply for a VHF Operator's License for U. S. vessels.

Taking Care of Finances

- **Banking and Bill-Paying** – Set up your accounts so that you will be able to receive and pay your bills as well as to manage your banking online.

- **Cash** – ATMs are readily available both in the U.S. and Canada but check with your bank(s) as to where and whether any additional bank fees might be applicable.

- **Credit Card** – Check with your credit card company about what its conversion charges are between Canadian and U.S. dollars. Also, be sure to notify your credit card company and your bank ahead of time that you will be traveling throughout the U.S. and Canada to avoid being locked out of your account for making suspicious purchases.

Mail

- A trusted neighbor or family member can collect and hold it and then open it at your request, or have that person send it along to your attention at a pre-chosen post office or marina where you know that you will stop, and have it held for your arrival.

An example of an addressee at a marina would look like this:

Hold for George and Pat Hospodar arriving aboard "Reflection"
Home Town Marina
100 Main Street
Some City, FL 12345
U. S. A.

or

- Sign up for a mail forwarding service that will scan your mail for you, allowing you to review it online and have only the mail that you want sent to you. These companies include:

  » **St. Brendan's Isle** (sbimailservice.com/index.html)

  » **Voyagers Mail Forwarding Service** (vmfs.com/index.html)

  » **MyRVMail.com** (myrvmail.com)

Computer Choices

A standard laptop computer performs well on a boat. As long as it is always kept out of the weather, its service life should be the same as if it was used in a waterfront home. No matter which type of electronic device you use onboard (i.e. computer, tablet, or phone), the less exposure it has to the elements, the better it will work.

Internet Access

Acquiring Internet access while traveling on the Loop can be a bit of a challenge. We use a RadioLabs USB Marine Wi-Fi antenna for improved reception (radiolabs.com/products/wireless/wireless-marine-antenna.php). The manufacturer claims that it has a range of 4 miles.

Using a Smartphone hot spot is also an option for Internet access; however, there will still be places on the Loop where cellphone reception can be iffy.

Phone Choices/Plans/and Access

Mobile phones will work most of the time on the Loop; however, you may find that in some remote places you may have no service unless you are moving. Even then, when you are able to get some degree of service, it might still be sporadic. So, if staying in touch 24/7 is vital to you, look into a satellite phone.

Before starting out, check that your mobile phone plan covers both the U. S. and Canada, or you might get a surprise when you get your bill!

Remember to bring any cords, chargers, and specialized batteries for these devices as well.

TV Access

If you want TV access 24/7, you will want to install a satellite system. If you don't want to go for the big bucks for satellite TV, bring along lots of DVDs. Few marinas on the Loop, especially when you leave the east coast of the U. S., will provide cable TV access. We use a Winegard Omnidirectional TV/FM antenna, which works reasonably well to capture both digital and analog TV signals through the air.

Clothing

Be prepared! Carry clothing for all seasons and types of venues. Good storm gear and outerwear is essential as well as are gloves, socks, hats, deck shoes, walking shoes, swim-suits and enough underwear. Though you will usually spend your time in seasonal casual clothing, ladies, remember to include a few "dress-up" outfits, and gentlemen, a blue blazer with khaki slacks and a dress shirt and tie will allow you entry to the finest locations you will encounter.

On the other hand, do not go to an extreme in carrying clothes. We met a couple on the Loop who thought that they would rarely be able to do laundry, so they took over a month's worth of clothes and underwear for each of them. After realizing that most marinas have laundries or that laundries are easily accessible near many marinas, they eventually packed up half their clothes and sent them home. Doing this freed up valuable storage space on their boat.

Medical and First Aid Supplies/Prescription Drugs

Carry a complete supply of the normal drugstore items that you have in your medicine cabinet at home (e.g. aspirin, acetametaphine, laxatives, stomach meds, band-aids, antibiotic ointments, gauze and gauze pads, tape, burn cream, cotton balls, alcohol, hydrogen peroxide, etc., as well as a first-aid instruction booklet). In addition:

- It is wise to see your doctor(s) or medical specialist(s) before you leave for a complete physical examination, if you haven't had one in a while, or if you have any specific health concerns. Also get a Tetanus shot (if overdue), as well as any other shots he or she might deem necessary.

- Ask the physician to prescribe any seasick medications, pain-killers, muscle relaxers, as well as a broad spectrum antibiotic for emergencies that you should carry onboard in case you can't get immediate medical help, and fill those prescriptions.

- If you are already on prescription medications for certain conditions, be sure, if you are from the U. S., that you have at least a six-week supply for the Canadian portion of your trip. For Canadians, make sure that you also can get your prescriptions refilled and sent to a U. S. address. For all travelers, it is also a good idea to confirm that the length of your prescription will not run out or that you will be able to have it easily filled or renewed, if necessary, along the way.

- Have a dental check-up, and ask your dentist for advice as to what you should carry in a dental emergency kit. Some travelers we know advocate the use of a product called "Soft Wax" until you can get to a dentist.

- See your eye doctor for an exam, and get a new prescription for glasses or contact lenses, if needed and about any eye drops, etc., that he suggests it would be wise for you to bring. Carry your eyeglass and/or contact lens prescriptions with you.

- Definitely have spare pairs of eyeglasses and sunglasses aboard.

- Sunscreen products, sun-burn sprays or ointments, insect repellants, antihistamines, bandages for sprains, and icepacks are also important items to have onboard.

Visitors and Crew Changes

As often happens when friends and/or family find out that you are going to make a trip of this magnitude (with the opportunity for visiting many wonderful stops along the way), you or they could make the suggestion about joining you on your boat at a particular location or for a special segment of the journey. Another kind of situation can also arise when you might have the unfortunate circumstance of having a family or business emergency which requires one of you to leave the boat for a period of time, and in order to continue the journey, you must take on different crew members for a period of time. What do you do?

Choose your ship-mates wisely!!! Here are some questions to ask yourself, and make sure you know the answers to these questions ahead of time:

- How well do you really know them and how amenable and boat-savvy are they?
- What are your expectations, and what are theirs?
- Do you have the same wake-up times, meal-times and bed-times?
- Do they get seasick? Do they have any food restrictions?
- Are they comfortable with spending lengthy days on the water, possibly in somewhat-confined quarters?
- Will they help with day to day activities, or will they expect to be entertained?
- Are they easily bored?
- How or will your expenses be shared?
- Be very careful with sharing expenses. Sharing expenses can be considered charging for passage. You may only charge for passage, if you are a licensed captain and have commercial insurance on your boat. Generally, if a visitor buys dinner for the owners of the boat on land, that is not considered charging for passage. However, if you split marina charges, it is. Do not accept any form of payment without seeking legal advice.
- How flexible is their travel schedule?
- Will their presence really contribute to the enjoyment of **your** adventure?

Remember that one of the biggest causes of stress on a trip of this kind is having a **deadline** imposed by the necessity of having to arrive at a particular place at a particular time. A popular phrase often being used in boating circles today is: "The worst thing that you can have on your boat is a schedule!" Whether a strict schedule is yours or someone else's, this kind of pressure can often cause you to make bad decisions like moving under adverse conditions when you normally wouldn't, rushing past places you really wanted to visit, or remaining at the helm for long hours in order to make up time due to some unexpected delays you have encountered. Keep in mind that a schedule on a trip like this is merely a "suggestion," and is often subject to change!

Family/Home/Taking a Break from the Trip

Having to take an emergency recess from your journey to return home due to family, business, or health issues may sometimes be an unfortunate necessity, but you may also find that a planned stop for a period of time can also provide the opportunity for you to take a travel breather from always being on the move.

It can also allow you some time to catch up with family, friends, and things at home, as well as give you the chance to take off or to replace items on the boat that you do not use or which are non-functional, and/or to bring on additional supplies that you forgot, ran out of, or wish you had. You will find that after each break that you take (which some seasoned "Loopers" suggest that you take at about 60 day intervals while on the move), you will look forward to returning to your boat and will feel rejuvenated and energized for the next segment of your passage. Always remember that your trip is an adventure and not a race, so take as much time as you want to complete it!

Important Papers to Carry and Stationery Supplies

- Passports, or Enhanced Drivers Licenses, or other Western Hemisphere Travel Initiative-Compliant documents
- Birth Certificates for Children
- Motor Vehicle Licenses
- Boat Operator's Licenses (if applicable)
- Captain's License (if applicable)
- Certificate of Completion of a Safe-Boating Course (if applicable)
- Boat Registration
- Boat Documentation papers (if applicable)
- Boat Insurance Policy
- Towing Insurance Card
- Copies of all other insurance policies: Home, Flood, Auto, Personal Umbrella, as well as Health Insurance Cards
- Automobile Insurance Policy

- Rabies Vaccination Certificate for your dog or cat noting breed, sex, color, weight, and age. It must also note name of the vaccination and duration of its validity.

- Important addresses and phone numbers

- Checkbooks and Extra Checks

Obviously, having some of these papers onboard is necessary for border cross-ings or, if you are ever stopped by the Coast Guard, Marine Police, or other law enforcement entities. However, having proof of boat insurance is also sometimes required by marinas, especially if you are there for a long-term stay. Also, having your insurance policies (or copies) with you can be of great help if you unfortu-nately find yourself having to handle a situation at home which may crop up. We can attest to that fact because when Superstorm Sandy damaged our home as well our cars in New Jersey, we were able to begin and continue the recovery process from aboard our boat in Florida.

Miscellaneous Items

- Stamps, postal and manila envelopes of various sizes, notepads, pens/ pencils/erasers, tape, elastic bands, a stapler and extra staples, paper clips, scissors, a ruler, calendar

- A printer for your computer(s) as well as paper and extra ink cartridges

- An auto GPS, for when you rent a car.

- Batteries for flashlights, etc.

Provisioning

Stocking up your boat with food-staple items, such as canned goods, spices and condiments, bottled water, soft drinks, liquor, paper products, cleaning supplies, toiletries, etc., that you know you will use is a good idea, but how much frozen and/or fresh food you can carry will depend on the size of your freezer and re-frigerator. However, don't overdo it! We have seen some boats that were so over-loaded with canned goods that they listed to one side! Do not be concerned that you will run out, since most times on this voyage you will never be more than 5 days from a port where you will be able to shop for groceries.

Shopping at different stops along the way gives you a good chance to sample and/or purchase local cuisine and area specialties. Many places will hold Farmer's Markets on the weekends, most displaying extraordinary fruits, fresh vegetables, and home-baked goods as well as butcher and deli items.

Brands will differ between the U. S. and Canada, and, depending on the size of the store, the variety of items which are available may be less that you might find at home. Also, "Loopers" from the U. S. can expect to pay higher prices in Canadian supermarkets than those to which they are accustomed.

On another note, if you love animals as we do, make sure to carry pet treats for all the "Looping" cats and canines you will have fun meeting along the way! We found that a number of dogs often chose our boat as one of their favorite places to visit, and one cat even had Thanksgiving dinner with us!

Laundry

Many boats today do have a washer/dryer aboard as either one single unit or as separate top and bottom entities. Some boaters also decide to give up these units in favor of more storage space. In many cases, they find that these appliances are only of sufficient size to wash small loads of items like underwear, but are not large enough to adequately wash or dry (unless vented) larger loads of towels and/or bed linens. If you would rather get your laundry done quickly and/or without hanging them outside on your boat to dry (not appreciated at some locations), keep in mind that laundromats are readily available at most marinas and in local towns. Just be sure to keep plenty of rolls of quarters on hand in the U.S. and one and two dollar coins in Canada. This can be one of your surprisingly larger expenses as you travel!

Your Proposed Itinerary

As a boater on a trip of this kind, you must learn to become flexible in your time expectations and to have the ability to quickly modify your plans due to the unexpected. Looking at alternative routes, anchorages, or places to stop is smart, since your schedule will always be subject to a variety of weather, situational, or boat repair problems that can arise, and/or health, family, or home issues that may need attention. Delays caused by flooding, bridge closings, excessive waits at locks, or waiting for mechanical parts may occur, so realize that your trip schedule is "merely a suggestion" and that it is often out of your control! You will also undoubtedly find places where you will want to spend more time than expected, and you are very likely to meet fellow boaters along the way with whom you may want to travel. These factors can also affect your schedule. You will find that you'll be a lot happier if you make adjustments as needed, and simply learn to go with the flow!

"Pet Onboard"

In making the decision whether or not to bring your beloved pet(s) along on this journey, evaluate ahead of time if they really enjoy being on the boat, or if they exhibit signs of discomfort like hiding out or often get seasick while underway. If you decide that they will be a part of your crew, besides their bed, favorite toys, food, treats, bowls, etc., carry a first-aid kit for them with up-to-date papers and shots' records along with current meds. Having a PFD for your pet is essential, as is also having a leash for your dog, and in some cases, also for your cat(s). There are collars that even come with a water alarm should your pet fall overboard.

Make sure that your animal is comfortable climbing both on and off your boat, and, if your pet is very large or infirm, you may even need a ramp or a special lifting device to assist them at certain venues.

Your cat should be accustomed to using a litter box, and your dog should be accustomed to riding in a dinghy for that same purpose to go for a walk on land when at anchor. In addition, it would also be wise to train your dog to use a specific onboard washable spot with astro-turf, sod in a box, or whelping pads for locations or times where or when he/she cannot be walked. Some examples of these might include places like the steep, rocky shorelines of some spectacular Canadian anchorages, when there is severe weather or a precarious outside situation exists, or if dockage or anchoring to get into shore is not only inconvenient, but almost non-existent. The last example is specifically found on the 249 mile run from Hoppie's Marina in Kimmswick, Missouri, to Green Turtle Bay Marina in Grand Rivers, Kentucky. This stretch is done over several days on the Mississippi, Ohio, and Cumberland Rivers where it may be extremely difficult for you to try to walk your dog or to dinghy into land because your only available options are to either wade ashore with your animal or to somehow dinghy him/her in to one of a few small public boat ramps on the route in river current conditions that are precarious at best. Instead, some boaters prefer to board their dogs in Alton, Illinois, over that period of time and then rent a car to drive back, retrieve their pets, and bring them back onboard afterwards.

Always call marinas ahead of time to see if they welcome pets. Most do, but there are some, particularly those at parks and wildlife areas, that do not allow pets ashore.

Dinghy and Engine

The choice of what type of dinghy (with or without an engine) you decide to carry with you is completely your choice, depending on the size of your boat. However, it should be easily accessible, not only for convenience sake, but also especially in the case of an emergency when you need to escape your boat quickly. Carry appropriate strong locking devices for both the dinghy and the engine to keep them safe from theft at marinas, when anchored, or tied up at landing areas. Also, be sure that if you carry your dinghy up against your boat's stern, your vessel's name is not obscured. Not being able to identify your vessel by name does not make bridge-tenders, lockmasters, law enforcement, or even other boaters (if they are trying to hail you on the radio) happy!

Bicycles

Having bicycles onboard are excellent for transportation and shopping, as well as for exercise, but make sure that you have adequate storage space for them, that they are well-secured while underway, that they have good locking devices, and that they are covered from the elements. However, also keep in mind that it is common for marinas to have them available for your use, as well as courtesy cars, if you decide not to bring any with you.

Head-Sets

Communication between the captain and the deck crew, especially when anchoring or pulling up the anchor, locking, or docking is of utmost importance. Many couples choose to use electronic head-sets as a means of talking to each other during these procedures, and many swear that they are "marriage savers." However, in our travels, we have also met those who have thrown these gadgets over-board in disgust, and we know of many who own them, but never use them because they prefer to communicate by the use of hand-signals and speaking directly to each other. Most "Looping" couples we have met have usually perfected their anchoring or docking procedures over time; they plan and discuss their maneuvers carefully before ever undertaking them, and they have not only their lines and fenders ready to go, but also their boat hooks, if necessary, in place before beginning.

Familiarizing Your Guests/Crew with the Boat

After you have welcomed them and stowed their bags (Hopefully you had warned them in advance that hard luggage is banned on boats!):

- Make sure that they know where the PFDs (life-vests) are kept aboard, and when they should be worn.

- Show them the location of all the fire extinguishers onboard and explain their operation.

- Introduce them to your on-board daily routine and to what tasks they may be assigned.

- Go over the operation and use of marine toilet(s) as well as paper usage.

- Go over the operation of the shower(s) and water usage.

- Go over the operation of your marine stove/oven as well as other appliances in the galley.

- Let them know that there may be some times when it might be better for them to stay out of the way and not attempt to assist you. You will advise them.

- Warn them that under no circumstance should they use one of their limbs to try to protect the boat from damage, and that jumping onto or off the boat is not advised.

- Familiarize them with the use of your VHF radio, and show them how to call for help in case of an emergency.

- If you are boarded by the Coast Guard, the Marine Police, or any other governmental entity, tell them to be calm and polite and to just respond to the questions they are asked without volunteering any additional information.

Boat Calling Cards

On the Great Loop, it is customary for you to carry business-size cards of your own design to distribute to fellow boaters on the trip with the following information:

- A photo or graphic of your boat
- The name of your vessel
- Your names
- Your cell phone number(s)
- Your email address
- Optional: Home Port or Home Address

It is amazing how many you will hand out to fellow "Loopers," and how many you will collect in return. They also become a wonderful remembrance of your trip, as well as a way to stay in touch on the water and to make new friendships!

Chapter 7

Association Memberships

We are members of the following associations and have found them to be of benefit to us before, during, and after our Great Loop journey.

America's Great Loop Cruisers' Association (AGLCA) – www.greatloop.org

An organization of people who share a sense of adventure and a curiosity about **America's Great Loop** and whose primary purpose is to disseminate information and enhance the overall experience for those dreaming of, learning about, or in the process of exploring and safely cruising the continuous waterways that circumnavigate the eastern portion of North America.

Marine Trawler Owners Association (MTOA) – www.mtoa.net

A non-profit, member-operated boating club, which offers trawler owners, as well as prospective owners, not only boat operation and maintenance tips, but a wealth of other marine advice and information, along with meeting events such as national rendezvous, and other local gatherings and cruises.

Boat Owners Association of the United States – www.boatus.com

An organization which provides savings, service, and representation for boats owners throughout the nation. Members are offered discounts on fuel, transient slips, and repairs. Other benefits include an online boating-safety course, on-the-water and on-the road towing services, boat insurance, and boat loans.

Yacht Club Membership

Remember that reciprocity can be a great advantage in your saving on marina fees, and it will also allow you to stay at wonderful locations with great facilities.

Membership in one can often be an idea worth exploring, but make sure that it is a member club listed in "The Register of American Yacht Clubs." We are proud to be active members of the Marathon Yacht Club in Marathon, Florida, since 2010.

Lighthouse on the Hudson River

Chapter 8

Websites and Apps

Here is a list of websites and smartphone applications that we have found to be very helpful while traveling on the Loop. They cover:

- Cruising related topics

- Free chart downloads

- U. S. and Canadian Customs regulations

- Specialized boating equipment

- Latest fuel prices around the Loop

- Mail-forwarding services

- Helpful organizations

- Tide and current predictions

- Information on waterways and locks

- Weather, waves, and wind predictions

WEBSITES

Cruising Related

ActiveCaptain – www.activecaptain.com

This is an interactive cruising guide that updates marina data, provides marina reviews, and supplies local knowledge on anchorages and hazards on a continual basis, plus much more information for the cruising boater.

Local Notice to Mariners – www.navcen.uscg.gov/?pageName=lnmMain

Published weekly by the United States Coast Guard, the local Notice to Mariners is the primary means for disseminating information concerning aids to navigation, hazards to navigation, and other items of marine information of interest to mariners on the waters of the United States. These notices are essential to all navigators for the purpose of keeping their charts, Light Lists, Coast Pilots, and other nautical publications up-to-date. Vessels operating in ports and waterways in several districts will want to obtain the Local Notice to Mariners from each district in order to be fully informed.

Marinas.com – www.marinas.com

This provides marina information (including nearby points of interest), maps and charts, aerial photos, weather conditions, and bridge and lock information for the U. S., Canada, and around the world.

Salty Southeast Cruisers Net – www.cruisersnet.net

Focused on the Atlantic Intracoastal Waterway, it provides valuable information on its changing conditions with detailed information on problem areas.

Waterway Guide – www.waterwayguide.com

This is a guidebook series which encompasses virtually all the navigable cruising areas along the East Coast, Gulf Coast and Great Lakes, including the interconnecting waterways that make up the Great Loop cruise.

Chart Downloads

NOAA Charts – www.charts.noaa.gov/InteractiveCatalog/nrnc.shtml

U. S. Army Corps of Engineers charts

Illinois River System

www.mvr.usace.army.mil/Missions/Navigation/Navigation-Charts/Illinois-Waterway/

Upper Mississippi River

www.mvr.usace.army.mil/Missions/Navigation/NavigationCharts/UpperMississippiRiver.aspx

Ohio River

www.lrl.usace.army.mil/Missions/CivilWorks/Navigation/Charts.aspx

Cumberland River

www.lrn.usace.army.mil/Missions/Navigation/Downloadable-Cumberland-River-Charts/

Tennessee River

www.lrn.usace.army.mil/Missions/Navigation/DownloadableTNRiverCharts.aspx

Tennessee Tombigbee Waterway

www.sam.usace.army.mil/Missions/Civil-Works/Recreation/TennesseeTombigbee-Waterway/Navigation/NavCharts/

Black Warrior Tombigbee Waterway

www.sam.usace.army.mil/Missions/Civil-Works/Navigation/Black-Warrior-and-Tombigbee-River/BWT-Alabama-Rivers-Navigation/River-Charts/

Customs

Canadian Border Services Agency

General Information – www.cbsa-asfc.gc.ca/menu-eng.html

Ships' Stores (Go to this website and copy and carry this information with you) –

- http://laws-lois.justice.gc.ca/eng/regulations/sor-96-40/FullText.html

(There is detailed information on bringing Ships' Stores into Canada in Chapter 14 "Border Crossings".)

Direct Reporting Sites for Marine Private Vessels

* www.cbsa-asfc.gc.ca/do-rb/services/drsm-dmsm-eng.html

Telephone Reporting Sites for Marine Private Vessels

* www.cbsa-asfc.gc.ca/do-rb/services/trsm-sdtm-eng.html

U.S. border documentation and procedures

* www.cbp.gov/travel/pleasure-boats-private-flyers

Equipment

* Landing Loop – www.landingloop.com
* RadioLabs USB Marine Wi-Fi antenna for improved reception – radiolabs.com/products/wireless/wireless-marine-antenna.php

Fuel Prices

* Waterway Guide Fuel Prices – www.waterwayguide.com/

Mail-Forwarding Services

* St. Brendan's Isle – sbimailservice.com/index.html
* Voyagers Mail Forwarding Service – vmfs.com/index.html
* MyRVMail.com – myrvmail.com

Organizations

* America's Great Loop Cruisers' Association (AGLCA) – www.greatloop.org
* Marine Trawler Owners Association (MTOA) – www.mtoa.net
* Boat Owners Association of the U. S. (Boat US) – www.boatus.com
* U. S. Power Squadron – usps.org
* U. S. Coast Guard Auxiliary – cgaux.org

Tides and Currents

- NOAA Tide Predictions for the tidal waters of the United States – co-ops.nos.noaa.gov/tide_predictions.html

- NOAA Current Predictions for the tidal waters of the United States – co-ops.nos.noaa.gov/noaacurrents/Regions

Waterways and Locks

New York State Canals

- New York State Canal System general information – www.canals.ny.gov/index.shtml

- New York State Canal System toll charges – www.canals.ny.gov/boating/tolls.html

- Champlain Canal navigation information – www.canals.ny.gov/wwwapps/navinfo/navinfo.aspx?waterway=champlain

- Erie Canal (eastern end) navigation information – www.canals.ny.gov/wwwapps/navinfo/navinfo.aspx?waterway=erieeastern

- Erie Canal (central) navigation information – www.canals.ny.gov/wwwapps/navinfo/navinfo.aspx?waterway=eriecentral

- Erie Canal (western end) navigation information – www.canals.ny.gov/wwwapps/navinfo/navinfo.aspx?waterway=eriewestern

- Oswego Canal navigation information – www.canals.ny.gov/wwwapps/navinfo/navinfo.aspx?waterway=oswego

Okeechobee Waterway

- Okeechobee Waterway (Blue Seas) routes information – www.offshoreblue.com/cruising/okeechobee.php

- Okeechobee Waterway (Blue Seas) locks information – www.offshoreblue.com/cruising/okeechobee-locks.php

- Lake Okeechobee navigational channel depth report (US Army Corps of Engineers) – www.saj.usace.army.mil/ (click on the Lake Okeechobee link)

Parks Canada Waterways

- Chambly Canal, Rideau Canal, and Trent–Severn Waterway information resource – www.pc.gc.ca/eng/index.aspx
- Chambly Canal National Historic Site visitors' information – www.pc.gc.ca/en/lhn-nhs/qc/chambly
- Chambly Canal National Historic Site lockage fees – www.pc.gc.ca/en/lhn-nhs/qc/chambly/visit/tarifs-fees
- Rideau Canal National Historic Site visitors' information – www.pc.gc.ca/en/lhn-nhs/on/rideau/
- Rideau Canal National Historic Site lockage fees – www.pc.gc.ca/en/lhn-nhs/on/rideau/visit/tarifs-fees
- Waterway Historic Site visitors' information – www.pc.gc.ca/en/lhn-nhs/on/trentsevern
- Trent-Severn Waterway Historic Site lockage fees – www.pc.gc.ca/lhn-nhs/on/trentsevern/visit/tarifs_fees_e.asp?park=102
- Trent-Severn Waterway Hours of Operation/Mobile Crew Availability www.pc.gc.ca/eng/lhn-nhs/on/trentsevern/visit/visit3.aspx
- Trent-Severn Waterway system all-encompassing resource – TrentSevern.com

River Locks (maintained by the US Army Corps of Engineers)

- Lock Performance Monitoring System (wait times at river locks) – corpslocks.usace.army.mil/lpwb/f?p=121:1:5305624834451

Saint Lawrence Seaway System

- Saint Lawrence Seaway System general information – www.greatlakes-seaway.com/en/
- Saint Lawrence Seaway Locks toll charges information – www.greatlakes-seaway.com/en/recreational/craft_tolls.html

Weather, Wind, and Waves

AccuWeather – www.accuweather.com

Local forecasts for everywhere in the United States and over two million locations worldwide

The Weather Channel – www.weather.com

National- and local-weather forecast for cities, as well as weather radar, reports, and hurricane coverage.

Weather Underground – www.wunderground.com (for cities) and www.wunderground.com/MAR/ (for marine)

Committed to delivering the most reliable, accurate weather information possible for locations across the world

NOAA Great Lakes Environmental Research Laboratory – www.glerl.noaa.gov/res/glcfs/

Great Lakes wave heights, wind speeds, and direction

NOAA's National Weather Service Marine Forecasts – www.nws.noaa.gov/om/marine/zone/usamz.htm

Marine weather forecasts for the Atlantic, Pacific, Gulf of Mexico, and Great Lakes.

Stormsurf (Gulf of Mexico) – www.stormsurfing.com/cgi/display.cgi?a=gom_height

Gulf of Mexico wave heights forecast

Stormsurf (Atlantic Ocean) – www.stormsurfing.com/cgi/display.cgi?a=eus_height

Atlantic coast wave heights forecast

National Weather Service – www.weather.gov

National and marine weather forecasts for the Atlantic, Pacific, Gulf of Mexico, and Great Lakes."

SMART PHONE APPLICATIONS (APPS)

AIS

- Boat Beacon
- Ship Finder Free

Cruising

- ActiveCaptain Companion

Charts and Planning

- Charts & Tides by Navimatics Corporation
- Garman BlueChart Mobile – Trip Planning
- Navionics Boating
- Skipper – NOAA Marine Charts

Tides

- Tides Near Me – Free
- USA Tides Free
- Tide Table by Tudormoble

Safety

- DragQueen Anchor Alarm

Weather

- Intellicast Boating
- Marine Weather by AccuWeather
- SeaStatus Marine Weather & Tides
- WeatherBug by Earth Networks

The "Thousand Islands" area of the St. Lawrence River

Chapter 9

Guidebooks, Books, and Periodicals

The following is a list of publications that we found to be most helpful during our Great Loop journey. Each provides detailed information about the various waterways, anchorages, and marinas along the Loop, plus information about the locales through which you will be traveling.

Dozier's Waterway Guides – Atlantic, Southern, Chesapeake Bay, Northern, and Great Lakes editions – www.waterwayguide.com

OnTheWaterChartGuides – Mark and Diana Doyle – CruiseGuide for the Intracoastal Waterway – www.onthewaterchartguides.com

Skipper Bob Publications – Atlantic and Gulf ICW guides, Canal guides, Great Lakes and Chicago to Mobile guides, and Planning guides – www.skipperbob.net

PORTS Cruising Guides – Lake Ontario & the Thousand Islands Guide, Georgian Bay, the North Channel & Lake Huron Guide, Trent-Severn & Lake Simcoe Guide, and the Rideau Canal and the Lower Ottawa River Guide – www.portsbooks.com

Quimby's Cruising Guide – Marinas, Locks, and Cruising on the Inland and Gulf Intracoastal Waterways – www.heartlandboating.com

Cruising Guides by Captain Rick Rhodes – Lake Michigan to Kentucky Lake, Florida's Big Bend, The Tidal Potomac

Richardson's Embassy Cruising Guides – Chesapeake Bay to Florida, Long Island Sound, New England Coast

The Great Book of Anchorages – compiled by Chuck Baier and Susan Landry – The Atlantic ICW from Hampton Roads to Key West

The Tenn-Tom Nitty-Gritty Cruise Guide – Fred Myers

Reflection on America's Great Loop – George and Patricia Hospodar

PassageMaker Magazine

Power and Motor Yacht Magazine

Soundings

Chesapeake Bay Magazine

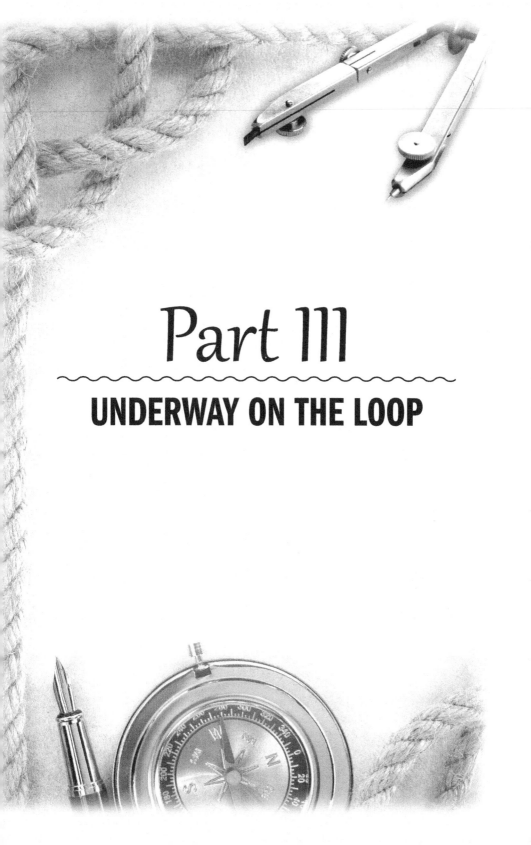

Part III

UNDERWAY ON THE LOOP

You have probably spent months, if not years, planning and preparing for your Great Loop Adventure. Now it is time to finally get underway, and it is a truly wonderful feeling to leave the dock at last for the start of your journey. The topics we have covered in the previous sections of the book have been centered on making your trip as safe and pleasant as possible, and that is our same goal in this next section.

Here we will discuss transiting under bridges, passing other pleasure craft and commercial vessels, dealing with various types of locks, reviewing the many waterways you will travel, handling open water crossings, passing through Canadian and United States Customs, and reviewing places that you may want to visit along the way.

The Trent-Severn Waterway, Campbellford, Ontario

Chapter 10

Boating Protocol

One of the numerous drawbridges between Miami and West Palm Beach, Florida

Bridges

It is important to understand the proper protocol when approaching a bridge. Bridge openings tend to be narrower than the channel leading to them, and if there is any current present, it may be accelerated at the bridge opening. As you approach a fixed bridge, if a vessel is coming from the other direction and you have a concern that there is not enough room for the two of you to pass safely together under the bridge, call the other vessel on the radio and establish who will pass under the bridge first. The general rule is that the vessel traveling with the current goes first.

When approaching a bridge that will have to open for you to pass under it, call the bridge tender to request an opening. This is generally done on either VHF Channel 13 or 9, (never on Channel 16), using the name of the bridge. For example, "14th Street Bridge Tender, this is the vessel *Reflection* requesting an opening." If you want a bridge to open, you must request the opening! Remember that just because your boat is sitting in front of a bridge is not necessarily an indication to the bridge tender that you want the bridge to open. He/she is not a mind reader!

We have also been in some situations where a bridge tender has not responded to our radio or cannot be sighted on the bridge. In those cases, we have used our cell phones to call the bridge, using the phone number that is usually posted in guidebooks.

If there is a boat waiting for an opening on the other side of the bridge, contact the other vessel and establish who will go first once it is open as in the earlier discussion.

On many of the waterways, there are also bridges that open on definite schedules. Their openings may vary from once an hour on the hour, to every half hour on the hour and half hour, to every half hour at quarter to and quarter after the hour, to every twenty minutes starting on the hour. Also some schedules are in force 24 hours a day, while others are on schedule only during certain hours. Once again, this is where your guidebooks come in handy.

Knowing when a bridge is scheduled to open and how long it will take you to get there can save you both time and fuel. We like to arrive at a bridge just before its scheduled opening time. We will set a waypoint on our GPS for the bridge in question, and then we'll monitor our progress to that point, always keeping track of our projected arrival time. We understand that if you are traveling on a waterway that zigzags to your target, the time estimate becomes a rather rough projection of when you will arrive, but you can always adjust your speed as you get closer to ensure that you will get there on time. It is better to arrive five minutes early than one minute too late at a bridge, and do not forget to call for the opening.

As we mentioned earlier, just because you are idling in front of a bridge even at its scheduled opening time, does not mean that the bridge will automatically open for you. We have heard many a conversation between a pleasure craft and a bridge on an opening schedule, where the captain did not understand why the bridge did not open automatically at that time. The reply from the bridge tender was always the same, "You didn't ask for an opening. I can't open the bridge unless an opening is requested."

After you are safely through a bridge, protocol also calls for you to quickly thank the bridge tender for the opening on your VHF radio. Here is an example: "This is the vessel *Reflection*. Thank you, 14th Street Bridge Tender, for the opening, and have a nice day!" You will be surprised how many charming responses you will get back!

Information about bridges can be found in the appropriate guidebooks for each waterway, including: the height of fixed bridges, the height of opening bridges in their closed position (Both heights are given at mean high water or at "normal" pool on inland waterways.), the name of the bridge, and if there is an opening schedule.

We are following behind "Silver Seas" after she gave us an expert "slow pass"

Passing – The "Slow Pass"

While on the Loop, there will be many times when you will overtake another boat and other times when one will overtake you. When boats are traveling in the same direction, the boat that is passing can make quite a wake, which can also create an uncomfortable and sometimes dangerous condition for the boat being passed. To prevent this from happening, it is courteous to conduct a maneuver called a "slow pass".

This is properly accomplished by the overtaking boat calling the boat to be over-taken on VHF Channel 16, then having both boats switch to an agreed-upon working channel to discuss the "slow pass". However, in reality, the "slow pass" request is almost always very quickly discussed on Channel 16 since the entire conversation can take place in only a few seconds.

Once the two boats have established communication, the trailing boat will say something like, "*Reflection*, this is *Fast Fish Freddie* behind you, and we would like to give you a slow pass on your port/starboard side." If we, as the lead boat, agree with the passing side, we will respond to the trailing boat with, "Come ahead, *Fast Fish Freddie*. We will slow down for you." However, if we disagree with the passing side, we will tell the trailing boat what we would prefer him to do.

Since we are still the lead boat, we will now slow down to the slowest speed at which we feel comfortable traveling, and the trailing boat should now slow to a speed just fast enough for him to pass us. Just after he passes our boat, and as soon as it is safe, we will now cross over the other boat's wake, allowing him, as the new leading boat, to increase speed without waking us. If this procedure works well, we will then contact him on the radio, and thank him for the "slow pass".

Though most boaters are polite, be mindful, however, that there are times when you will come in contact with those who do not know how to perform a slow pass as either the lead boat or the trailing boat! In our travels, we have encountered everything from stubborn slow sailboat captains who refuse to move over in tight areas so that you can safely go around them; sport-fishing boat delivery captains in a hurry who refuse to slow down for any reason, even if it means throwing a huge wake; as well as some ego-maniacs on "go fast" vessels who are either too ignorant or who really just don't care about the damage they can do to others. Often some of these vessels do not respond to radio communications or pretend not to hear you. Keep a camera, your cell phone, and/or pen and paper at the helm to record any instance of aggressive boating behavior, call ahead to other boaters warning them of the particular offending boat that is on the way, and then notify the local authorities. On several occasions, we were delighted to see that they were waiting for and had stopped the offending boat(s) at a spot up ahead!

 It is important for the name of your boat to be clearly visible on the stern of the vessel so that other boaters can call you on the radio! If the name is obstructed in any way or is written on your boat's side, it becomes difficult to read from behind, so you may want to have an inexpensive banner made with the name of your boat on it and display the banner in a conspicuous place across your stern. This will also keep bridge tenders and lockmasters, who often have to keep records of the names of vessels and their home ports passing through their passage areas, happier!

Passing Commercial Traffic

During your Great Loop journey, you will be passing a considerable amount of commercial traffic in the form of towboats pushing long lines of barges on the midwest rivers and waterways as well as some commercial traffic along the intra-coastal waterways. It is important to understand correct protocol when in a passing situation, including a familiarity with "whistle signals."

Whistle signals were developed before the advent of VHF radios for communication between passing vessels so that there would be no misunderstanding between them about on which side the vessels would pass each other. For example, if two boats were meeting head on and they agreed to pass port to port, they would pass on one whistle. In the same situation, if they agreed to pass starboard to starboard, they would pass on two whistles, which seems simple enough, right?

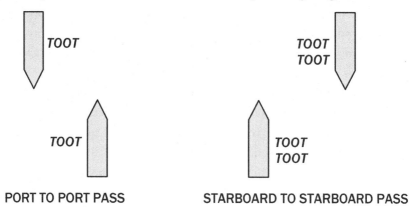

Here is where it gets a little tricky! When one vessel is overtaking another and the trailing vessel wants to pass on the leading vessel's starboard side (passing it on the trailing vessel's port side), that is a one-whistle pass. If the situation is reversed, where the trailing vessel is going to pass on the port side of the lead vessel (passing it on the trailing vessel's starboard side), that is a two-whistle pass.

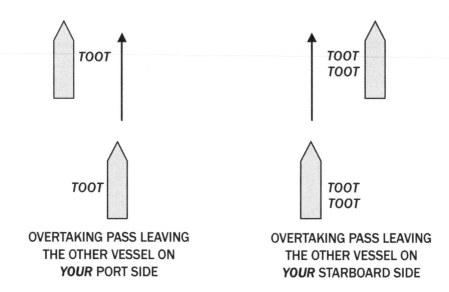

OVERTAKING PASS LEAVING
THE OTHER VESSEL ON
YOUR PORT SIDE

OVERTAKING PASS LEAVING
THE OTHER VESSEL ON
YOUR STARBOARD SIDE

This is how we have come to remember whistle signals. In either a head to head or overtaking situation, if you are going to LEAVE the other vessel on YOUR port side, it is a one-whistle pass. If you are going to LEAVE the other vessel on YOUR starboard side, it is a two-whistle pass.

Although we now use VHF radios to communicate between vessels to establish on which side we will pass, towboat captains still refer to the pass as either a one-whistle or two-whistle pass.

Here is an example of a passing situation on the Mississippi River if you are heading downstream and spot a towboat pushing barges heading upstream. If you can identify the towboat through your AIS system, call it by name on VHF Channel 13, but if you do not know the name of the boat, call the boat using a landmark reference. For example, "This is the vessel *Reflection* calling the towboat heading upstream near Portage Island." (On the intracoastal waterways, if you do not know the vessel's name, identify the boat using the nearest navigation marker number.) Once contact has been established, ask the captain on which side you should pass his boat. He will come back with instructions to pass him on one or two whistles.

Today, most passing situations between vessels are discussed via the boats' VHF radios. Use your boat's horn for signaling only if for some reason you get no radio response.

Here is one more note about passing towboats on the rivers and waterways. Towboats pushing barges around curves will almost always take the outside of the curve for two reasons: first, the water tends to be deeper on the outside of curves, and second, it allows the towboat to make a wider turn. If you see a towboat pushing barges in a curve, you will most likely be passing it on the inside of the curve.

In our experience, we have found that towboat captains especially have always been very helpful in assisting us in safely passing their tows. By following their advice, we thankfully have never had a problem.

Good Docking Procedures

The following are some suggestions on how to make your experience a bit less hectic:

- Call the marina well ahead of time by radio or mobile phone to let them know how soon you will be arriving.
- Find out if you will be put at a floating or a fixed dock and where it is located.
- Ask if marina staff will be there to take your lines.
- Check if you will have any issues with wind or current.
- Ask if it is a slip or a side tie-up. If it is a side tie, which side of your boat will be against the dock?
- If it is a slip, determine whether you will be bow or stern-in, depending on the length and location of their finger piers.
- In all instances, secure your lines at all the appropriate locations on the boat from where they will be thrown to the dock.
- If it is a floating dock, have your fenders secured vertically at a height that will cushion your boat from the pier(s).
- If it is a fixed dock, have your fenders ready to be deployed horizontally, but do not hang them overboard until you are sure that they will not get caught on the pilings.
- Have a boat hook or a Landing Loop handy.
- Make sure that everything on deck is ready before proceeding in.
- **Proceed in slowly**.

Chapter 11

Locking

The Coffeeville Lock on the Tombigbee-Black Warrior Waterway

Be Prepared

If you haven't done much locking before starting out on your Great Loop journey, you may have some apprehensions about the locking process. Before we started our trip we had only previously traveled through two locks in the Dismal Swamp on the intracoastal waterway between North Carolina and Virginia. There, the change in water level was only eight feet, and we had crew onboard to help us with the process. However, on the Great Loop, we would mostly be just by ourselves while passing through over one hundred locks and some with water level changes as much as 80 to 90 feet!

Although at first this prospect seemed a bit daunting, once we set up a system for passing through the various types of locks that worked for us, it became routine. Before entering a lock, there are several things you can do ahead of time to make the passage through a lock go smoothly.

1. **Have your fenders in position on both sides of your boat before entering the lock.** It is essential to have them ready on both sides, because once you begin entering the lock, you may be directed by the lockmaster to secure your boat to the opposite side than the one which you had planned on using.

   Use as many fenders as you wish to ensure your comfort and safety. It is important that you know where to best locate your fenders to protect your boat while locking. We found this out the hard way.

   Prior to owning our current boat, the majority of our boating experience was on sailboats. As we started our Great Loop journey, we had really only gotten a few weeks of experience in operating our twin-engine power boat (with no bow thruster), so we were very much still on the learning curve. Upon entering the Troy Lock on the Hudson River (our first serious lock), we had our fenders positioned on both sides of the boat where we thought they would work best – one towards the bow, one about amidships, and a third near the stern. The amidships and stern fenders were placed just fine; however, the bow fender was not in its optimum position, so we hit the concrete lock wall with the bow rub-rail. We then noted where we bumped the wall with the rub-rail, and then placed a fender in that spot each time we entered a lock afterwards. This was a lesson well-learned because we never scraped the rub-rail again!

2. **Have your lines ready on both sides of the boat before entering the lock.** Where the lines should be placed will be discussed later when we describe the various types of locks.

3. **Have your life vests on before coming to the lock.** Many of the lock-masters require you to wear a life vest during the locking procedure. We have found that inflatable vests work well because they are not bulky and allow a great deal of freedom of movement. When purchasing such a life vest, be sure that they are Coast Guard approved. Also, be aware that some vests are designed to inflate automatically when a person enters the water, so they might also inflate in a heavy rain. That could be a funny, but not very pleasant experience for your boat's line handler (especially if it blows up quickly)!

Pat wearing her inflatable life vest during locking

4. **Have your boathooks ready.** In virtually every locking situation, you will use boathooks. It is a good idea as you approach a lock to have one boathook ready near the bow and one ready near the stern. You will be using them to grab lines hanging from the locks, to hook cables attached to lock walls, to place lines over bollards, and to keep your boat steady during the locking process.

5. **Have a very sharp knife ready.** We have never had to use ours; however, you will most definitely want to have a sharp knife close at hand to cut lines if the need arises. Here is what can happen: If a line securing your boat to the lock gets fouled while a lock is emptying, your boat can get hung up (literally) in the lock, causing considerable damage to your vessel. If the lock is filling, the fouled line will try to pull your boat under. If either of these situations should happen, do not try to free the line, just quickly *cut it!* This never happened to us or to anyone else we met on the Loop, but be prepared just in case.

6. **Put on your work gloves.** Lock walls, securing cables and pipes, lines provided by locks, and just about everything else associated with locks (except the lock operators) are covered in slime. We recommend that whoever is working the deck lines, before securing to a lock, put on a pair of inexpensive work gloves before entering the chamber. It will protect their hands and provide a more secure grip.

(There are toll charges on the New York Canal System, Parks Canada Waterways, and the St. Lawrence Seaway. Tolls can be paid at the first lock of the New York Canal System and Parks Canada Waterways for the entire transit of each system. Tolls on the St. Lawrence Seaway are paid at each lock. See the "Websites and Apps" chapter for information on how to contact each canal system for their toll charges.)

Locking Etiquette

Knowing the proper protocols for contacting the lock, entering the lock, securing to the lock, and exiting the lock will save you time and possibly some embarrassment. There are some general rules that apply to all locks, some that apply to Parks Canada locks, and others that apply to certain locks in the United States. We will look at all of them.

1. **Requesting passage through a Lock**

    When approaching a lock in the U. S., call the lock by name on VHF Channel 13 to let the lockmaster know that you want to pass through the lock. If you are on one of the river systems in the Midwest and Southern United States, you may also call on Channel 16. Frequently at these locks there will be a sign at the lock entrance with the VHF Channel displayed that the lockmaster is monitoring. Once the lock doors are fully open and a green traffic light is on, you may enter the lock. Do not enter until you get a green light.

    At Parks Canada locks, on the Rideau Canal call the lock by name on VHF channel 13 to let the lockmaster know you wish to enter the lock. On the Ottawa River and Chambly Canal, call the lock on VHF channel 68 to request permission to enter the lock. However, if you are on the Trent-Severn Waterway, things are done a bit differently when you request to pass through a lock. The lockmasters do not communicate via radio. Instead, they know that you want to enter their lock by either the fact that you have positioned your boat in front of the closed lock doors, or that they have spotted you tied up at the "Blue Line". At locks where there are traffic control lights, wait for a green light before entering the lock. If there is no traffic control light, enter the lock only when the doors are fully opened.

    The "Blue Line" is an area of a wall located outside a lock which is painted blue, and delineates a spot where several boats can tie up while waiting for the lock to open. Due to cutbacks in staff, one lockmaster may have to operate multiple locks, so wait times may be considerable at a particular lock. It is suggested that you tie up at the "Blue Line" to wait for the doors to open, and then follow the lockmaster's instructions that will be broadcast over a loudspeaker. See Illustration 1 on page II of the color insert. At all Parks Canada locks you may tie up at the "Blue Line" while waiting for the lock doors to open.

    To request passage through a St. Lawrence Seaway lock, tie your boat up at the small craft boat basin near the end of the lock. Climb up the steel staircase and call the lockmaster on the phone at the top of the stairs.

2. **Entering the Lock**

   Once you see a green light or have been instructed to enter the lock, proceed into the lock at idle speed only. If you have a choice, pick a side to secure your boat and go as far forward into the lock as possible; this will allow other boats to fill in behind you.

3. **Securing to the Lock**

   Do not rush to secure your boat to the lock. Remember, everyone else will be dealing with the same issues that you are in securing their vessel. Not only is this process not a race to see who can get ready first, rushing to secure your boat will leave you open to mishaps. The lockmaster does not care how long you take to get your boat ready for locking since he is going to be there all day. Always think safety first.

   Once secured to the lock, in the U. S. call the lockmaster on your VHF radio, identify your boat by name and let him know you are ready. In Canada, the lock master will watch you and can see when you are secured.

   Shut down your engine(s). Not all lockmasters require you to shut down your engine(s); however, since many do, we make it a practice to turn them off during the locking process.

4. **Leaving the Lock**

   Only leave the lock when the doors are fully opened. Some locks have an audible signal to let you know when you may leave the lock. If you leave too soon, you may get a scolding from the lockmaster!

   Exit at "Idle" speed. Do not pass other boats in the lock. The general rule is "First In, First Out", but there is an exception to this rule when locking with commercial traffic. As a matter of safety, all pleasure craft locking with commercial vessels leave the lock first.

New York State Canal System Locks

On America's Great Loop you will encounter three to four major lock systems: the New York State Canal System, the Parks Canada System, the Army Corps of Engineers Locks on the Midwest and Southern River Systems, and (depending on your route) the St. Lawrence Seaway. Each has its unique differences when locking. We will first discuss the locks on the New York State Canals that are on the Great Loop route. The canals you may travel are: the east and west branches of the Erie Canal, the Champlain Canal, and the Oswego Canal.

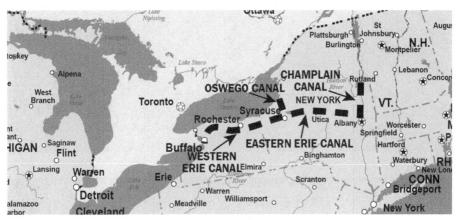

The New York State Great Loop Canals

There are three ways of securing your vessel to a lock in the New York State Canal System:

1. With weighted lines hanging from the lock wall

2. With pipes recessed in the lock wall

3. With rigid cables recessed in the lock wall

Most locks have hanging lines and either pipes or cables to secure your boat. The first illustration on the next page shows a lock wall with cables recessed in it, and the second with pipes.

Lock 2 – Erie Canal

Lock 12 – Champlain Canal

In order to secure your boat to a cable or pipe, the helmsman should bring the boat's amidships cleat alongside the recess. Whoever is working on the deck will now pass a line, which has already been attached to the cleat, around the cable or pipe, and will then secure it back to the same cleat. Be sure to leave some slack in the line because the line must slip its way up or down the cable or pipe, and you do not want to get it hung up.

Once secured to the lock wall, both of you (one near the bow and one near the stern) will use boathooks, or some other device of your choosing, to keep the boat relatively steady during the locking procedure.

When you are ready to leave the lock, release the top of the line from the cleat (leaving the bottom section still attached to the cleat), and pull the line back around the pipe or cable. You are now ready to exit the lock.

After you have done this a few times, it will become routine.

Usually locks will also have lines available for securing your vessel. They are at-tached from the top of the wall, and are hanging down using weights at the bottom to keep the lines in place.

Lock 17 – Erie Canal

To secure your boat using these lines, the helmsman should bring the boat's bow cleat alongside the line. Whoever is working on the deck will now bring the line and weight onboard using a boathook, and then cleat the line near the bow.

WARNING: Do not overreach with a boathook to retrieve a line! You can lose a boathook this way, or you can even be injured. Always allow the helmsman to bring the boat close to the line before attempting to retrieve it.

Once the line is secured, he or she will move to the stern area and retrieve a second line and weight and then cleat it there. Now when the helmsman comes on deck, each of you can take up a position at either the bow or stern where both lines can be released and re-attached as shown below.

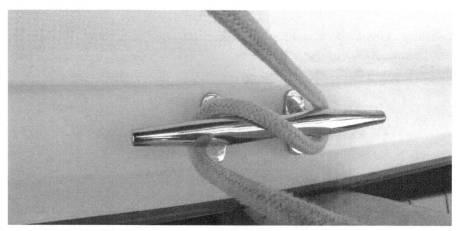

Holding the line in this manner will allow you to control the boat by taking in or letting out line as the boat moves up or down the lock wall, and there is little chance of fouling the line.

When you are ready to leave the lock, re-cleat both lines. Start your engine(s), then when ready, release the stern line first, followed by the bow line, and you are on your way again.

It is just that easy!

Parks Canada Locks (Trent-Severn Waterway, Rideau Canal, and Chambly Canal)

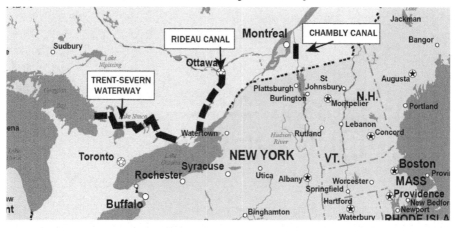

Parks Canada Great Loop Canals

Securing your vessel to the locks of Parks Canada differs from the New York Canal System locks as follows: The majority of the locks on the Trent-Severn Waterway and Rideau Canal have covered cables hanging from inside the lock wall which are attached at both the top and bottom. Because the cables are not rigidly mounted like the ones in New York, they have a considerable amount of fore and aft flex.

To secure to these locks, lines are first attached to the bow cleat and the stern cleat. The helmsman now positions the boat's bow cleat near a cable. Using a boathook (and not overreaching), the cable is hooked and the bow line is looped around it, and then it is secured to the bow cleat. The process is now repeated in the stern, leaving some slack in the lines, so that the lines can easily slip along the cables during the locking procedure.

When you are ready to leave the lock, release the top of the stern line from the cleat (leaving the bottom section still attached to the cleat), and pull the line back around the cable. Repeat the process in the bow, and you are on your way.

Kingston Mills Lock 47 – Rideau Canal

On the Chambly Canal, you will be handed lines from the lock tenders to secure your boat.

Lock tender waiting to hand off a line at Lock 3 – Chambly Canal

There are two unique types of locks on the Trent-Severn Waterway: the Peterborough and Kirkfield Hydraulic Lift Locks and the Big Chute Marine Railway. Each is a unique locking experience.

When approaching one of the hydraulic lift locks, have an amidships and a stern line secured to a cleat on both sides of the boat. You will enter what is called a "pan". Once in the "pan", you will secure the amidships line to a horizontal rail and then snug it up leaving *no* slack. If possible, attach a second line around the rail to another cleat near the stern. The lockmaster will raise the gate behind you, sealing in the water and your boat. The pan, the water, and your boat will all move as one, as if you are in an elevator to the next water level.

Once you are at the new level, the gate in front of your boat will be lowered. Wait for the lockmaster to instruct you as to when you may leave the "pan". Now simply slip your lines from the horizontal rail and exit the lock.

The Peterborough Hydraulic Lift Lock

The gate is raised and locked behind us

Room for only two boats on this lift

"Reflection" is secured tight to the lock

Looking astern after the lift

Looking ahead while waiting for the gate to be lowered

The gate is being lowered and soon we will be on our way

The next unique lock on the Trent-Severn Waterway is the Big Chute Marine Railway. The way this lock operates is that your boat, possibly along with several others, will be loaded onto a massive submerged railway apparatus. Using hydraulic rams and straps to hold the boat steady, your vessel will be taken for a ride up a hill, then down the other side. The apparatus will submerge once more, and you will float away.

There are some things you will want to do to prepare your boat for this ride. First, you will want to know the fore and aft position of your propeller(s) from a fixed mark on your deck. For example, on *Reflection* there is a cleat located on each side of our boat near the stern that marks the aft most location of the propellers. You will want to know this because, depending on the size of your boat, the Big Chute operators may want to hang the aft section of your boat, including the propellers, off the end of the apparatus. Also, they will want to know if your boat has a keel and, if so, whether the propellers sit above or below it. Believe us, the operators are extremely professional, and they make every effort to ensure the safety of your boat.

Since your boat will be coming out of the water, all your seawater connections will drain. To prevent problems with your air conditioning pumps loosing prime, it is advisable to close their seacocks ahead of time.

The procedure for passing through Big Chute is as follows:

1. Wait at the blue line to be called to approach the submerged apparatus. (Vessels will not necessarily be called in order of arrival, but in order of how best they will fit on the apparatus.) You will not need any lines for this locking.

2. Follow the instructions of the Big Chute operators. They will let you know when your vessel is secured, and when you can shut down your engine(s).

3. Get your camera ready, find a good viewing spot on your boat, and go for a ride!

4. Once the apparatus begins to submerge on the other side of the hill, you will be instructed when to start your engine(s) by the operator. You then just pull away!

The Big Chute Marine Railway – boats heading southbound

The carriage about to be submerged

Getting ready for another load of boats

Our turn to go for a ride

Of all the locks on the Trent-Severn Waterway – the Peterborough and Kirkfield Hydraulic Lift Locks and the Big Chute Marine Railway – are by far the most memorable and the most fun to pass through.

Federal Locks (those run by the Army Corps of Engineers)

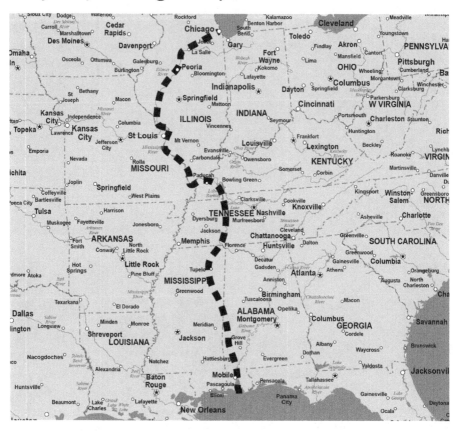

The majority of the Federal Locks on the Great Loop are located on the run from Chicago to Mobile

The federal locks are quite different than those on the New York State Canal System or the Parks Canada Waterways, and in comparison they are massive in size. You will also encounter a considerable amount of commercial traffic, and you may experience substantial wait times at the locks.

Vessel Priority at Federal Locks

These wait times are in direct relationship to the vessel transit priority system that has been set up by the Army Corps of Engineers. Military vessels always have the highest priority when passing through locks, and next in priority are commercial passenger vessels. On our Great Loop, journey we did not encounter either of those types of vessels; however, we did come upon many commercial cargo vessels, especially towboats pushing lines of barges, which are third in the priority hierarchy. Unfortunately, the rest of us all fall into the lowest priority category, pleasure craft or PCs, which are what we are called by both towboat captains and lockmasters.

The Wilson Lock on the Tennessee River – it takes approximately 35,000,000 gallons of water to raise vessels about 95 feet in a matter of minutes. IMPRESSIVE!

Reducing Your Wait Time at Federal Locks

Because of our low status among vessels, you may be asked to wait, sometimes for hours, to pass through a particular lock. However, there is some possible negotiating that you can do to get you through a lock faster, and/or a procedure to use that will at least give you some advanced warning so that you will not be holding in place with your engine(s) and wasting fuel in front of a lock while you are waiting.

When you are starting your day, call the first lock through which you want to pass on the phone (Your guidebooks have all the numbers, or you can get them from the internet.) and ask the lockmaster if he is expecting any commercial traffic, and, if so, at what time. Based on his answer, you may want to stay where you are for a while or get ready to move swiftly to the lock.

A similar strategy is that once you have passed through a lock, call the next lock and find out what conditions are at that lock so you can adjust your speed accordingly. If, for example, the lockmaster tells you, "If you can be here in an hour, I can get you through.", but you are not really sure that you can make it on time, tell him that you will be there anyway. Then proceed as fast and as safely as you can. If you find that are going to be late, call the lockmaster and tell him, "I will be there in a few minutes. Will you hold the lock?" They usually will.

If you pass a towboat heading in the same direction that you are, it is going to have priority over you at the next lock, even though you will arrive at the lock first. If you are still several miles away from the lock, call the towboat captain on VHF 13 and ask if he would allow you to go through the lock first. If he agrees, head to the lock as fast and safely as you can to get some distance between the two of you. When you have reached the lock, call the lockmaster and tell him that you have already spoken to the towboat captain (giving him the name of the towboat) and that the captain said it was alright for you to pass through the lock ahead of him. The lockmaster will call the towboat captain to confirm your story, and you will then be allowed through the lock.

If you arrive at a lock and a towboat is waiting to enter with a line of barges that is less than three barges wide, and it is not carrying explosive material (red flag cargo), call the lockmaster and ask if you can pass through the lock with the towboat. The lockmaster will contact the towboat captain to ask for his "Okay!", and then he will then let you know if you can lock through with the commercial traffic. We were always given permission.

The towboat and barges will enter the lock first. Wait for instructions from the lockmaster to tell you when you will be allowed to enter the lock and where in the lock to secure your boat.

Here, when leaving the lock, the "First in, First out" rule does not apply. All pleasure craft will leave the lock first; then the towboat and barges will leave.

Caution: If you are invited to a lock with a short tow that is three barges wide, where you will be placed in the back of the lock with the towboat, wait for the next locking. If you are locking through with a towboat that will be pushing barges ahead of you, the wash from the tow while in the lock can be overwhelming and cause your boat slam against the lock wall.

The Army Corps of Engineers has established the Federal Lock Status and Wait Time Website – *corpslocks.usace.army.mil*. Although this website is useful, we prefer to speak directly to a lockmaster to get the latest lock status.

Securing Your Boat to the Federal Locks between Chicago and Mobile

Although the size of these locks may seem daunting, it is relatively easy to secure your boat to them. Have a line secured at the amidships cleat before entering the lock. Once you are inside the lock, the helmsman should bring the boat's amidships cleat alongside a floating bollard. Whoever is working the deck lines uses a boathook to loop the line over the floating bollard and then secures the line back to the same cleat with some slack in it to allow the boat to move up or down the wall freely. When the water level changes, the floating bollard will move up or down with you.

When you are ready to leave the lock, release the top of the line (leaving the bottom of it secured to your cleat), then pull the line back around and off the floating bollard. You are now ready to exit the lock.

Floating Bollard

Special Locking Etiquette on the Illinois River System

When traveling through locks on the Illinois River System, you are expected to ask the lockmaster for permission to secure your boat to a floating bollard, even though we were always given permission to do so. If all floating bollards are occupied, the lockmaster will lower lines for you to use. On all other river systems it is simply assumed that you will secure your boat to a floating bollard.

The first lock on the Illinois river system south of Chicago, the Thomas J. O'Brien Lock, has no floating bollards because of its short drop. There you will secure your vessel to a fixed bollard at the top of the lock wall. If you are the only boat in the lock, the lockmaster may tell you, "Float in the middle." This means that he wants you to keep your boat in the center of the lock, using your engine(s) to do so during the entire locking process.

St. Lawrence Seaway Locks

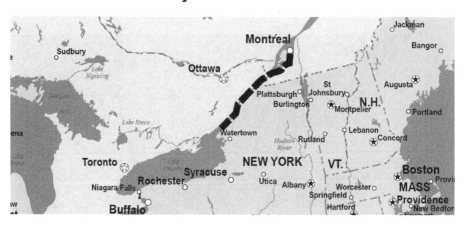

St. Lawrence Seaway Locks

The U. S. locks are similar to the Federal Locks on the rivers: commercial traffic has priority over pleasure craft, and vessels are secured to the locks using floating bollards. At the Canadian locks the lock tender will lower lines for you to secure your boat.

Chapter 12

Negotiating the Variety of Waterways

Atlantic Intracoastal Waterway – Fort Lauderdale, Florida

As you journey along America's Great Loop, you will travel through a wide variety of water passages including: the winding intracoastal waterways along the east coast of the United States and the west coast of Florida, the sometimes narrow, but always scenic Parks Canada Waterways, and the mighty rivers of America's Midwest. All of them have their own unique differences and challenges. What we want to accomplish in this section of the book is to supplement the information in your guidebooks by highlighting some of the more notable features on each body of water; for example, recurring problem areas on the Atlantic Intracoastal Waterway, passages on the Erie Canal that must be completed in one travel day, areas of the Trent-Severn Waterway that require a security (pronounced 'say-cure-ee-tay') call, obstructions on the Mississippi River, and many more.

The Atlantic Intracoastal Waterway (AICW)

While traveling America's Great Loop, you will pass through some of the most historic and beautiful waterways and rivers in North America. The longest of these on this trip is the AICW which extends for over 1,200 miles from Key West, Florida, to Norfolk, Virginia.

This waterway is made up of natural inlets, saltwater rivers, bays, sounds, and artificial canals. The original route began in Manasquan, New Jersey, and went south through what is now known as the New Jersey Intracoastal Waterway (NJI-CW), through the Cape May Canal, then north up the Delaware Bay and River, through the Chesapeake and Delaware Canal, then south on Chesapeake Bay to the Elizabeth River in Norfolk, Virginia, where the current AICW now begins.

The idea for an inland waterway began in 1787, when a national policy was established for the development of coastal rivers and inland waters for transportation use. In 1808, when the first federal government report on possible routes along the Atlantic Coast that were deemed worthy of improvement for transportation was presented to Congress, it included much of what is now the ACIW. Then, at the request of the Senate, an overall plan was written for future transportation developments of national importance and scope.

During the War of 1812, the effect of a British blockade showed the continued need for such a waterway in order to provide a secure route for transportation along the coast. Since the original plan for the waterway was based on routes with known advantageous natural geographic features, many of these proposed locations were authorized for improvement starting with the 1824 General Survey Act.

However, following the Civil War, development of the waterway system fell out of favor with government funding instead moving toward railroads. Eventually in 1882 and 1884, Congress passed the Rivers and Harbors Appropriations Acts and again decided to improve the waterways to stimulate competition among transportation modes.

In 1909, the Rivers and Harbors Act laid out a national policy for an Intracoastal Waterway that was proposed to run from Boston to the Rio Grande, and between 1910 and 1914, channels were indeed widened and deepened. Following this period, Congress then decided to incorporate the Inland Waterways Corporation, and this became the first legislation to treat the ICW as a continuous waterway.

During World War II, with the threat of German submarines stalking merchant ships along the east coast of the United States, the need for a safe route to transport materials became vital for national security. This prompted the government to pass legislation to maintain the Waterway at a minimum depth of 12 feet for much of its length. Unfortunately today, due to funding cutbacks, many areas of the waterway have not been maintained, and are greatly in need of maintenance dredging.

Despite that, it is still possible to carefully travel its full length without many of the hazards of the open sea. Although today's Waterway is used mostly by recreational boaters, there is still a good deal of commercial activity along its route with barges hauling petroleum products, rock and sand, and a wide assortment of manufactured goods.

Atlantic Intracoastal Waterway, Great Bridge, Virginia

Because of the lack of dredging, many areas of the waterway now have mean low water depths of 4 feet or less. Although these problem areas are constantly changing, we will point out some of the most common offenders. To find the latest on AICW problem areas, go to: the *Waterway Guide* website at waterwayguide.com/waterway-updates/nav, the *Salty Southeast Cruiser's Net* at cruisersnet.net and click the "AICW PROBS." on the top of the page, or visit the *ActiveCaptain* website at: activecaptain.com/index.php and click on: "The ActiveCaptain Companion" at the top of the page.

When looking at charts of any of the intracoastal waterways, you will observe a magenta-colored line that will define the waterway's route. In theory, it will mark the deepest water; however, as stated earlier in this book, following it exactly can lead you into trouble! (See Illustration 2 on page II of the color insert for an example of the Magenta Line and the Intracoastal Waterway Mile Markers)

We will point out some of the most notable areas where you must be cautious on the AICW; however, there is no substitute for your own personal observations as you travel its waters. Buoys are often moved, especially near inlets. As an additional aid to you, we have included the NOAA tide chart references that we feel most closely correspond to each problem area where depths may be of concern. Before using any of these tide charts, verify to your satisfaction that they correspond to the particular problem area. The waterway is in a constant state of change, so stay vigilant!

The AICW has its own unique rules for marking its route. The mainland side of the waterway is marked with red placard triangles mounted on poles or red buoys, each with yellow triangles on them signifying that they are intracoastal waterway markers. The Atlantic Ocean side of the waterway is marked with green placard squares or green buoys, each with yellow squares on them. (See Illustration 3 on page III of the color insert.)

There are, however, some exceptions to this rule. Where there is a major navigation channel that is shared with the Intracoastal Waterway, such as the Cape Fear River in North Carolina, the "Red on the right when returning from the sea" rule is observed, which may reverse the marker colors. In this case, look for the small yellow triangles or squares on the markers to identify the waterway. (See Illustration 4 on page III of the color insert.)

Besides these areas of concern, we have also included some of the anchorages we have personally used along the AICW. Be sure to check with your guidebooks for more details on each anchorage as well as on the many additional anchorages that can be used on this section of the Loop.

Please note that when you are traveling on any inland waters, if your boat is equipped with a holding tank with an overboard discharge, be sure that the valve between the holding tank and the discharge pump is always in the closed position. If you should be boarded for an inspection, especially by local law enforcement, one of the first things they will want to see is the holding tank shut-off valve. If it is found to be open, you can expect a heavy fine.

Key West to Biscayne Bay, Florida – Mile Marker 1241.5 to 1095

Since most " Loopers" travel from south to north, we will begin our journey up the waterway from Key West, Florida, to Norfolk, Virginia, noting some of the most well-known problem areas, as well as some of our favorite anchorages along the way.

Heading north from Key West, the most direct route on the waterway travels up Hawk Channel which is well-marked, wide, and deep, and is located on the Atlantic side of the island chain. After traveling for just over 40 miles, the waterway now enters Moser Channel where it crosses under the Seven Mile Bridge near Marathon, Florida, to the Gulf of Mexico side of the Keys, and then enters Florida Bay.

Be extremely careful since the entire waterway from Key West through Biscayne Bay is located in an environmentally-sensitive marine area, so going aground here can become very costly, not just with towing fees but with fines that can run into the thousands of dollars for disturbing sea grass beds or coral. If you should go aground in the channel, the officials are usually lenient with the fines. However, if you happen to go aground outside of the channel, your fines can be severe!

Dolphins following "Reflection" north in Florida Bay

In between Marathon and Biscayne Bay there are areas where the waterway is relatively wide and deep with markers that are widely-spaced, but where the channel becomes narrow there are numerous markers to guide you safely through the area. In this stretch of the waterway, low water depths can run between 5 to 6 feet in places. Our boat, *Reflection*, draws 4 feet of water, and we have never had a problem going through this area. The tides along this section of the Loop vary from about 1 to 2.5 feet with light current. Also, be on the lookout for numerous crab and lobster trap floats throughout the Florida Keys portion of the AICW.

Anchorages

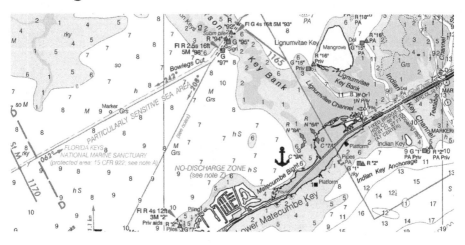

Matecumbe Bight Anchorage

We have three favorite anchorages between Marathon and Biscayne Bay. The first is between Mile Mark 1170 and 1165, and is known as Matecumbe Bight. There is good holding here and wind protection from east to south.

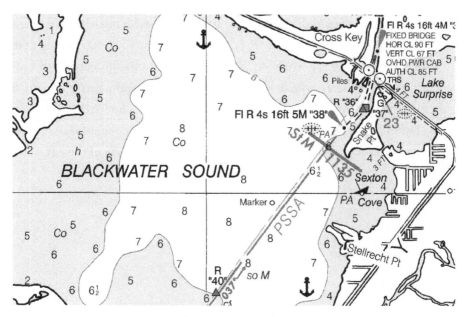

Blackwater Sound Anchorages

The next two anchorages are near Mile Marker 1135 in Blackwater Sound. Both have good holding. The northern anchorage has good wind protection from the north to the northeast, and the southern anchorage has good wind protection from the east to southeast.

Consult your guidebooks for additional anchorages along this section of the waterway.

Biscayne Bay to North Palm Beach, Florida – Mile Marker 1095 to 1010

Biscayne Bay (Mile Marker 1010) to North Palm Beach is a distance of approximately 85 miles. The waterway in this section is relatively easy to follow with good depths in all but one area. You will pass some of the most luxurious and expensive homes in the U. S. and some of the largest private yachts you may ever see. Along this route, you will encounter many "No Wake" zones and numerous bridges; the lowest fixed bridge is in the Miami area with a clearance of 56 feet. The many drawbridges along the waterway, with few exceptions, all have scheduled openings. Your guidebooks will provide you with the name, location, and opening schedule of each bridge.

Tides between Biscayne Bay to North Palm Beach, Florida run between 2.5 to 3 feet with a light current.

The AICW through Miami

Problem Area

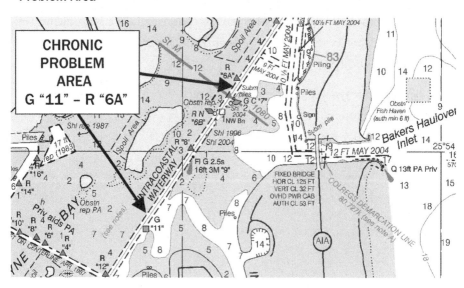

AICW/Bakers Haulover Inlet Intersection

In the North Miami part of the waterway, there is one chronic trouble spot near mile marker 1080, close to Bakers Haulover Inlet. Sandbars tend to build up on the inlet side of the waterway (the "Green" side), and buoys are often relocated to mark the best water. For the tide chart we use in this area, go to: co-ops.nos.noaa. gov/tide_predictions.html, click on: "Florida" in the left column, and then on the next page click: on "Bakers Haulover Inlet (inside)" to find the tide predictions.

Anchorages

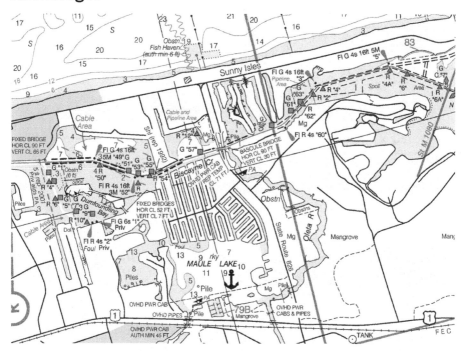

Maule Lake Anchorage

We have two favorite anchorages along this area of the waterway. The first is near mile marker 1078 in "Maule Lake", which has good holding and good wind protection from all directions.

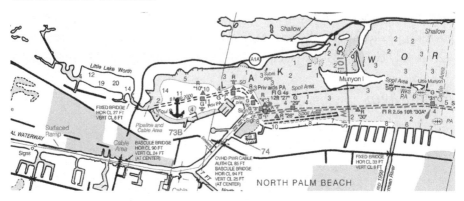

Lake Worth Anchorage

The second is just north of mile marker 1015 in Lake Worth, with good holding and good wind protection from all directions except southeast to southwest.

Consult your guidebooks for additional anchorages along this section of the waterway.

North Palm Beach to Fernandina Beach, Florida – Mile Marker 1010 to 715

In the approximately 300 miles from North Palm Beach to Fernandina Beach, Florida, the waterway becomes more rural. It is well-marked, relatively deep for cruising boats, and the number of drawbridges on opening schedules is greatly reduced.

As you travel north tide levels range from 3 feet near North Palm Beach to 7 feet near Fernandina Beach with current speeds increasing as you travel north.

Island off the AICW – Florida

Jupiter Inlet Lighthouse

Problem Areas

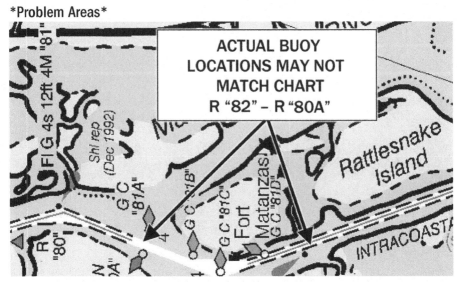

Matanzas Inlet

There are two problem areas: one south of Saint Augustine, and one at Saint Augustine Inlet where you will want to pay close attention to the markers. The first is near Mile Marker 793, just north of Red "82" near Matanzas Inlet. Here, the channel has moved so far to the west that your GPS may show your vessel traveling over land! Be sure to follow the buoys and not your chart!

The second area to watch out for is at Saint Augustine Inlet itself. Many of the charts and chart plotters show the magenta line passing west of Red "60". Be sure to round it on its east side, leaving it to port as you head north. (See Illustration 5 on page IV of the color insert)

Anchorages

We have four anchorages in this section of the waterway that we like. Three of them are located in the Titusville area near the Kennedy Space Center, and one is about 18 miles north of Saint Augustine.

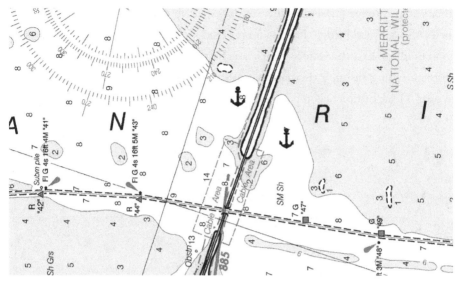

NASA Parkway Anchorages

The first two anchorages are near Mile Marker 885, and each has good holding. For protection from northerly winds, exit the waterway just north of marker G "47", head east, and then anchor near the NASA Parkway. For protection from southerly winds, exit the waterway at marker R "44", head east and then south, and anchor near the NASA Parkway.

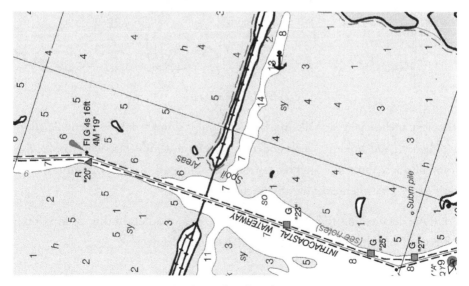

NASA Railroad Anchorage

The next anchorage that is a favorite of ours is at Mile Marker 876.5, just south of the NASA railroad bridge. It provides protection from the northwest to east with good holding. Exit the waterway just south of the bridge, and head east along the railroad. Going through the narrow unmarked entrance; water depths can drop to near 5 feet, but once you get inside you will be able to anchor in 13 to 14 feet of water.

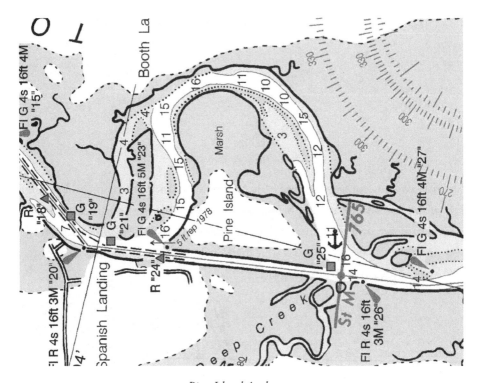

Pine Island Anchorage

The next anchorage is at Mile Marker 765, and is known as Pine Island Anchorage. It has good holding with moderate current and moderate wind protection from all sides. Enter the anchorage from the south off of R "26", and stay well clear of G "25" when entering this anchorage.

For more detailed information on this anchorage and others in this section of the waterway, consult your guidebooks or activecaptain.com.

Fernandina Beach, Florida to Savannah, Georgia – Mile Marker 715 to 575

This section of the waterway winds through the vast marsh lands of Georgia, with only one drawbridge at a height of 25 feet along its route. Unfortunately, it also has only a few good anchorages, a sparse amount of marinas, and some of the most problematic areas along the AICW. Tides can run from 7 to 10 feet or more on the Georgia section of the AICW, resulting in some strong currents when the tide is changing.

It also has a reversal of waterway marker colors when you pass through the Saint Marys River as you enter Georgia. After passing buoy R "2" at Mile Marker 714.5, the waterway markers reverse color, starting with buoys R "24" and G "25", and they stay reversed to Kings Bay Navy Base at buoy R "44A". (See Illustration 4 on page III of the color insert.)

Range markers along the Georgia AICW

Problem Areas

The first problem area in Georgia comes at Mile Marker 704, at Cumberland Dividings, where the "Magenta Line" takes you on the wrong side of Markers R "60A" and R "60". In addition, shoaling of the waterway is often reported in this section. Be sure to get the latest updates on this area, and follow the markers, not the "Magenta Line." (See Illustration 6 on page IV of the color insert) For the tide chart that we use in this area go to: co-ops.nos.noaa.gov/tide_predictions. html, click on: "Georgia" in the left column, and then on the next page click on: "Crooked River, Cumberland Dividings" to find the tide predictions we use.

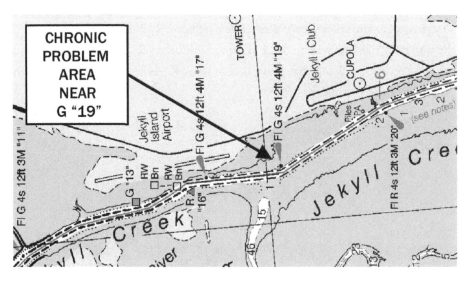

Jekyll Creek

The next area to watch out for is in Jekyll Creek by R "19" near Mile Marker 683. This again is a chronic area where shoaling occurs, so be sure to get the latest information on its condition before passing through this location. For the tide chart that we use in this area go to: co-ops.nos.noaa.gov/tide_predictions.html, click on "Georgia" in the left column, and then on the next page click on "Jekyll Island Marina, Jekyll Creek" to find the tide predictions.

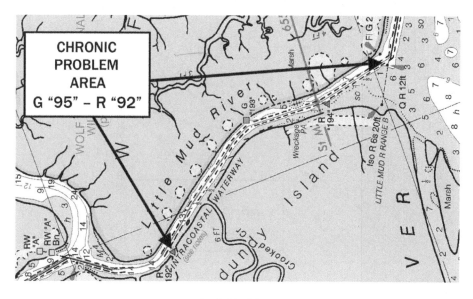

Little Mud River

After Jekyll Creek, be careful passing through Little Mud River at Mile Marker 655. This section of the AICW, particularly the section just north of the waterway's intersection with Altamaha Sound, is frequently considered the worst area of the entire AICW. Before transiting this area, get the latest information on its condition through the Salty Southeast Cruisers' Net, ActiveCaptain, or some other source. For the tide chart we use in this area go to: co-ops.nos.noaa.gov/tide_predictions.html, click on "Georgia" in the left column, and then on the next page click on "Wolf Island, south end" to find the tide predictions.

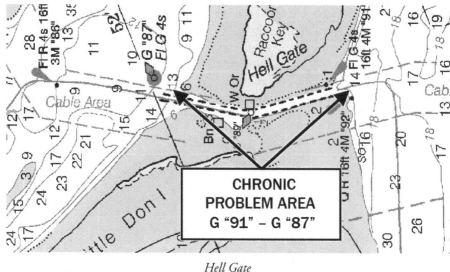

Hell Gate

The next and final trouble spot in Georgia is Hell Gate at Mile Marker 602. This again is an area where shoaling is a constant problem. Have the latest updates on this section of the waterway before proceeding through it. For the tide chart that we use in this area go to co-ops.nos.noaa.gov/tide_predictions.html, click on: "Georgia" in the left column, and then on the next page click on: "Egg Islands" to find the tide predictions.

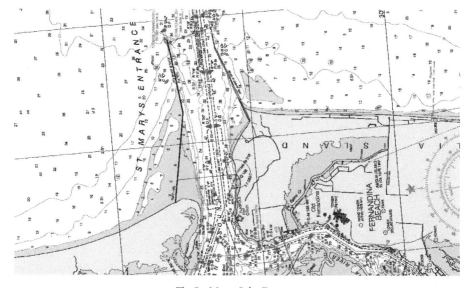

The St. Marys Inlet Entrance

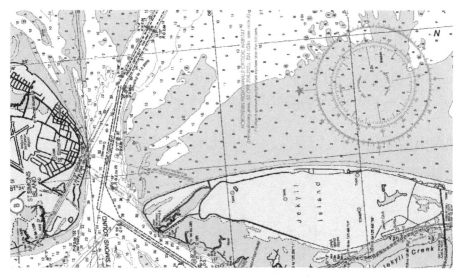

Saint Simons Sound

Because of the numerous trouble spots in the Georgia AICW, if the weather is favorable, you can take the ocean route from Saint Marys Entrance/Cumberland Sound near Mile Marker 714 on the AICW to Saint Simons Sound near Mile Marker 678 on the AICW. The ocean route is 8 miles longer; however, you will bypass two recurring problem areas on the waterway at Cumberland Dividings and again at Jekyll Creek. We prefer to take this outside route whenever the weather is favorable for us to do so.

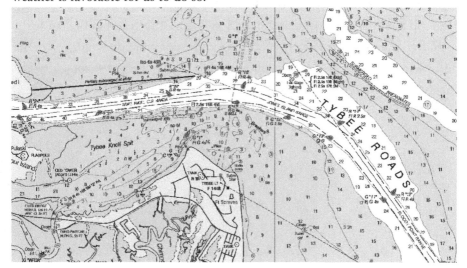

Tybee Roads (Entrance to the Savannah River)

If the weather continues to be favorable, you can then again take the ocean route from Saint Simons Sound to Tybee Roads (Savannah River) and reenter the Waterway near mile marker 575. The ocean route is approximately 98 statute miles long compared to the 103 mile trip on the AICW, plus you will eliminate two of the worst trouble spots on the AICW at Little Mud River and Hell Gate.

Anchorage

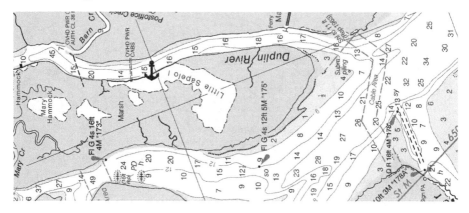

Duplin River Anchorage

There is only one anchorage along the Georgia AICW that we can personally recommend. It is located on the Duplin River just past Mile Marker 650. The holding is very good; however, the current can be strong when the tide is changing. Head up the unmarked river, anchoring just south of the overhead cables in 14 to 16 feet of water. There is very good wind protection from the southwest to the northwest, as well as good protection in the remaining directions. For additional anchorages, consult your guidebooks or activecaptain.com.

Savannah, Georgia to the South Carolina – North Carolina Border – Mile Marker to 757 to 342

This section of the waterway runs through the "Low Country" of South Carolina, passing through vast marshes and scenic tree-lined rivers. Bridges are fixed at 65 feet, or they open on signal. The waterway for the most part is deep and is well-marked; however, there are several problem spots here also that require your attention. Tides run from 10 feet near Georgia to about 3 feet as you near North Carolina.

Waccamaw River in the South Carolina Low Country

Problem Areas

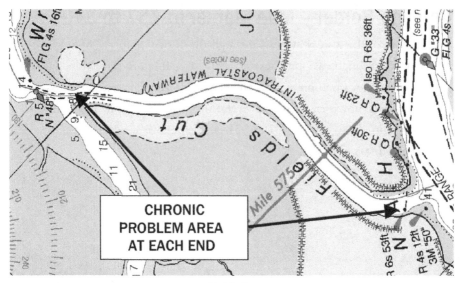

Fields Cut

The first of these is in Fields Cut just north of the Savannah River at Mile Marker 575. Shoaling is frequently a problem on the southeast side of the waterway as you enter the Cut from the Savannah River. The Cut is in the shape of a curve, and like many other areas of the waterway, where it curves the deepest water is usually found on the outside of the curve. Fields Cut is no exception.

The northern end of Fields Cut, where it intersects with the Wright River at Mile Marker 574, is also a chronic problem area with frequent shoaling. Do not enter Fields Cut without the latest information on its condition. For the tide chart that we use for Fields Cut go to: co-ops.nos.noaa.gov/tide_predictions.html, click on "South Carolina" in the left column, and then on the next page click on "Fields Cut, Wright River" to find the tide predictions.

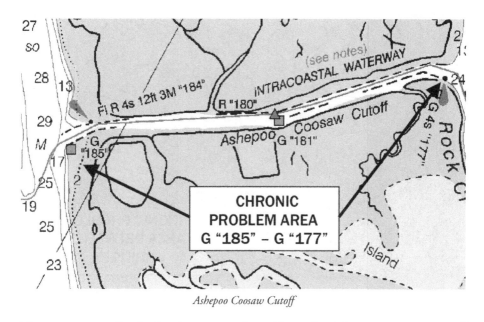

Ashepoo Coosaw Cutoff

The next area in South Carolina to watch out for is the Ashepoo Coosaw Cutoff into the Coosaw River at Mile Marker 517. Here shoaling continues to reoccur generally between G "185" to G "177". For the tide chart we use for this area, go to: co-ops.nos.noaa.gov/tide_predictions.html, click on "South Carolina" in the left column, and then on the next page click on "Ashepoo-Coosaw Cutoff, ICWW" to find the tide predictions.

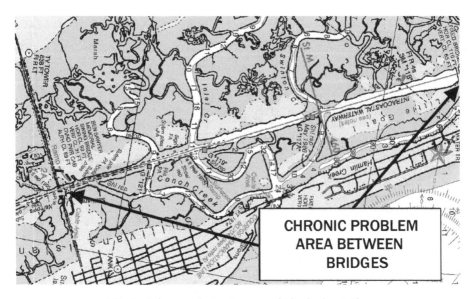

The AICW between the Ben Sawyer and Isle of Palms Bridges

After this area the next one of concern is a few miles north of Charleston at Mile Marker 460 between the Ben Sawyer and Isle of Palms Bridges. This area of the waterway tends to shoal along its southern and southeastern flank. For the tide chart we use for this area, go to: co-ops.nos.noaa.gov/tide_predictions.html, click on "South Carolina" in the left column, and then on the next page click on "Hamlin Creek, Isle of Palms" to find the tide predictions.

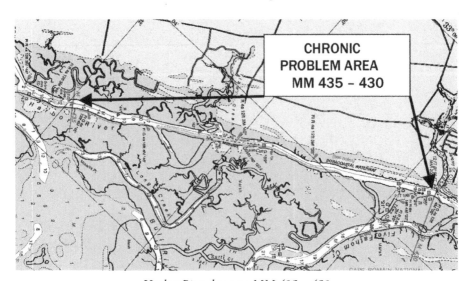

Harbor River between MM 435 – 450

The next problem spot in South Carolina is 25 miles north, starting at Mile Marker 435 near Awendaw Creek on the Harbor River and continuing to Mile Marker 430 at the intersection with Jeremy Creek and McClellanville. Travel this section of the AICW with maximum caution, stay in the middle of the channel, and do not cut corners. For the tide chart that we use for this area, go to: co-ops.nos. noaa.gov/tide_predictions.html, click on "South Carolina" in the left column, and then on the next page click on "McClellanville, Jeremy Creek" to find the tide predictions.

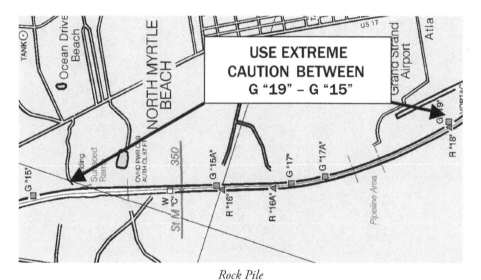

Rock Pile

The last area of concern in this section of the waterway is the "Rock Pile" in the Myrtle Beach area of South Carolina. Shoaling is not the issue here. This was the last section of the AICW to be built, and it was cut through solid rock where at low tide the rock edges can be clearly seen. As work proceeded, the Army Corps of Engineers apparently got tired of blasting their way through, so as a result the last section that they built between Mile Marker 352 and 349 is very narrow. Before entering the "Rock Pile", call a security warning on VHF Channel 13 and 16 and announce that you are heading northbound, entering the "Rock Pile", and asking all concerned traffic to respond. Believe us, you do not want to meet a southbound tug pushing a barge in this area! You will not be able to pass, and turning around will be difficult, if not impossible.

While on our Great Loop trip, we let another cruising boat pass us in the "Rock Pile". Unfortunately, in doing so, we went too far to the starboard side of the channel and "touched" the rock ledge. As a result we bent our starboard propeller and shaft, so learn from our mistake and STAY IN THE MIDDLE!

Before passing through these problem areas in South Carolina be sure to get the latest information on their condition.

Anchorages

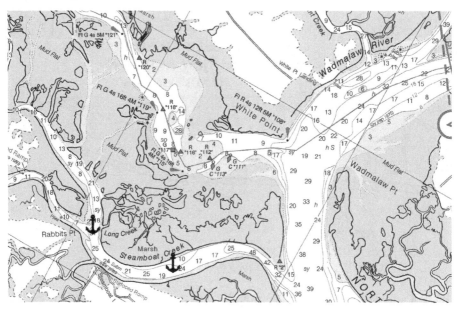

Steamboat Creek Anchorage

There are three anchorages we have used in this area of the waterway. The first is Steamboat Creek off the North Edisto River near Mile Marker 496.5. It has good holding with moderate current, and although the surrounding land is marsh, the protection from wind-driven waves is good. There is plenty of room for several boats to anchor well up the creek.

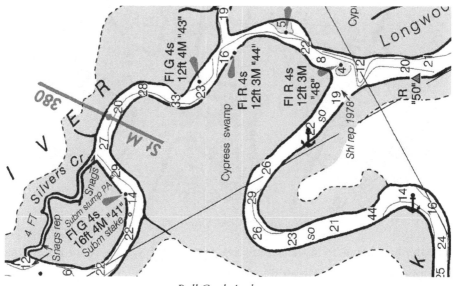

Bull Creek Anchorage

The next anchorage is in Bull Creek near Mile Marker 397. Here again, the holding is good with light current. The area is wooded resulting in very good wind protection, and like Steamboat Creek, there is room for several boats.

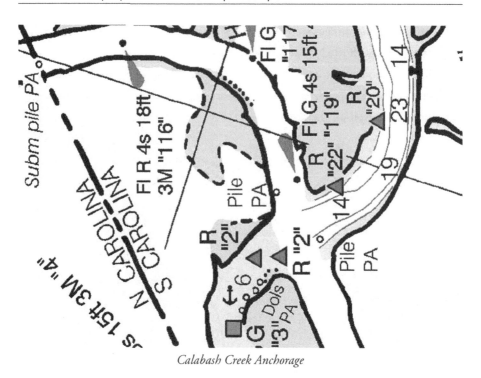

Calabash Creek Anchorage

The third anchorage is in Calabash Creek at the South Carolina/North Carolina border across from Little River Inlet near Mile Marker 342. Holding is good with moderate current, and there is wind protection from the north, west, and south. There is room for only a few boats in about 7 feet of water, and it is a bit tight for boats over 40 feet in length.

Check your guidebooks or ActiveCaptain for more anchorages in this section of the AICW and for more information on the three mentioned above.

North Carolina to Norfolk, Virginia – Mile Marker 342 to 0

This section of the waterway, like most of the AICW, is well-marked and is relatively easy to navigate. Much of it travels through low marshlands and past thousands of homes set on high ground with long straight docks ending on the waterway. In traveling through this area, be mindful of the numerous "No Wake" zones that pop up along the populated areas along the route.

You will pass through some wide bodies of water along the way including: the Cape Fear River (where the Marker colors will reverse) and the Neuse River. Then you will cross the Pamlico River, travel through the Pungo River (where once again Marker colors will reverse), pass through the Alligator River, and finally cross Albemarle Sound where the waterway splits, with one way heading toward the Virginia Cut main route and the other heading to the Dismal Swamp.

Most of the drawbridges along this section of the Waterway are on schedules. Tides vary widely from 3 feet near the Little River Inlet at Mile Marker 342, to 6 feet in the Cape Fear River at Mile Marker 308, to 0 feet near Coinjock, North Carolina, at Mile Marker 50, and then to 3.5 feet at Norfolk, Virginia, at Mile Marker 0. Check your guidebooks for bridge locations and schedules.

Problem Areas

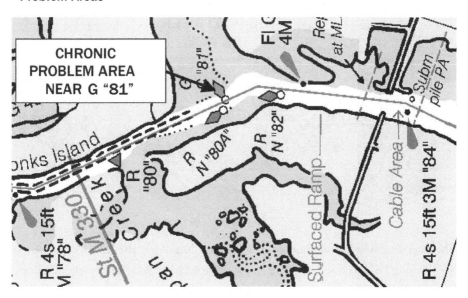

AICW/Shallotte Inlet

In this part of the waterway, there are some areas that we would like to bring to your attention. The first is at the Intersection of the AICW and Shallotte Inlet near Mile Marker 330. The area near G"81" frequently shoals. When transiting past this inlet or any other inlet in North Carolina, you will generally find more water on the mainland (red) side of the waterway. Also be on the lookout for additional buoys or buoys that have been moved and follow them, not the Magenta Line. For the tide chart that we use for this area go to: co-ops.nos.noaa.gov/ tide_predictions.html, click on "North Carolina" in the left column, and then on the next page click on "Shallotte Inlet (Bowen Point)" to find the tide predictions.

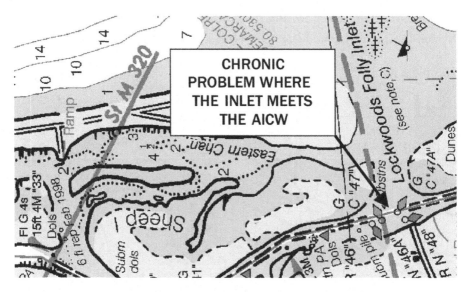

AICW/Lockwoods Folly Inlet

The next area where you should be mindful is located at the intersection of the AICW and Lockwoods Folly Inlet near Mile Marker 321. Here, like Shallotte Inlet, the waterway frequently shoals on the ocean side of the channel, and, once again, the deeper water is usually found on the mainland side. Buoys here are also sometimes moved, differing from the charted course. For the tide chart that we use for this area go to: co-ops.nos.noaa.gov/tide_predictions.html, click on "North Carolina" in the left column, and then on the next page click on "Lockwoods Folly Inlet" to find the tide predictions.

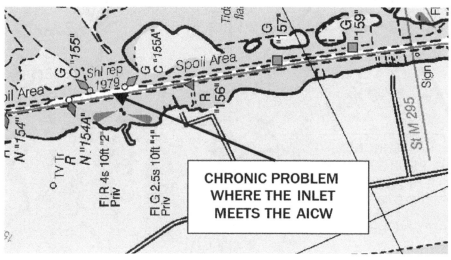

AICW/Carolina Beach Inlet

The next problem area is at the junction of another inlet at Carolina Beach near Mile Marker 293.5. Here, as we've mentioned earlier, shoaling is often reported on the eastern side of the waterway. Again, the deeper water is usually found on the western side of the waterway near the red markers, and the buoys are frequently moved to mark the best channel. For the tide chart that we use for this area go to: co-ops.nos.noaa.gov/tide_predictions.html, click on "North Carolina" in the left column, and then on the next page click on "WRIGHTSVILLE BEACH" to find the tide predictions.

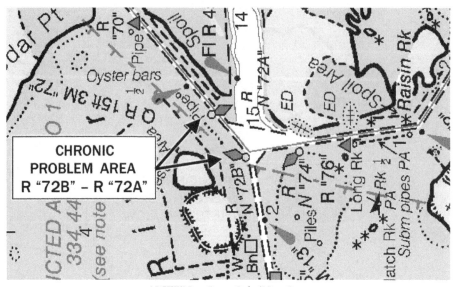

AICW/New River Inlet/New River

After Carolina Beach Inlet, the next area of concern is the intersection of the AICW and the New River and New River Inlet near Mile Marker 246. Shoaling is frequently reported at this four-way intersection in the vicinity of R "72B" and R "72A". Like all the previous problem spots mentioned at North Carolina inlets, the best water is usually found on the "red' side of the waterway; be sure to follow the buoys and not the Magenta Line. For the tide chart that we use for this area go to: co-ops.nos.noaa.gov/tide_predictions.html, click on "North Carolina" in the left column, and then on the next page click on "New River Inlet" to find the tide predictions.

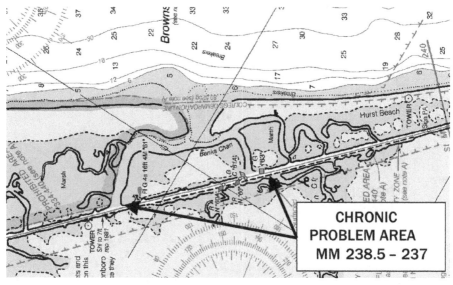

AICW/Browns Inlet

The next problematic section is another inlet area at the intersection of the AICW and Browns Inlet between Mile Markers 238.5 and 237, just north of the Onslow Bridge. Shoaling here at times has been extreme. The same suggestions that apply to the other inlet problem areas also apply here. The "red" side is usually better, and buoys are frequently added or moved. For the tide chart we use for Browns Inlet as well as for the following trouble area at Bogue Inlet, go to: co-ops.nos.noaa.gov/tide_predictions.html, click on "North Carolina" in the left column, and then on the next page click on "Bogue Inlet" to find the tide predictions.

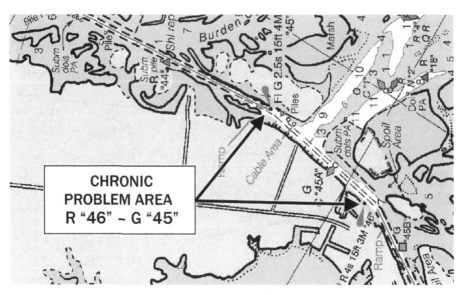

AICW/Bogue Inlet

The last inlet that is a habitual problem area is at the intersection of the AICW and Bogue Inlet near Mile Marker 227, in the area extending from R "46" to G "45". In this section of the waterway, we have often found that staying near the docks along the mainland side of the waterway will keep you in the best water depths.

When traveling through any of these areas of North Carolina, be sure to get the latest updates on conditions from Waterway Guide, Salty Southeast Cruisers Net, or ActiveCaptain.

There is one additional area to note in North Carolina. It is located where the Alligator River intersects with Albemarle Sound, just south of Mile Marker 80. In recent years the markers leading from the River to the Sound have been moved, and on some older charts, if you follow the Magenta Line, you will be traveling outside the channel. Follow the markers!

The Alligator River Pungo River Canal – North Carolina

Magenta Line Note

In Illustration 7 on page V of the color insert, notice how the Magenta Line curves between G "7" and G "5" toward marker R "6". It does this for a very good reason which is to keep you centered in the channel. If you were to travel in a direct line from G "7" to G "5", there is a pretty good chance that you would find the bottom of your boat also touching the bottom of the waterway. Except where noted in problem areas, it is always wise to stay in the middle of the channel honoring all markers.

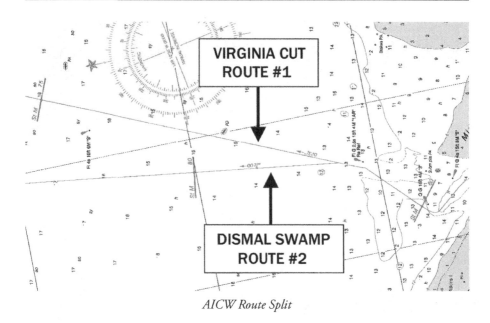

AICW Route Split

Route Split

After entering Albemarle Sound, the waterway divides at G "1AR" near Mile Marker 79. The starboard route is the main AICW route (Route #1) that heads through the Virginia Cut to Norfolk, Virginia, while the port route (Route #2) goes through the Pasquotank River and on through the Dismal Swamp (with a target control depth of 6 feet), and then rejoins the main route just south of Norfolk. The Dismal Swamp route, despite its name, is the more scenic of the two routes.

Construction on the Dismal Swamp Canal was started in 1793, but it was not fully operational until 1814. George Washington was one of its original financial backers, and it is rumored that he was the original surveyor; however, there is no proof of this. It was dug entirely by hand to an original width of 40 feet and a depth of 4-1/2 feet, and many years later it was widened and deepened. When you travel on this Waterway you are literally traveling through a piece of American history.

Anchorages

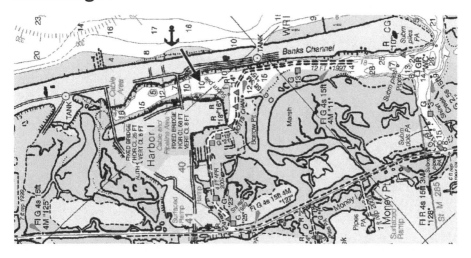

Banks Channel Anchorage

There are eight anchorages we have used along this section of the waterway. The first is Banks Channel near Mile Marker 283.5 in Wrightsville Beach, North Carolina. Holding is good with some current, and there is good wind protection except from the southeast to southwest. There is room for several boats in about 10 feet of water.

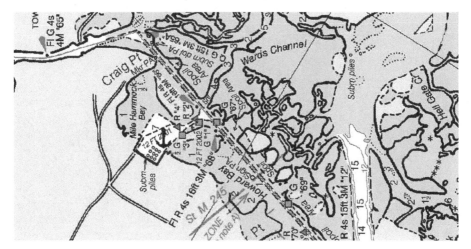

Camp Lejeune Anchorage

The next anchorage is located at Mile Marker 244.5 in the Camp Lejeune Marine Base. There is good holding and room for several boats in 12 feet of water with no current.

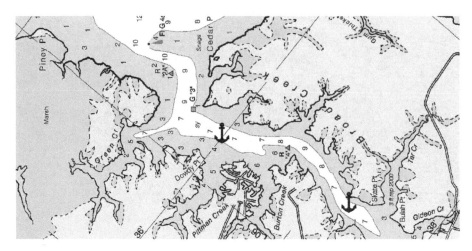

Broad Creek Anchorage

The third anchorage, in Broad Creek, is located off the Neuse River near Mile Marker 175. Holding is good in 7 to 8 feet of water, and it has no significant current plus generally good wind protection from all sides in either location marked on the chart. There is room for several boats.

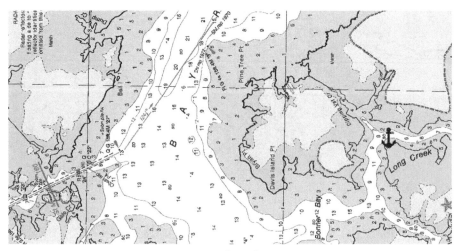

Long Creek Anchorage

Not far from Broad Creek is Long Creek, located 4 miles off of Bay River near Mile Marker 161. Holding is good in 9 feet of water with room for a few boats. Wave protection is good from all directions except from the northwest to southwest, and there is little current.

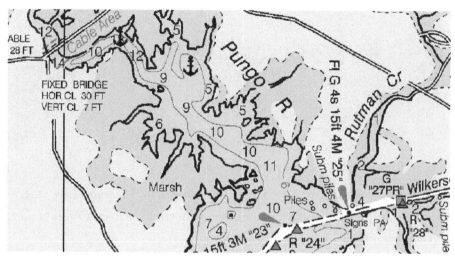

Pungo River Anchorage

The next anchorage is on the Pungo River near Mile Marker 127.5. The northern location has room for only 1 to 2 boats in 10 feet of water with good holding, no current, and all around wind protection. The more southern spot has room for several boats in 7 feet of water with good holding and no current. Wind protection here is good in all directions except southeast to southwest.

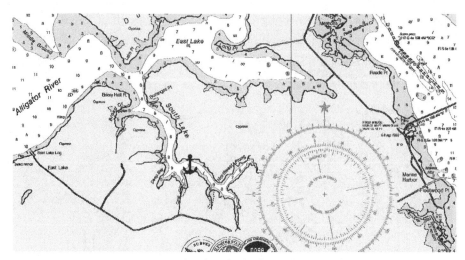

South Lake Anchorage

Seven miles off the Alligator River near Mile Marker 81.5 is South Lake anchorage. It has nearly all around wind protection with good holding in 7 feet of water with room for several boats and no current.

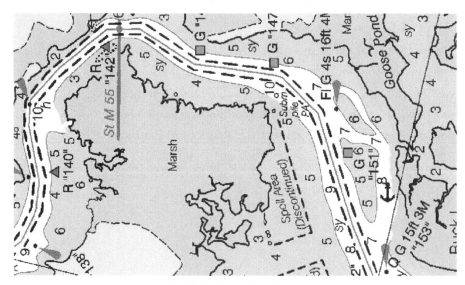

Buck Island North Anchorage

Just off the waterway on the Virginia Cut Route (Route #1) near Mile Marker 53.5 is a spot to anchor just north of Buck Island. Wind protection is good only from the southeast to the southwest, and there can be some wake action from the AICW. Holding is good in about 8 feet of water with no current and room for only 1 to 2 boats.

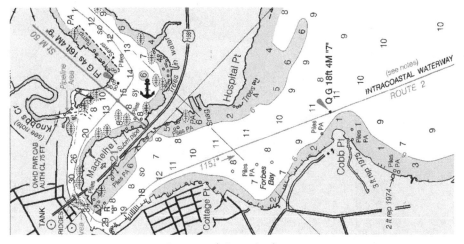

Pasquotank River Anchorage

On the Dismal Swamp Branch (Route #2) of the AICW there is a good place to anchor just past Mile Marker 50 on the Pasquotank River. Both the holding and wind protection are good with room for a couple of boats in 7 feet of water.

AICW Northern Terminus

Mile Marker 0, at the intersection of the Elizabeth River's eastern and southern branches in Norfolk, Virginia, is the AICW's northern terminus. From here to the New Jersey Intracoastal Waterway (NJICW), channel markers follow the "Red Right Return" rule. There are no bridge concerns in this section of the Loop until you reach the NJICW.

Norfolk, Virginia to Chesapeake Bay

The Great Loop route heads north up the Elizabeth River for about 9 miles (with the red markers on your port side). The river is wide and deep with considerable commercial and naval traffic, and at its northern end, it enters Hampton Roads.

*Passing the **CMA CGM New Jersey** on the Elizabeth River*

 During the American Civil War, Hampton Roads became famous for the first battle between two Ironclad warships, the USS Monitor and the CSS Virginia (ex-USS Merrimack). The battle took place over two days, March 8-9, 1862, with neither vessel ever able to claim victory since their iron cannon balls just kept bouncing off of each other. However, later that year the Union forces eventually took control of the area.

After a short 3-mile trip through Hampton Roads, you will enter the vast Chesapeake Bay.

Chesapeake Bay to the Chesapeake and Delaware Canal

The Chesapeake Bay Bridge just north of Annapolis, Maryland

There are more than 150 rivers, creeks, and streams that flow into the bay. It is approximately 200 miles long and 30 miles wide at its widest point near the Potomac River, with an average depth of 46 feet and a maximum depth of 208 feet. We have traveled throughout the bay for almost 40 years, and throughout that time, because of its immense size, we have only been able to see a small portion of it.

You will see an abundance of commercial traffic of all types and sizes while traveling the bay; however, because of the bay's size, there is plenty of room to stay safely out of their way. The red markers will now be on your starboard as you travel north, and you may encounter up to 2 knots of tidal current with an average tide change of only 1 foot.

One thing you will want to be cautious of when boating on the Chesapeake is the crab trap (pot) marker floats. They are not found in the main channels, but they frequently crowd the side channels. Be sure to stay clear of them as their lines can easily get fouled on propellers and rudders.

This is a region of the Loop where you may want to slow down and explore a bit. The numbers of anchoring opportunities are considerable and most have little to no current. We will mention some of our favorites; however, there are so many that you will want to consult your guidebooks for a complete list of them.

Anchorages

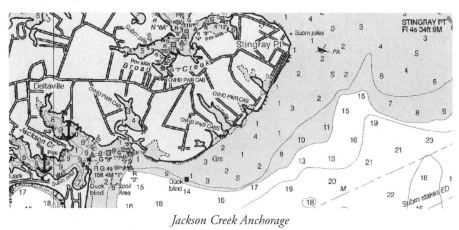

Jackson Creek Anchorage

The first anchorage is at Jackson Creek on the western shore of the Bay off of the Piankatank River in the area of Sting Ray Point located at 37°32.8' north, 76°19.7' west. Carefully follow the marked channel into the creek, and anchor in either branch in 8 to 9 feet of water with good holding and good wind protection. There is room for several boats.

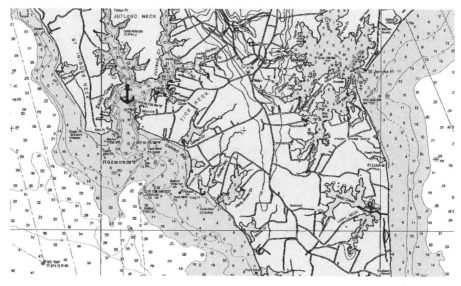

Smith Creek/Jutland Creek Anchorage

The next anchorage is on the western shore of the Bay off the Potomac River in Smith and Jutland Creeks, located at 38°06.6' north, 76°21.8' west. Follow the marked channel into Smith Creek, and after Jutland Creek splits off, find a spot to anchor in either creek. Holding and wind protection are good in 8 to 15 feet of water with room for many boats.

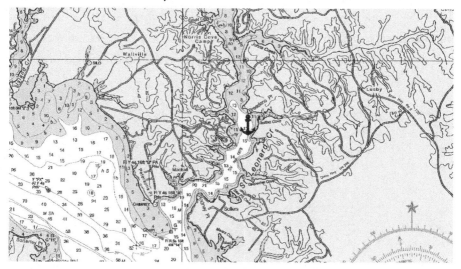

Saint Leonard Creek Anchorage

Off the Patuxent River is Saint Leonard's Creek on the western shore of the Bay at 38°23.31' north, 76°30.12' west. This is one of the most scenic creeks off the Chesapeake. The creek is lined with plantations and farms on hills. Holding and wind protection are good, so anchor almost anywhere along the creek in 7 to 15 feet of water. There is room for many boats in this picturesque anchorage.

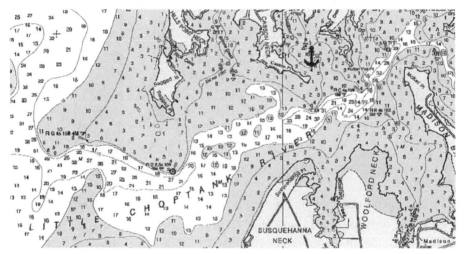

Hudson Creek Anchorage

On the eastern shore of the Chesapeake at 38°32.5' north, 76°14.8' west, off the Little Choptank River is Hudson Creek. This is a lightly populated area of farms and woodlands. Anchor in 7 to 9 feet of water off Casson Point. Holding is good, and there is good wind protection from the southwest to northeast with room for several boats.

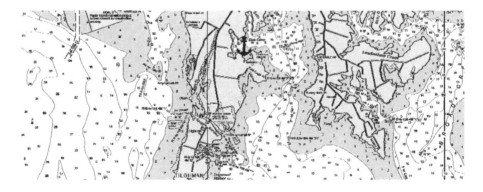

Dun Cove Anchorage

Another favorite eastern shore anchorage is Dun Cove at 38°44.46' north, 76°19.04' west, off Harris Creek which is off of the Choptank River. Again, this anchorage is in a rural farmland setting with good holding in 8 to 10 feet of water, and there is wind protection from all but easterly winds as well as room for several boats.

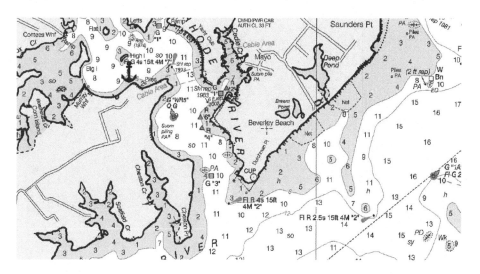

Rhode River Anchorage

Along the western shore of Chesapeake Bay, south of Annapolis, is the Rhode River anchorage located at 38°52.95' north, 76°32.00' west. Holding is good in about 8 to 9 feet of water with room for several boats. The wind protection is good from all directions, so just anchor near a lee shore. Watch out for the crab trap floats as you enter the river.

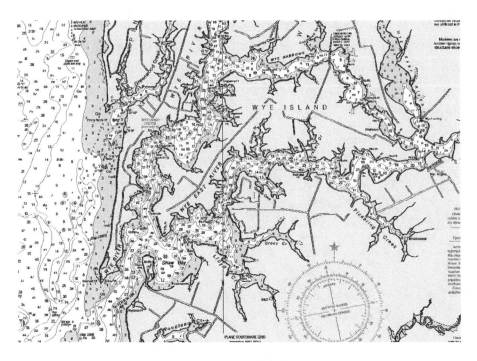

Wye River Anchorages

On the eastern shore, the Wye River anchorage areas are numerous and are located in a rural setting among farms and woods with room for lots of boats. The anchorages are approached from Eastern Bay to the Miles River and then by proceeding to the Wye River entrance at 38°50.79' north, 76°12.20' west. Anchor almost anywhere along its branches and adjoining creeks in 8 to 25 feet of water with all around wind protection in many locations.

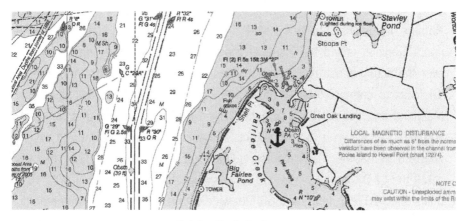

Fairlee Creek Anchorage

On the eastern shore, Fairlee Creek's anchorage at 39°15.80' north, 76°12.59' west is popular with the locals, especially on weekends. Follow the marked channel from R"2F" along the beach, taking a hard turn to starboard to enter the anchorage. You may experience some current as you enter the narrow opening, and there may be even some slight current inside the anchorage. Anchor your boat in about 7 to 8 feet of water outside the channel near R "8". There is room for several boats with good all around wind protection.

Consult your guidebooks for more details on these anchorages and information on the many more that you may want to explore along Chesapeake Bay.

Chesapeake and Delaware Canal (C&D Canal) to the Delaware River

At the top of Chesapeake Bay, you will enter the Elk River and then Back Creek that leads into the 14-mile long sea-level C&D Canal.

In the early 1600s, a mapmaker working for the Dutch proposed a canal connecting Chesapeake Bay to the Delaware River, but it wasn't until 1764 that a survey of possible water routes across the Delmarva Peninsula was made, and a route from the Chester River to the Delaware River was proposed.

Nothing happened until 1788, when regional businessmen, including Benjamin Franklin, raised the issue of constructing the waterway again. However, the actual construction of the canal didn't begin until 1804, including 14 locks to connect the Christina River in Delaware with the Elk River in Maryland, but the project was halted again for 20 years due to a lack of funds. (When it comes to civil projects, things really haven't seemed to have changed all that much!) Construction finally got going again in 1824, and by 1829 the C&D Canal was opened for business. When completed, it was 14 miles long, 10 feet deep, and 66 feet wide with 4 locks. Through numerous improvement projects, the canal today is at sea level, and is 35 feet deep with a width of 450 feet. Further improvements are said to be in the works.

The canal carries commercial traffic, including ships and tugs with barges, between Chesapeake Bay and the Delaware River. Red markers will be on your starboard until the railroad lift bridge over half-way through the canal. There the red markers will switch to the port side. The canal is very easily navigated, but be sure to consult your current charts beforehand, because the current can run up to 3 knots with a 2.5 foot tide change.

Once you leave the canal at its eastern end on the Delaware River, there are no anchorages that we would really recommend until you reach Cape May Harbor in New Jersey. The total distance from the western end of the C&D Canal to Cape May Harbor is about 68 miles.

Anchorage

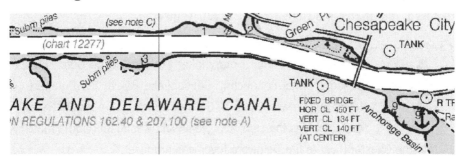

Chesapeake City Anchorage Basin

There is only one anchorage on the C&D Canal. It is located in Chesapeake City at 39°31.55' north, 75°48.50' west, near the canal's western end at the anchorage basin indicated on the chart. Holding is good, and there is no significant current in about 9 feet of water with very good wind protection from all sides. There is room for just a few boats.

Hug the shores at the entrance, as there is some shoaling in the center.

Delaware River and Bay to the Cape May Canal

Upon entering the Delaware River, the red buoys will now be on your port side since you will be heading toward the Atlantic Ocean. The river/bay carries large commercial traffic including various types of ships and tugs pushing or pulling barges. There is plenty of depth outside of the main channel for maneuvering to stay out of the way of any large vessels.

The river/bay can carry strong tidal currents well over 3 knots with 6 feet of tide. However, because the trip from the C&D Canal to the Cape May Canal is about 52 miles and you will be heading toward the ocean, you will probably pass through 2 full current cycles. If the current is moving strongly against you in the river, it will be with you in the bay, and vice versa.

Before heading into the Delaware River, check the weather. If the forecast is for strong winds from the northeast or southwest you will experience steep chop when the wind and current are opposing. This can make for a very uncomfortable trip down the river and the bay!

When we travel down the Delaware River and Bay to the Cape May Canal, we follow along the edge of the ship channel just inside the markers, and then move outside the channel when any large vessels approach. When we get to Miah Maull Shoal lighthouse at 39°07.60' north, 75°12.49' west, we leave the lighthouse to port, and then head directly to the Cape May Canal. This is the most direct route to Cape May, and it will keep you in deep water without running into fish traps or crab trap floats.

The Cape May Canal to Manasquan Inlet, New Jersey

The Cape May Canal is a three-mile long sea level waterway with a control depth of 7 feet that connects the NJICW and the Atlantic Ocean, through Cape May Harbor, to the Delaware Bay. At the Delaware Bay end of the Canal, there is a ferry terminal where ferries the size of small ships pull in and out, so be sure to stay alert. There are two fixed bridges at a height of 55 feet along its route as well as a railroad bridge that is usually open. Tides here are 6 feet and the current in the canal can run over 3 knots especially at the narrow opening of the railroad bridge.

The United States Army Corps of Engineers constructed the Cape May Canal during World War II to provide a protected route in order to avoid German U-boats operating off Cape May Point. It is the final link which connects the NJICW starting in Manasquan, New Jersey, to Delaware Bay.

Anchorage

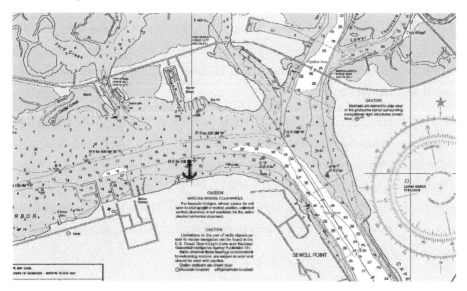

Cape May Harbor Anchorage

There is only one anchorage we can recommend in Cape May Harbor. It is located just past the U. S. Coast Guard Station at 38°57.02' north, 74°53.03' west. Holding is good in 7 to 10 feet of water with room for several boats. It is subject to wakes and wind from all directions but the south, and unfortunately it is the only place to anchor in the Harbor.

Between Cape May and Manasquan, New Jersey, there are two routes you may take. The inside route will travel through the marshland of the NJICW and the outside route will follow along the New Jersey coastline on the Atlantic Ocean. Both have their advantages. First we will look at the NJICW.

Here are some guidelines for a trouble-free and enjoyable trip through the NJICW:

- Do not follow the magenta line or the buoys on your chart plotter – they are merely general guides. If you do follow the magenta line or the buoys on your chartplotter, you will definitely go aground.

- Do follow the buoys and day markers you see in front of you – they mark the best water. In areas where buoys are used, they are often moved, and additional ones are added as necessary. Follow the numbers and colors. For example: if your chart shows three green buoys in a line, but you observe that one is way off to one side, it is most likely there for a reason. It is also a wise idea before starting out on the NJICW to call the Coast Guard or TOWBOATUS ahead of time and ask if there are any markers that are off-station, or if they know of any recent shoaling.

- Do not cut corners.

- Do not pass buoys on the wrong side.

- Do stay in the middle of the channel except when passing other boats. If your depths are looking shallow, look behind your boat at the last mark you have passed, and make sure that you are in the channel.

- Avoid traveling the waterway on weekends or holidays. New Jersey is the most densely populated state in the U. S., so it is not surprising that it also has the greatest boating density in the country. The boat traffic on weekends can be considerable, and it is highly likely that you will find yourself being passed very closely by vessels traveling at high speeds with little regard for fellow boaters. As locals who live just off the NJICW, take our advice, weekdays are much better for travel!

- Don't let the charted depths north of the Route 37 Bridge in Barnegat Bay scare you. There is considerably more water in the channel than the chart shows.

- The last bridge on the NJICW heading north is a railroad bridge which crosses the Manasquan River. Use caution when transiting this area as it can be congested with boats. The opening at the bridge is narrow, and the current can run strong. Before entering the bridge, be sure that you have a clear view through the bridge.

- If you draw 4 feet of water or less, you should be fine traveling the NJICW. However, we suggest that you travel between mid and high tide to ensure plenty of water below your keel. If your draft is over 4 feet, take the ocean route!

- The majority of the bottom on the NJICW is soft mud, so if you are going slowly and find yourself touching the bottom, you can usually get yourself off with little problem.

Like the AICW, the NJICW red markers will be on your port side with small yellow triangles, and the green markers will be on your starboard side with yellow squares. Tides at the extreme southern and northern ends of the waterway run about 5.5 feet, while in Barnegat Bay between Mile Markers 30 and 5 the tide is only about .5 feet. The maximum tidal current runs from 2 knots near Cape May in the south to 3.5 knots near Manasquan in the north, but there is virtually no current in Barnegat Bay. The waterway between Cape May at Mile Marker 114 and Atlantic City at Mile Marker 65 twists and turns its way through low marsh lands with several low drawbridges (on opening schedules) through which you must pass, and on hot summer days it can be quite buggy. There are no anchorages that we can personally recommend in this area of the waterway. Check your guidebooks for detailed information on this section of the NJICW.

Between Atlantic City and Manasquan Inlet at Mile Marker 0, the waterway continues to wind its way through marshlands, then passes several shore communities on Long Beach Island, and eventually enters Barnegat Bay. Except for a railroad bridge that is usually open near Mile Marker 0, there are five drawbridges, all with a minimum closed clearance of 30 feet. Some are on opening schedules.

Anchorages

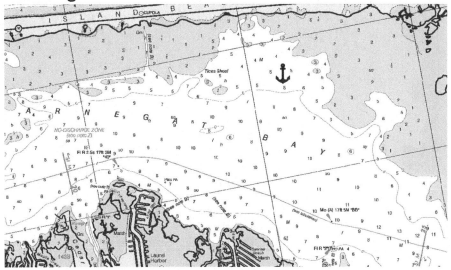

Tices Shoal Anchorage

There are two anchorages in Barnegat Bay on the NJICW where we have stopped numerous times. The first is at 39°49.59' north, 74°06.46' off Mile Marker 24. Head just north of east from marker "BB" to Tices Shoal. Holding is fair to good with no current in 5 feet of water, but wind protection is only from the northeast to southeast. There is room here for a great number of boats, and on summer weekends it can be crowded with lots of "partying" people in attendance!

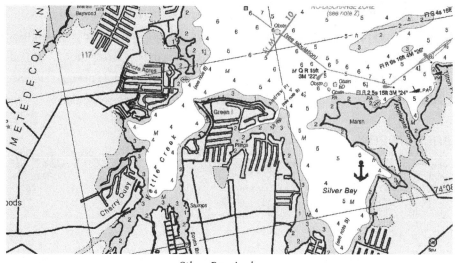

Silver Bay Anchorage

The next anchorage, Silver Bay, is just before Mile Marker 10 at 39°59.45' north, 74°07.53' west. Holding is good in 5 feet of water with no current, and wind protection is only from the southeast through the southwest. Although there is room for many boats, this anchorage can also get crowded on summer weekends.

Be sure to consult your guidebooks for more detailed information on negotiating the NJICW.

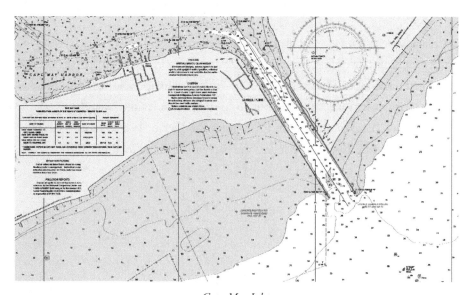

Cape May Inlet

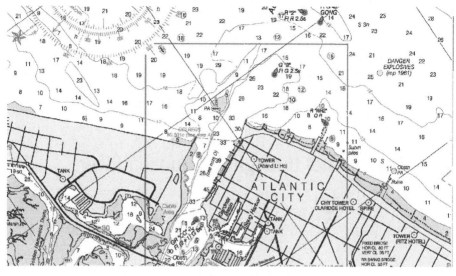

Absecon Inlet

As an alternate to taking the inland route, we recommend your taking the ocean route, especially between Cape May and Atlantic City (Absecon Inlet). (See "Crossing Open Water" later in this book.) The ocean route is 41 miles from harbor to harbor, which is 8 miles shorter than the NJICW route, and there are no bridges to slow you down and there is very little chance of your going aground.

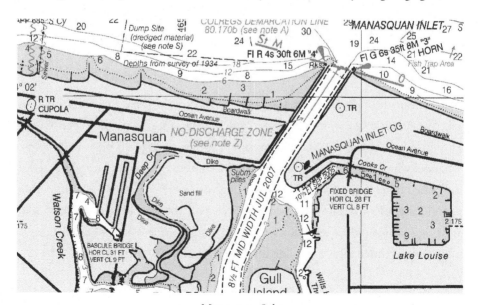

Manasquan Inlet

The ocean trip from Atlantic City's Absecon Inlet to Manasquan Inlet is 59 miles, which is 6 miles shorter than the inland route, plus you will be able to travel in deep water all the way. However, no matter which route you take, you will most likely pass through Manasquan Inlet. As a word of caution; we again want to remind you that Manasquan Inlet can be extremely congested on spring and summer weekends. Avoid transiting this inlet at these times.

Manasquan Inlet through the Hudson River

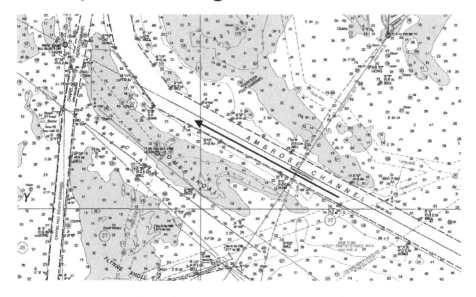

Ambrose Channel (Entrance to New York Harbor)

At Manasquan, New Jersey, the NJICW ends. Now you have no choice but to take the Atlantic Ocean route to New York Harbor. (See "Crossing Open Water" later in this book). From Manasquan head up the coast for 28 miles to Ambrose Channel which will lead you into New York Harbor. This is an area with a great deal of commercial traffic. It is best to time your approach to New York Harbor and all of your travels on the Hudson River with the incoming tide. The 5 foot tidal range can produce a 3.5 knot current throughout this area, either making it a big help, if timed wisely, or a big hindrance, if not.

From Ambrose Channel it is about a 17 mile trip into New York Harbor off Liberty Island. (Red markers will be on your starboard side.) From here the Hudson River runs north for about 150 miles to Waterford, New York, where the Erie and Champlain Canals begin. (There is a free dock at the Waterford Harbor Visitors Center with room for many boats.) The Hudson is deep and wide with plenty of room to negotiate around any commercial traffic you many encounter. The lowest bridge along the route is 25+ feet at Troy, New York. Once you pass the Troy Lock, which is just 2 miles south of Waterford, you will not return to sea level until you pass through the Coffeeville Lock in Alabama over 2,500 miles away!

Anchorage

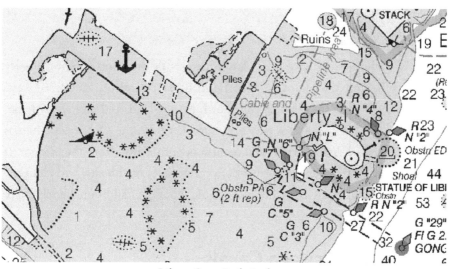

Liberty State Park Anchorage

The view from Liberty State Park Anchorage

The only anchorage we have used along this part of the Loop is off of Liberty State Park behind the Statue of Liberty at 40°41.70' north, 74°03.78' west. From G "29" follow the channel south of Liberty Island, and after passing between R "6" and G "7", follow the private markers into the anchorage. There is good holding with little current and good wake protection from the Harbor. It also has good all around wind protection, room for several boats, and an excellent view of New York City. Check your guidebooks for additional anchorages along this part of the Loop.

The Erie and Oswego Canals

At Waterford, New York, the Great Loop route splits with the northern route which goes through the Champlain Canal, Lake Champlain, the Chambly Canal, and the Richelieu River to the Saint Lawrence River, and the western route which travels through the Erie and Oswego Canals to Lake Ontario. We chose to take the more popular Erie Canal Route. For complete information on all the New York State Canals, visit: www.canals.ny.gov/index.shtml.

On inland waterways such as the Erie Canal, there are no tides, so all measurements (bridge heights, water depth, etc.) are taken at what is known as "normal" pool. Knowing how this was established is not as important as your knowing if the pool is at, above, or below normal. For example, if the pool is 1 foot above normal, the charted depths will be 1 foot deeper, and bridge heights will be 1 foot lower.

According to the New York State Canal Corporation that runs the canal system (www.canals.ny.gov/navinfo/navinfo.cgi?waterway=erieeastern), the eastern Erie Canal, which runs for 160 miles to the Oswego Canal, has a control depth of 14 feet unless otherwise noted, and the minimum bridge height clearance is 21 feet at "normal" pool. (The actual minimum bridge clearance is 20 feet at "normal" pool. We will explain this discrepancy later in this section of the book.) Before arriving at the Erie Canal, contact the New York State Canal Corporation at: 1 800 422 6254 (1 800 4CANAL4) to check on the current pool level.

Prior to entering the first actual lock (E2) on the Erie Canal at Waterford (There is no E1 lock on the Erie Canal because the Troy Lock is considered to be the first lock.), take a walk to the lockmaster's office to purchase your lock pass and to watch the lock operation. You may find it to be quite informative.

You can get the latest toll prices at: www.canals.ny.gov/boating/tolls.html. The pass is good for both the Erie and Oswego Canals, and a 10 day pass should be more than sufficient to get you through both canals.

Red markers will be on your starboard side on both the Erie and Oswego Canals, but after the last lock (Lock 8) on the Oswego Canal, the marker colors will switch, and the red markers will then be on your port side. Speed limits on both canals can run as slow as 5 miles per hour, so stay alert!

The Erie Canal between Canajoharie and Little Falls, New York

There are 22 locks on the Erie Canal between Waterford and the start of the Oswego Canal. Once you enter Lock E2 at the start of the Erie Canal, you must travel through Lock E6. This is known as the Waterford Flight; between E2 and E6 there is no place to stop. You must pass through all five locks in one travel sequence. It is a good idea to start the Waterford Flight early in the day because, depending on traffic in the locks, it can take several hours to complete the flight. Consult your guidebooks for anchorages and marinas beyond Lock E6.

 Proposed in 1808 and completed in 1825, the Erie Canal links the waters of Lake Erie in the west to the Hudson River in the east. It is an engineering marvel dug by hand (Oh, my aching back!) to an original depth of 4 feet and a width of 40 feet, and when it was built some called it the Eighth Wonder of the World.

Before we began our trip through the Erie Canal, we contacted the New York State Canal Corporation to request pool information. We were told that the canal was at "normal" pool. Based on this information, the minimum bridge clearance should have been 21 feet. The height of our boat is 20 feet and 2 inches to the top of our anchor light. According to our chart, the CSX railroad bridge (E-40) at Mile Marker 94.92 just before lock E19 has an air clearance of 22 feet at "normal" pool. Yet, WE HIT THE BRIDGE! Luckily, our damage was minor. We did break the anchor light from its mast, but we didn't break the lens, and the light still worked! Because of this event, I estimate that the clearance on this bridge at "normal" pool is actually just over 20 feet. So, be aware!

The bridge that did the damage

The picture speaks for itself!

Once you arrive at Three Rivers, New York, the route then turns north into the Oswego Canal for 24 miles to Oswego, New York, and Lake Ontario. The route passes through seven locks, O1 through O8. (There is no lock O4.) According to the New York State Canal Corporation, the control depth in the channel is 14 feet and the bridge clearance is 21 feet at "normal" pool. We had no problems in this Canal, because after the incident at the railroad bridge, we lowered our radar arch which dropped our air clearance to about 17 feet.

We cannot personally recommend any anchorages along these two canals; however, we did stay at several free docks along the way at Waterford, Amsterdam, and Canajoharie. Check your guidebooks for a complete list of the current free docks on the Erie and Oswego Canals. For free or low-cost dockage on the Erie Canal visit: www.100megsfree3.com/wordsmith/publictieups.html.

The Free Dock at Sylvan Beach (no services)

Lake Ontario

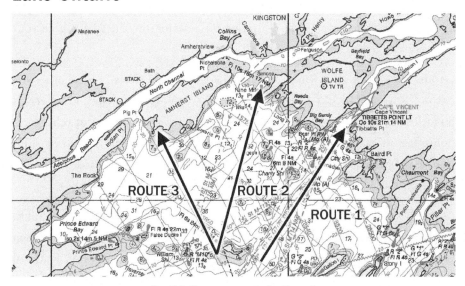

Possible Routes across Lake Ontario

From Oswego, there are four routes that can be taken through Lake Ontario. The first crosses Lake Ontario and passes between Main Duck Island and Galloo Island, then goes between Wolf Island and Tibbetts Point, and into the Saint Lawrence River and the Thousand Islands. The second route crosses Lake Ontario, passes between Psyche Shoal and Main Duck Island, and then passes to the northeast of Amherst Island and on to Kingston, Ontario. The third route again crosses Lake Ontario, passes between Psyche Shoal and Main Duck Island, then passes between Indian Point and Amherst Island, and heads southwest into Adolphus Reach. Whichever of these three routes you take, eventually you will head through Adolphus Reach on your way to the Bay of Quinte and the Trent-Severn Waterway. A fourth route takes you along the southern shore of Lake Ontario to the Welland Canal and Lake Erie.

The Champlain Canal Route

At Waterford, if you decide to take the Champlain Canal route, there are a few things of which you will want to be aware. The lowest bridge height listed on the route is 17 feet at "normal" pool, and in Lake Champlain you are required to physically disconnect the hose from your holding tank to the overboard seacock, in order to ensure that you will not pump black water into the lake. Check your guidebooks for the latest information.

Depths are 12 feet at "normal" pool on the Champlain Canal, unless otherwise noted. There are 11 locks on the 60 mile long Canal, C1 through C12. (There is no lock C10.) Lock passes can be purchased at Lock C1 as well as at other locations. See: www.canals.ny.gov/boating/tolls.html. A 2 day pass should be sufficient to get you through the canal. There are free docks along the canal with water and electric at Mechanicville, New York, and at Ft Edward, New York.

As you head north on the Canal, red buoys will be on your starboard side until north of lock C12 where the buoys colors will switch, and the reds will now be on your port side all the way through to the Saint Lawrence River. For navigational information on the Champlain Canal, visit: www.canals.ny.gov/navinfo/navinfo. cgi?waterway=champlain.

Once you pass through the Champlain Canal, you will enter the wide and deep Lake Champlain, which is over 100 miles long. From here the route takes you to the Richelieu River and the Chambly Canal with its nine locks, a control depth of 6 ½ feet, and an air clearance (under a power line) at 29 feet. Lock passes for the Chambly Canal and all the locks operated by Parks Canada can be purchased at the first lock. Depending on your route choice you may find it more economical to purchase a season pass for all Parks Canada locks rather than a one-way pass for just the Chambly Canal. For detailed information on the Chambly Canal, go to the Parks Canada website at: www.pc.gc.ca/lhn-nhs/qc/chambly/visit.aspx.

You will exit the Richelieu River into the Saint Lawrence River at Sorel, Quebec. The total distance from Waterford to Sorel is about 243 miles. From Sorel the route takes you southwest down the Saint Lawrence Seaway to Kingston, Ontario, a trip of about 239 miles. The seaway has a considerable amount of ocean-going traffic that has priority over pleasure craft at the locks. This can possibly cause you extensive delays. Tolls are collected at each lock through which you pass. Along the seaway, red markers will be on your starboard side. For complete information on the seaway, go to: www.greatlakes-seaway.com/en/.

Taking the Champlain Canal to the Saint Lawrence Seaway route will add about 260 miles more to your Great Loop journey in comparison to your taking the Erie Canal/Oswego route. Consult your guidebooks for detailed information on this route.

You may also want to add a side trip up the Ottawa River to visit the scenic and historic city of Ottawa, the capital of Canada. If so, leave the Saint Lawrence Seaway at St Anne de Bellevue, and head northwest up the Ottawa River with red buoys on the starboard side, a control depth of 9 feet, and a minimum air clearance of 38 feet. Once you arrive in Ottawa, there is dockage downtown near restaurants and shopping. Upon leaving Ottawa, head through the Rideau Canal with red buoys on port. There are a total of 47 locks from the Ottawa River to Kingston, Ontario including 9 groups of flight locks the longest a series 8 locks between the Ottawa River and the city of Ottawa. The canal has a control depth of 5 feet, and a minimum air clearance of 22 feet. For detailed information on the Rideau Canal, go to the Parks Canada website at: www.pc.gc.ca/lhn-nhs/on/rideau/visit.aspx.

After the War of 1812 the British were concerned that the United States might someday blockade the St. Lawrence River south of Montreal. To circumvent this, in 1826 they began construction of the Rideau Canal, connecting the Ottawa River to the St. Lawrence River, thus giving the British an alternate route from Montreal to Upper Canada and the vital naval dockyard in Kingston. The Rideau Canal opened in 1832 and was hailed as one of the greatest engineering accomplishments of the 19th century

The Rideau Canal today is used exclusively by pleasure craft. It is the oldest continuously operating canal in North America and has been named by the United Nations Educational, Scientific, and Cultural Organization (UNESCO) as a World Heritage Site.

Taking the Champlain Canal route to the Saint Lawrence Seaway and then onto Ottawa will add about 310 miles more to your Great Loop journey instead of your taking the Erie Canal/Oswego route. Consult your guidebooks for detailed information on this passage.

Adolphus Reach and the Bay of Quinte

Whether you take either the Erie/Oswego Canal route and then cross Lake Ontario, or the Champlain Canal route down the Saint Lawrence, you will wind up passing through Adolphus Reach and the Bay of Quinte on your way to the Trent-Severn Waterway. These two bodies of water are wide and deep with red markers on the starboard side and no low bridges.

The Trent-Severn Waterway

 This waterway is listed as one of the National Historic Sites of Canada, and on this passage you will lift to a height of 840 feet above sea level (the highest point on the Loop) and travel through 44 locks. The Trent-Severn had formerly been used for commercial purposes, but is now used exclusively for pleasure boats, connecting Lake Ontario at Trenton to the Georgian Bay area of Lake Huron at Port Severn. Its construction began in the Kawartha Lakes region in 1833 with the building of the lock at Bobcaygeon. Originally the canal system was intended to be a defense route, but it soon became a major transportation pathway. It took over 87 years to complete the Waterway with two "temporary" marine railways installed at Big Chute and Swift Rapids. Only by 1920 could a boat travel the whole route. Some argue that the canal is not yet really finished since only the Swift Rapids Marine Railway was ever replaced by the intended conventional lock in 1965, while the Big Chute Marine Railway today still continues to operate having never been replaced by a conventional lock.

The Trent-Severn Waterway, possibly the most beautiful waterway on the Great Loop, extends for 240 miles from Trenton to Port Severn, Ontario. The official minimum bridge clearance along the main channel is reported to be 22 feet; however, high water levels can reduce that clearance, especially at the bridge at Mile 87. Also, the Gannon Narrows Bridge at Mile 130 was recently rebuilt, and its clearance is now reported to be is just over 20.5 feet at its lowest point in the middle of the span. We understand that the port and starboard sides of the bridge have a clearance of just over 21 feet. The minimum depth along the waterway is 6 feet, and there are many slow speed zones at 10 kilometers per hour (about 6 miles per hour). If you are concerned about bridge heights or depths in the waterway, call the Trent-Severn Waterway at 705 750 4900 for the latest information on bridge heights and waterway minimum depths before you start out.

There are a total of 44 locks on the waterway (There is no Lock 29.); 41 gate locks (including two pair of flight locks, Locks 11 and 12 at Ranney Falls and Locks 16 and 17 at Healey Falls); two lift locks (Lock 21 at Peterborough, and Lock 36 at Kirkfield); and one marine railway lock (Lock 44 at Big Chute).

 The Kirkfield Lift Lock is situated at the highest section of the Waterway as well as on the Great Loop route. At 840 feet above sea level, its construction took place between 1900 and 1907. A hydraulic lift lock had never been put into operation in the harsh Canadian climate prior to the building of this lock and the Peterborough Lift Lock, and at the time, the successful completion of the locks was considered to be a major technological breakthrough.

The Trent-Severn Waterway between Trenton and Frankford, Ontario

You can stay at a lock for from one to five nights, depending on the lock. There are areas to tie up at the bottom or at the top of the lock or both. Water and electric can be extremely limited. You can tie up anywhere other than the "Blue Line" on a "First come, First served basis." If you arrive after the lock has closed for the day, you may then tie up at the blue line; however, you will be expected to leave when the lock opens the following morning. There is a fee for mooring at all locks.

We cannot personally recommend any anchorages on the Trent-Severn Waterway; however, we did stay at lock walls on several nights and recommend them as an alternative.

Ranney Falls Lock – mooring space is available along the wall to the right of the triangle marker

Red markers are on your starboard side as you travel from Trenton until you pass through the Kirkfield Lift Lock at Mile 170. Here they reverse with the red markers now on your port side.

The buoys used on the waterway are a "spire" type. (See Illustration 8 on page V of the color insert.) Except for a small triangular shape on the top of the red buoy, the physical characteristics between red and green buoys are identical, and in times of poor visibility, it can be difficult to distinguish the red from the green buoys.

NEVER cut corners. On our Great Loop adventure, a boater unfamiliar with the Waterway was traveling at high speed, missed a buoy, went outside the channel, and tore both propeller shafts out of his boat. It sunk in minutes.

When traveling on any Canadian waterways, if you spot a white object floating, it has most likely been placed there by someone who is a "local," and it usually marks an uncharted rock, so STAY CLEAR.

At Mile 163, before entering the Trent Canal between Balsam Lake and Mitchell Lake, call a "security" on VHF Channel 16. Announce the name of your vessel, say that you are about to enter the Trent Canal heading westbound, and request that all interested parties respond. You will want be sure that no one is coming the other way because this canal is extremely narrow, unforgiving, and there is no room to turn around. Dug through solid rock, the depth in this land cut is only 6 feet. Go slowly.

The cut between Balsam Lake and Mitchell Lake

On our own Great Loop journey, before we entered the cut between Balsam Lake and Mitchell Lake, we called for a "security" on the marine radio to notify any vessel that was entering from the other end that we were about to come through. When we did, we received a call back that three boats had just entered the cut. Since there was no place for us to pass in the canal, we waited for about 45 minutes for the boats to come out at our end so that we could enter. Again, we called a "security" stating that we were about to enter the cut, but this time we got no response in return, so we headed in. Once we were on our way, it was obvious that except for a very small boat, no one would be able to pass us.

The channel was so narrow, because of the sheer rock walls on both its sides, that we didn't pass through the water as much as we felt that it was pushed around us. It was like we were going through a long, thin water trough, forcing us to travel very slowly at about five knots, and it seemed like it would take forever to get to the other end of the cut.

When we got about three quarters of the way through, suddenly a boat appeared that was coming the other way! We turned to each other and shook our heads in disbelief with Captain George exclaiming, "Great! Look at this idiot coming straight at us! I'm not giving up the middle of the channel at this point. He'll just have to squeeze past us!" Fortunately, that boat was able to slip between us and the rock ledge without incident, proving that God not only protects us, but also the "clueless"!

Be sure to check your guidebooks before starting out each day for any other narrow passages you may encounter along the way where you might possibly have to announce a "security". Also, there are certain areas of the waterway that can become choked with weeds, so make sure you check your raw water strainers often.

It is a good idea to travel on the Trent-Severn on weekdays as this waterway is very heavily used by locals on summer weekends. Its locks and the waterway itself can be very congested at these times, so find a good place to stop on Friday and stay there until Monday morning.

Your trip on the beautiful Trent-Severn Waterway will not only be scenic, but it will also be very safe as long as you pay attention to what you are doing and use your common sense.

The Trent-Severn Waterway – a house on a rock

Stoney Lake

There are more than 1,000 islands of every size and shape in Stoney Lake, from red granite rock to rounded hills of dense green foliage. This lake is touted as the best one for fishing in all the Kawarthas, and many species of fish abound, including walleye, bass, muskie, and perch, to name a few. Like most lakes in Ontario, it was created during and after the last Ice Age, and many Indian tribes eventually lived here. During the 16th century, the famous French explorer Samuel de Champlain passed through Stoney Lake, as well as almost every other lake and river along the Trent-Severn Waterway. When you visit certain historical places on the eastern seaboard of the United States, you frequently hear the phrase, "George Washington slept here." Similarly, in this part of Ontario, the often-used expression is, "Champlain passed through here."

For detailed information on the Trent-Severn Waterway, visit: TrentSevern. com or www.pc.gc.ca/eng/index.aspx, and consult your guidebooks for more detailed information.

Georgian Bay and the North Channel

Georgian Bay is about 120 miles long and 50 miles wide. Covering about 5,800 square miles, it is almost 80 percent of the size of Lake Ontario and is sometimes called "The Sixth Great Lake." The eastern shore of the Bay, where you will most likely be traveling, is composed of granite bedrock which was exposed by glaciers at the end of the last Ice Age.

As a result of its formation, tens of thousands of islands have formed, leaving channels that are, for the most part, deep. However, be aware that in areas outside of the channels the bottom can be unforgiving. This region is absolutely beautiful with granite rock formations and windswept Eastern White Pines growing on islands and along the shore.

There are as many as a 1,000 anchorages in Georgian Bay. It is like the Chesapeake Bay on "steroids," except instead of having low rolling farm land and woods as your boating scenery, here you see magnificent granite rocks and cliffs. We will mention a few anchorages at which we stayed, and you will also want to consult your guidebooks for a complete list of additional ones. Some anchorages are extremely crowded on the weekends, so it is always wise to have alternate options in your plans.

The Small Craft Route, where you will do most of your traveling, has plenty of depth in most areas, and is well marked with red markers (similar to the size and shape of those on the Trent-Severn Waterway) on your starboard side as you head northwest along its route. Like the Trent-Severn Waterway, it can also be crowded with locals on weekends, and similarly, if you spot anything white floating in Georgian Bay, stay clear of it since it most likely marks an uncharted rock.

Upon leaving the last lock on the Trent-Severn Waterway at Port Severn, you will enter the Georgian Bay Small Craft Channel. As you exit the last lock, call a security. The channel beyond the lock is very narrow! Also, just before Mile 3 on the Small Craft Channel, the route goes through the approximately 1,000 foot long Potato Channel. This channel is only 6 feet deep, and about 50 feet wide. Before entering Potato Channel, again call a "Security", since you do not want to meet another boat coming the other way. There is no room to turn around and very little room to pass. Proceed slowly, follow the markers, and stay in the middle of the channel!

At Mile 5 in Severn Sound, we suggest that you turn off the Small Craft Channel and head west southwest to Midland Bay to the Bay Port Yachting Centre, which is about 5 miles away. This is an excellent place to get cruising information on Georgian Bay and the North Channel. The very friendly staff will go over your charts with you and will also show you the best anchorages and the routes to get to them, so it is well worth the stop!

After leaving Bay Port Yachting Centre, follow the secondary Small Craft Channel between Beausoleil Island and Present Island, and then rejoin the main Small Craft Channel near Mile 10. The scenery here is almost otherworldly - with homes built on islands (rock boulders) in the middle of the water which is so clear that you can actually see the rock ledges along the channels.

Making the best of a "rocky" situation

Longuissa Bay Anchorage

Just before Mile 17 is Musquash Channel. Following that channel for three miles will lead you to Longuissa Bay anchorage at 44°58.08 north, 79°53.43 west. There is good holding in 10 to 25 feet of water with room for many boats. This location has no current with good all-around wind protection. Check your guidebooks for additional details on this and other anchorages in the area.

At Mile 40.6 on the Small Craft Channel is "Henry's Fish Camp." It is popular for the good food served at its restaurant along with reasonably-priced dockage. Don't be surprised to see sea-planes in the water nearby since they, too, stop here for lunch/dinner!

 When traveling in Georgian Bay and the North Channel, it is possible to see the Aurora Borealis on clear nights. It will appear during the summer at these latitudes as a blue green glow, like a false sunrise, in the northern sky. We saw it in the Benjamin Islands in the North Channel at about 2 a.m.

Kineras Bay

At Mile 42.4, the Small Craft Channel splits, with the preferred channel that has less hazards and deeper water to starboard, going around the north side of Perry Island. At Mile 47.6 is Kineras Bay at 45°15.2' north, 80°07.9' west. It is an excellent anchorage with good holding, has room for a large number of boats, as well as good wind protection from all directions except southeast. Check your guidebooks for additional details on this and other anchorages in the area.

Just before Mile 54 is a 15 foot high swing bridge that opens on the hour from 6 a.m. to 10 p.m. Just past the bridge is Parry Sound Harbor with several marinas, a selection of restaurants, and nearby shopping. Also, at Parry Sound Harbor the Small Craft Channel mileage markers start again at 0, and the red markers switch sides and will now be on your port.

At flashing red buoy P30, just past mile 10, the channel once again splits. The route to starboard goes through Canoe Channel. This route is not recommended for boats over 40 feet. If you do take this route, call a security before entering Canoe Channel. If your boat is over 40 feet, take the route around Squaw Island to the south.

At Mile 28.5 is Hopewell Bay anchorage at 45°30.8' north, 80°25.3' west. From the Small Boat Channel, head northwest to the Bay. It has room for many boats and is an excellent anchorage in all but southeast winds. Check your guidebooks for additional details on this and other anchorages in the area.

Killbear Point Light along the Small Boat Channel

Just past Mile 37 near Pointe au Baril, the Small Boat Channel turns sharply to starboard and enters Hangdog Channel. **DO NOT TRAVEL THROUGH HANGDOG CHANNEL UNDER ANY CONDITIONS!** It is very winding and narrow with numerous shoals. It should only be traveled by those with local knowledge; instead go into Georgian Bay. If the conditions in Georgian Bay are unfavorable, wait for a better day to travel. We had fellow "Loopers" who took Hangdog Channel and regretted making that decision. They observed unforgiving rock ledges along the edge of the channel and told us that any misstep could have been disastrous for them and their vessel.

Pointe au Baril Lighthouse

Byng Inlet

From Pointe au Baril to Byng Inlet 45°44.0' north, 80°44.8 west, is about 18 miles through Georgian Bay. Follow the inlet to the community of Britt with a couple of good marinas and the Little Britt Inn, one of the more unique dining experiences on the Great Loop.

Beaverstone Bay anchorage

From Byng Inlet, it is about another 14 miles heading northwest to the Bustard Islands at 45°53.1' north, 80°55.0' west. This is a very popular anchorage area. From there, it is about 30 miles heading west northwest to Beaverstone Bay at 45°58.2' north, 81°11.1' west, another scenic anchorage and the entrance to Collins Inlet.

In both the Bustard Islands and Beaverstone Bay, there are many anchorage possibilities with room for many boats, so choose the location that gives you the best wind protection. Check your guidebooks for details about these areas.

Collins Inlet

From Beaverstone Bay, the route passes through Collins Inlet, a magnificent fjord. It has a narrow low water area near its entrance which is about a half-mile long with the deepest water clearly marked by buoys. The channel is frequently deeper than is indicated on the charts, but use caution. The fjord is scenic, deep, and somewhat narrow, but two boats have enough room to pass easily.

Covered Portage Cove

From Collins Inlet follow the Small Craft Channel to Killarney Inlet at mile 54. At the village of Killarney the Small Craft Channel mile markers start again at 0. The channel now enters Killarney Bay, followed by Badgeley Point Channel, and then enters the North Channel. This area has many sheltered and scenic anchorages including: Covered Portage Cove at 40°00.0' north, 81°32.7' west; Snug Harbor at 45°57.5 north, 81°38.4' west; and "The Pool" at 46°02.7 north, 81°29.4' west. Check your guidebooks for details on these and other anchorages in this area.

At about Mile 24.5 on the Small Craft Channel is a swing bridge with an 18 foot clearance. Timing is important at the bridge, because it only opens for 15 minutes on the hour. Just past the bridge is the town of Little Current. (For details about Little Current see: Many of the Great Stops on America's Great Loop on page 302.)

From Little Current you have multiple route options, so consult your guidebooks for possible scenic opportunities. One of them is about a 19-mile trip to the Benjamin Islands which offer several anchorage choices. Some are completely protected; they can be crowded in the summer, even during the week, so get there early. After leaving Little Current, follow the Channel west, and then turn north along the eastern side of Clapperton Island, and now across the Main Passage to the Benjamin Islands, at 46°05.0' north, 82°14.5 west.

From here the North Channel is wide and deep all the way to the marked channel between Cedar Island and Drummond Island on Potagannissing Bay. This channel will take you to Drummond Island Yacht Haven. Once you pass red buoy "8" on the port, follow the buoyed channel to the marina where you will clear U.S. Customs as you are now back in the United States.

Lakes Huron and Michigan

From Drummond Island, follow the route across Sturgeon Bay to De Tour Passage (Both are wide and deep with red markers on your port side.) and enter Lake Huron. (See "Open Water Passages" for more information.) The route heads to the Les Cheneaux Islands about 30 miles from Drummond Island. At G "1" 45°56.9' north, 84°17.1' west, follow the route through the island chain with red markers on your starboard until you come to the west side of La Salle Island. The markers will now switch, and the red markers will be on your port side. The route carries about 6-½ feet of water; follow it to Marquette Bay where you will re-enter Lake Huron.

Anchorage

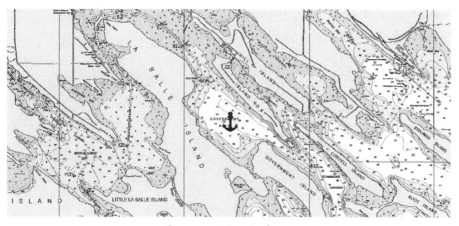

Government Bay Anchorage

There is a popular anchorage at Government Bay, 45°58.4' north, 84°12.3' west, with good holding and no current, in 10 to 20 feet of water with room for many boats but with only fair wind protection.

After entering Lake Huron, go around either side of Mackinac Island to the Straits of Mackinac heading westerly until White Shoal Light in Lake Michigan. Now head south through Grays Reef passage. From here, follow either the western or eastern shore of Lake Michigan to the Chicago area.

 The Straits of Mackinac is the strip of water that connects Lake Michigan and Lake Huron, and it is a shipping lane which provides passage for commercial vessels traveling between Lake Michigan and ports on the other Great Lakes and beyond. At its narrowest point (five miles), it is spanned by the Mackinac Bridge, which connects the Upper and Lower peninsulas of Michigan. Envisioned since the 1880s, the bridge was completed in 1957, and is the third longest in total suspension in the world.

The eastern side of the Lake has some advantages because it has a Harbor of Refuge every thirty miles. So, if the Lake kicks up, you will be no more than 15 miles from a safe harbor. Also, these harbors have a policy of not turning anyone away. Even if all the dock spaces are filled, they will raft boats together in order to accommodate everyone. The harbor entrances are clearly marked with lights on the end of jetties. See "Crossing Open Water" later in this book.

Entrance to Betsie Lake from Lake Michigan

 Lake Michigan is an inland sea. It is the fifth largest lake in the world with a length of 307 miles, a maximum width of 118 miles, and an average depth of 279 feet.

Lake Michigan has the distinction of sometimes generating its own weather, and it can be somewhat unpredictable at times. On our Great Loop trip, we crossed Lake Michigan from Holland, Michigan, to Chicago, Illinois, which is a distance of about 95 miles. The marine weather forecast was for waves of about 2 feet coming from our port side. When we were about 20 miles out, the waves began coming from the bow at about 4 feet and stayed that way until we were about 20 miles from Chicago, where the waves finally began to flatten and then came on our stern. The middle of the lake can surprise you!

The Midwest and Southern Rivers

The rivers on which you will travel in the midwest and south carry considerable commercial traffic in the form of lines of barges being pushed by towboats. (Towboats pushing barges travel at about 6 miles per hour.) Stay in the center of the channel, unless you are passing or being passed by another vessel. Use the "sailing line" on the chart as a general guide; however, observe the buoys, since many of them are not charted.

The Illinois River System

As described earlier in "Route Planning", the Illinois river system can be entered from Lake Michigan in two ways, either from the Chicago River with minimum bridge heights of 17 feet or through Calumet Harbor with a series of bascule bridges. Both routes take you to the very industrial, heavily-used by commercial traffic, and narrow Chicago Sanitary and Ship Canal which has a minimum bridge height of 19.7 feet. This is the lowest bridge on the Great Loop, and there is no alternative route you can take to bypass it!

Waiting for a tow to pass on the narrow Chicago Sanitary and Ship Canal

The canal empties into the Des Plaines River that eventually joins the Illinois River. Depending on your route from Lake Michigan, you will pass through between 7 to 8 Federal Locks along this river system. As you head down-stream toward the Mississippi River, red buoys will be on the port side. The buoys, although charted, are *not* numbered.

A car-ferry on the Illinois River

Anchorages and Free Dockage

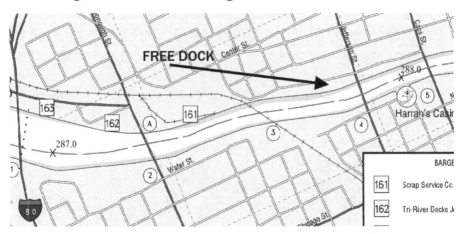

Free Dock in Joliet

There is a free dock with room for several boats at Joliet, Illinois, on the Des Plaines River. It is at a park on the starboard side immediately after the Jefferson Street drawbridge which is just past Mile 288. When we stopped there, there was free 30-amp electric. This is an unsecured dock in the city of Joliet, so be aware of your security.

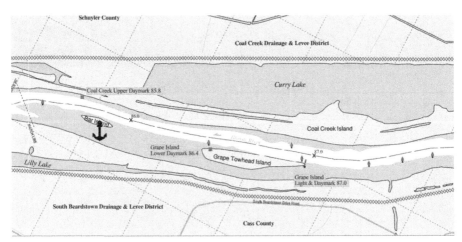

Bar Island Anchorage

Just past Mile 86 is Bar Island anchorage. Go past the island, then turn up-stream and go behind the island. There is room for a few boats in about 8 feet of water. Holding is good. Under normal conditions, the current is not strong and there is good protection from the wakes of passing tows.

Marinas are few on the Illinois river system, so be sure to consult your guidebooks for their locations as well as for free docks and anchorages.

Mississippi, Ohio, and Cumberland Rivers Overview

Mississippi River

Grafton, Illinois is at the confluence of the Illinois and Mississippi Rivers. The Mississippi River is wide and deep, and on your route you will pass though two locks.

 The Mississippi deserves its characterization as "mighty" because it is 2,320 miles long, comprises the largest river system in North America, it's the fourth longest river in the world and the 10th most powerful river in the world! Along with its tributaries, it drains all or parts of 31 states stretching from the Rocky Mountains in the West to the Appalachian Mountains in the east, and runs from Canada in the north to the Gulf of Mexico in the South.

The red buoys will be on your port side as you head down the river. Be aware that none of the buoys below Alton, Illinois, (Mile 202) are charted, and that none of them have numbers on them. In general, follow the sailing line on your chart, stay in the middle of the channel, and be on the lookout for buoys which will guide you through the deepest water, possibly away from the sailing line. Buoys on the Mississippi River are constantly being moved to mark the best channel.

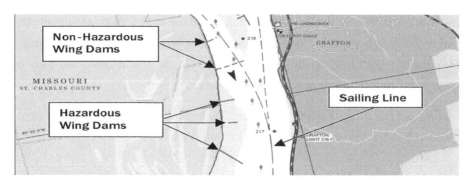

Do not travel near the shores of the Mississippi River. The Army Corps of Engineers has built wing dams along its banks to control the flow of the river. Be aware that there are two types of wing dams: hazardous and non-hazardous. Hazardous wing dams frequently cannot be seen, and are hiding just below the surface of the water. Striking one of them can sink your boat! Non-hazardous wing dams are 9 feet below the surface under normal conditions. Non-hazardous wing dams are shown on the charts as dashed lines, and the hazardous wing dams are shown as solid lines. (See the illustration above.)

The Mississippi River has very heavy commercial traffic traveling on it. We saw one towboat pushing as many as 45 barges down the river! They tend to move very slowly, so you should have no problem maneuvering around them. Stay alert! There are some staging areas on the Mississippi where the river seems covered with barges; however, there is always a safe way to get past them, and it is generally near the sailing line.

A lazy day heading down the mighty Mississippi River

Ohio River

From the Mississippi River, the best route takes you up the Ohio River to the Cumberland River. Like the Mississippi River, the Ohio River is wide and deep. The buoys on it are charted; however, like the ones on the Mississippi River, they are not numbered. Red buoys will be on your starboard side as you travel upstream on the river.

Again, like the Mississippi River, the Ohio River also has a great deal of commercial traffic. Just a few miles upriver from the Mississippi is a large staging area where small towboats push barges around, breaking up and assembling large barge flotillas. Make sure that you carefully negotiate through this area, remembering that the best route may be near the sailing line.

There are three locks between the Mississippi River and the Cumberland River. Just after Mile 965 is the Olmstead (duel chamber) Locks and Dam that has been under construction for over 30 years. It is scheduled to be fully operational in October of 2018. When it is completed, it will replace the next two locks, Locks 53 (duel chamber) at Mile 963 and Locks 52 (duel chamber) at mile 939.

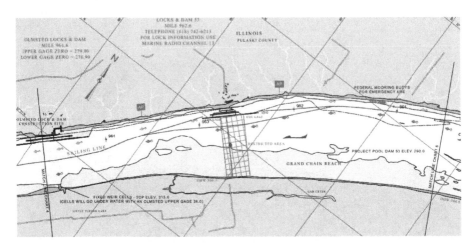

Locks 53 and its Wicket and Weir Dam

Notice in the illustration above that the sailing line at Locks 53 splits, with one route going through the locks and the other appearing to go over the dam. This is not an error. The crossed hatch area shown on the chart is a combination Wicket and Weir Dam. The Weir Dam is fixed; however, the Wicket Dam is moveable. There are times when the Army Corps of Engineers manipulates the height of the Ohio River so that the water level on both sides of the dam is equal. At these times they will lower the Wicket Dam which will allow vessels to cross over the dam and thus avoid the locks.

These types of dams are at both Locks 53 and 52. When you contact the lock-master at either lock, he will advise you if you will pass through the lock or over the dam.

Olmstead (dual chamber) Locks on the Ohio River – overdue and over-budget

Cumberland River

From the Ohio River, the best route takes you up the Cumberland River to Lake Barkley. The buoys on the Cumberland River are charted; however, like the ones on the Mississippi and Ohio Rivers, they are not numbered. Red buoys will be on your starboard side as you travel upstream on the river.

The Cumberland River is considerably narrower than either the Mississippi or Ohio Rivers, yet it is still deep enough for commercial traffic. Nonetheless, it is considerably less traveled by towboats and barges than the other two rivers, and there is only one lock on the Cumberland River at Lake Barkley.

Cruising up the Cumberland River

Traveling Down the Three Rivers from Alton, IL to Grand Rivers, KY

Alton Marina, at Alton, Illinois, on the Mississippi River at Mile 202.5, is about 17 miles south of the confluence of the Illinois and Mississippi Rivers. On our last Great Loop journey in 2015, it was the last place for provisions for 293 miles until we arrived at Grand Rivers, Kentucky. In good weather, it took us six days to travel from Alton to Grand Rivers. In 2017 the city of Paducah, Kentucky on the Ohio River opened the Paducah Transient Boat Dock, thus shortening the distance where you can find the next provisions to 250 miles.

From Alton, we first traveled 44 miles to Hoppie's Marine Service in Kimmswick, Missouri, at Mile 158.5. Hoppie's simply is a series of barges secured to the land by cables where you can safely stay overnight, and it is your last stop for fuel and water for the next 206 miles. Here, one of the owners will be glad to advise you on the current conditions along the Mississippi and Ohio Rivers. Be sure to do so before continuing down the river, since this will be your last chance to get local information for hundreds of miles.

Hoppie's Marine Services

When approaching Hoppie's, call them on VHF Channel 16. After switching to a working channel, Fern Hopkins, or one of her staff, will give you instructions to guide you safely alongside their dock (barge). Follow their instructions to the letter because they have a lot of experience at their location and they definitely know what they are doing.

One obnoxious captain apparently did not like getting docking instructions from a woman and made the mistake of telling Fern in a pompous manner that he "knew" how to dock his boat. So, she simply stood by, let the mighty Mississippi current have its "way" with him, and allowed the stubborn captain to bang his way into her dock. Remember, there is no substitute for local knowledge!

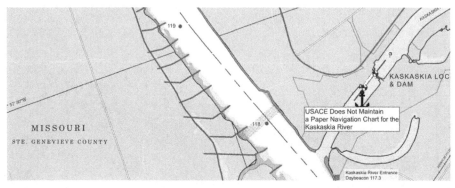

Costello Lock and Dam

From Hoppie's, we traveled 41 miles to the Costello Lock on the Kaskaskia River, just off the Mississippi River at Mile 117.5. The best way to enter the Kaskaskia River is to go past it, turn your boat around, and head into the current on the Mississippi River. This will give you control of your boat when entering the Kaskaskia River. Once inside the Kaskaskia River, call the lockmaster on VHF Channel 14, and ask him if you can tie up at the outer lock wall for the night. He will want to know your vessel's registration or documentation number, and where you are heading. Do not tie up without asking permission.

There is room for several boats. Do not tie your vessel to the railings on the wall unless there are no cleats in that section of the wall. If this is the case, ask the lockmaster if you can tie your boat to the base of the railing. If you have a dog to walk, ask the lockmaster where you can walk the animal. Generally they do not like anyone walking on the lock wall except to secure your boat.

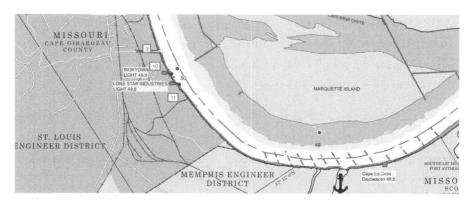

Little Diversion Channel Anchorage

Little Diversion Channel
Our boat, "Reflection," tied stern to stern with "Falkor," a 36 foot Grand Banks — We each have a bow anchor deployed preventing us from swinging in this narrow channel.

The next safe place to stop on the Mississippi River is sixty-nine miles downriver at Little Diversion Channel just past Mile 49. Just like the Kaskaskia River, the best way to enter Little Diversion Channel is to go past it, turn around into the current, and then enter the channel.

The Little Diversion Channel is very narrow, but the holding is good with two anchors, one from the bow and one from the stern, to prevent your boat from swinging. There is no current in this spot, very good wind and wake protection, room for several boats, and good depths.

"Falkor" at Little Chain Bar Anchorage – Notice the slight current.

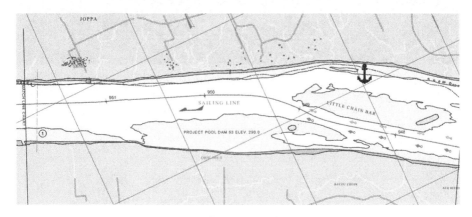

Little Chain Bar Anchorage

The following day we traveled 81 miles to Little Chain Bar Anchorage at Mile 949 on the Ohio River. Anchor as close to the northwest shore as you are comfortable because there is a coal dock up-river on the northwest shore, and towboats pushing coal barges pass between Little Chain Bar and the shore. You will want to give them as much room as possible to pass by you safely.

There is room for several boats with good holding in moderate current and good depths. As you can see from the previous illustration, the anchorage is away from the main channel in an area where the current is weaker. Wind protection is good from the north to the west and wakes are not a problem. It is not a perfect anchorage; however, we found it to be quite satisfactory. It is also a good idea to leave the anchorage the same way that you entered.

In 2017, Paducah, Kentucky, at Mile 935 on the Ohio River, opened its 340 foot Paducah Transient Boat Dock with power, water, and fuel. For more information, visit the Paducah Transient Boat Dock website at paducahky.gov/paducah-transient-boat-dock.

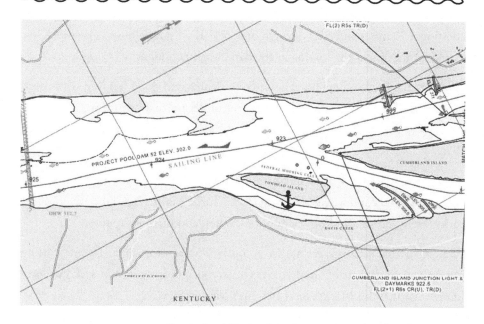

Cumberland Towhead Anchorage

Cumberland Towhead Anchorage

From Little Chain Bar Anchorage, we traveled 26 miles to Cumberland Towhead anchorage, just past Mile 924 on the Ohio River. The reason for such a short trip was that we were held up at Locks 52 for about 4 hours because of very heavy commercial traffic. By the time we reached the Cumberland Tow Head, it was already early afternoon. To reach our final destination on this leg of the trip, which was Green Turtle Marina on Lake Barkley, we would have had to travel an additional 32 miles and pass through one lock. If we got held up at that lock, we would be arriving at the marina in the dark, not a good idea!

Cumberland Towhead anchorage has good depths and good holding with room for several boats. There is very little current under normal conditions, and it has good wind and wake protection. Enter and exit the anchorage from the Ohio River.

From Cumberland Towhead anchorage, we traveled 32 miles up the Cumberland River into Lake Barkley and arrived at Green Turtle Marina in Grand Rivers, Kentucky. Here you can find provisions, fuel, water, and marine supplies.

Remember that these rivers are in a constant state of change. Before starting out on your journey to Grand Rivers check your guidebooks and seek out local knowledge at Alton Marina or at Hoppie's Marine Services.

The Tennessee River

From Lake Barkley, enter the Barkley Canal that takes you to the Tennessee River for your 190 mile trip to the Tennessee-Tombigbee Waterway. Red buoys will be on your starboard side, and, although they are charted, they are not numbered.

The amount of rain that has fallen up-river affects how much current will be running against you. (We experienced about 2 knots of current against us.) Just before Pickwick Lake, off of which is the beginning of the Tennessee-Tombigbee Waterway, you will pass through one lock.

The Barkley Canal

Rock formations along the Tennessee River

Anchorages

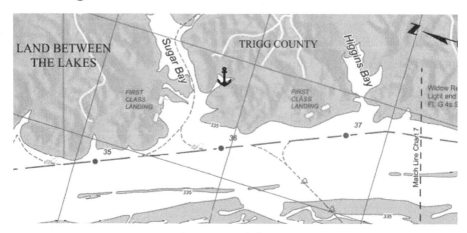

Anchorage just off of Sugar Bay

Anchorage off of Sugar Bay

There are two anchorages that we can personally recommend. The first is in Kentucky Lake (Tennessee River) near Mile 35.5 just off Sugar Bay. The unnamed cove, despite its appearance on the chart, has an easy entrance with room for several boats in this much-protected anchorage. It has good holding with no current, has plenty of depth, and is an excellent place to go for a swim!

Kentucky Lake is a major navigable reservoir along the Tennessee River that was created in 1944 by the Tennessee Valley Authority with the construction of The Kentucky Dam's confining of the River. It is the largest artificial lake by surface area (160,309 acres) in the United States east of the Mississippi River. When the lake was created, many farms, homes, towns, roads, and railroads had to be relocated, and other homes and buildings that were flooded at that time still lay below the water surface today. Some of the roads that at one time crossed the valley where the lake now stands can be seen along the shore entering the water, and serve today as public boat launch ramps.

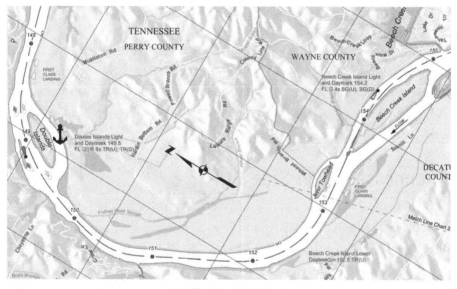

Double Islands Anchorage

Double Islands Anchorage – Notice the current moving past the boat.

Double Islands anchorage is at Mile 149 on the Tennessee River. Enter the anchorage from downstream, and anchor outside the channel behind the island. There is good holding in moderate current, room for several boats, good wind and wake protection, and sufficient depth.

A Tennessee River Side Trip

If you have the time, before continuing your Loop trip down the Tennessee/Black Warrior Tombigbee Waterway, you may want to consider a trip farther up the Tennessee River to Chattanooga, Tennessee. The 500 mile round trip will take you through some of the most beautiful waters in the United States. There are numerous protected crystal-clear deep water anchorages along the way and plenty of excellent marinas. Consult your guidebooks for detailed information.

The Tennessee/Black Warrior-Tombigbee Waterway

At Mile 215 on the Tennessee River (Pickwick Lake), you will turn to starboard and enter the Tennessee-Tombigbee Waterway (Tenn-Tom). You will travel down the Tenn-Tom for 234 miles to Demopolis, Alabama, and then you will go an additional 217 miles down the Black Warrior-Tombigbee Waterway to Mobile, Alabama.

The connecting of the Tennessee River with the Tombigbee River, a 12-year, $2 billion Army Corps of Engineers earth-moving project, moved more soil than the building of the Panama Canal. It was the building of this man-made waterway that has made the Great Loop journey around the Gulf Coast, East Coast, and Canadian and Midwest waterways possible.

The Tennessee-Tombigbee Waterway, commonly known as the Tenn-Tom, was first proposed in America's Colonial period. However, it wasn't until 1875 that engineers surveyed a potential canal route, but they also issued a negative report at that time, emphasizing that prohibitive cost estimates made the project economically unfeasible.

The construction of the Pickwick Lock and Dam on the Tennessee River under the Tennessee Valley Authority in 1938, however, helped decrease the Tenn-Tom's potential economic costs and increased awareness of its potential benefits. In 1971 President Nixon authorized $1 million for the Army Corps of Engineers to start construction of the Tenn-Tom. Funding shortages and legal challenges again delayed the start of construction until December 1972, and in 1984 the project was finally completed two years ahead of schedule.

Although its $2 billion dollar price tag was called a pork-barrel project by many at the time, since 1996, the United States has realized a positive economic impact of over $43 billion due to the existence and usage of the waterway, which has directly created more than 29,000 jobs.

Red buoys will be on your port side as you travel the waterway, and you will be moving downstream for the first time since leaving the Mississippi River. You will encounter towboats pushing barges along the waterway, although the traffic is much lighter than that which you see on the Mississippi or Ohio Rivers. The waterway passes through 10 locks until you reach Demopolis, Alabama. You will then continue on the Black Warrior Tombigbee Waterway to Mobile, Alabama, passing through 2 more locks and finally reaching sea level again after passing through the Coffeeville Lock. This will be the first time you will be back at sea level since the Troy Lock on the Hudson River, which is now at least 2,500 miles astern of you!

When traveling along the Tombigbee Waterway, be very careful of your speed. Do not "wake" small fishing boats as they will likely call the local constable, and you risk getting fined.

A friend of ours told us a story about a boater who was moving fast along the waterway, and was paying no attention to his wake. When he reached the next lock on his journey, he entered it, the doors closed behind him, and then nothing happened. He was told by the lockmaster that he would have to wait in the lock until local law enforcement arrived. He was not one of the area's "good 'ole boys", so things did not go well for him.

To prevent problems such as this, we were very observant as we traveled and always kept a camera ready. If we had a concern about our wake as we passed a small boat, we would wave to the fisherman and take a picture of the boat showing the wake we made. This seems to discourage false claims about excessive wakes.

The following is a list of areas along the Tennessee/Black Warrior-Tombigbee Waterway where wakes from passing boats can cause possible damage. Slow down when passing these areas, or risk a fine. These "No Wake" zones are taken very seriously by the locals. Also watch out for:

- Small fishing boats in nearby waters

- Small boats tied to the shoreline at hunting areas

NAVIGATION MILE	DESCRIPTION
450.0-449.0	Boat Ramp, Docks
447.0-446.0	Boat Ramp, Marina
443.6	Boat Ramp
435.5	Boat Ramp
433.0	Barge Fleeting Area
419.6	Boat Ramp
412.5	Boat Ramp
409.8	Barge Fleeting Area
407.3	Boat Ramp
404.0-403.0	Marina, Campground, Docks
402.0-401.0	Docks
400.0-398.0	Boat Ramp and Docks
396.0-392.0	Ramps, Docks, Campground, Marina
390.0-389.7	Barge Fleeting Area

NAVIGATION MILE	DESCRIPTION
387.1	Boat Ramp
381.2-380.6	Private oat Docks
379.3-378.8	Docks
376.8-376.2	Boat Ramp and Marina
372.8-371.0	Boat Ramps and Docks
370.0-369.0	Ports, Boat Ramp
360.5-358.0	Recreation Area and Docks
356.8-356.0	Arberdeen Port
355.5	Boat Ramp
349.4	Boat Ramp, Dock
343.7	Docks
342.8	Docks
341.7-341.5	Campground and Boat Ramp
340.3-339.8	Campground and Boat Ramp
338.7	Marina/Barge Fleeting Area
338.0	Boat Ramp
335.1-334.8	Marina
332.8	Boat Ramp
331.4	Boat Ramp
324.5-323.5	Boat Docks
316.5-314.0	Boat Docks and Boat Ramps
311.0-308.1	Campground and Boat Docks
307.4	Marina
303.2	Boat Ramp
294.7-294.3	Boat Ramp, Campground
292.7-292.3	Barge Fleeting Area
283.3	Boat Ramp
281.8	Boat Docks
280.1-280.0	Docks
279.0-278.0	Docks
274.5-274.2	Boat Ramp
272.0-271.7	Boat Ramp
259.5	Barge Fleeting Area
251.7	Boat Ramp
247.5	Bathe Fleeting Area/Boat Ramp
219.1	Recreation Area
217-216	Marina, Boat Ramps, Recreation Area
215.8-213.2	Barge Fleeting Area
201.6	Barge Fleeting Area

NAVIGATION MILE	DESCRIPTION
186	Boat Ramp
170.4	Boat Ramp
168.6	Boat Ramp
165.1	Ezel Landing
156	Barge Fleeting Area
145.2	Recreation Area
141.5	Boat Ramp
136.3	Recreation Area
125.7	Recreation Area
125.1	Recreation Area
118.8	Bladen Springs Landing
117.5	Recreation Area
114.6-114.8	Ramp
103.1	Peavey's Landing
98.8	Boat Ramp
92.4	Boat Ramp
91.8	Arge Fleeting Area
80	Lady's Landing
75	Oven Bluff
60.3	McIntosh Landing
63.9	Three Rivers Lake
54	Bates Lake
41	Boat Ramp
31.2	Boat Ramp
30.6-29.8	Barge Fleeting Area
25.6	Boat Ramp
19	Dead Lake Marina
8.5-8.2	Swing Bridge
5.0-0.0	Barge Fleeting Areas

The Tenn-Tom Waterway area is very sparsely populated, yet in this rural setting it is still possible to find a good anchorage or marina no farther than 60 miles apart. Following is a list of anchorages where we stopped on the waterway. Consult your guidebooks for a full list of anchorages and marinas, and check with the local marina operators about their knowledge of any change to the condition of an anchorage which you wish to visit since the waterway is in a constant state of change.

Anchorages

Since the Tombigbee Waterway is manmade, there is the possibility of submerged tree stumps in all the anchorages; therefore, we recommend the use of an anchor trip line wherever you anchor.

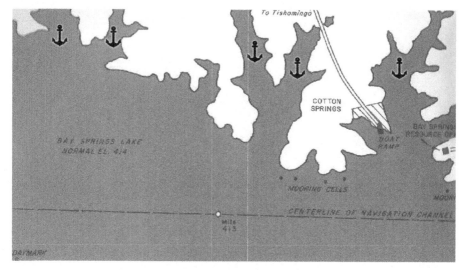

Five Fingers Anchorage

There are three places at which we anchored along the Tenn-Tom. The first is known as Five Fingers anchorage on the port side off Mile 413. There are several places to anchor here, and although there are no depths marked on the chart, the coves are all about 10 feet deep. There is room for many boats with good holding, good wind and wake protection, and no current.

Enter the area slowly, and pick your spot. You may find that you will be anchoring literally off the chart. Use a trip line on your anchor because as stated earlier, there is the possibility that you might snag a tree stump that was not removed when the waterway was built. If you can, pick up a fishing chart available at local marinas. They often have more details about areas off the main waterway.

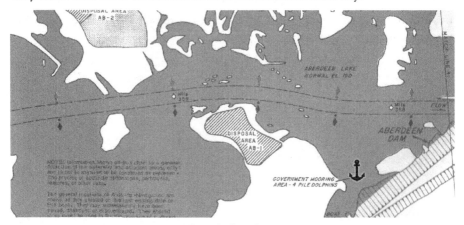

Blue Bluff Anchorage

The next anchorage is Blue Bluff Anchorage which is on your starboard side just before Mile 358. Follow the marked channel through 5 to 6 feet of water into the basin. Tie up at the free dock (no services), or anchor in 10 to 12 feet of water. The holding is good (you may want to use an anchor trip line here), there is room for several boats, it has good wind and wake protection, and there is no current.

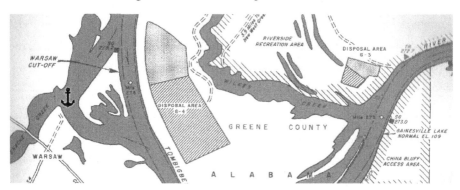

Warsaw Cut-Off Anchorage

The next anchorage where we stopped is located at Mile 272.2 in the Warsaw Cut-Off. The area is wide and deep (depths range up to 30 feet) with room for several boats. Anchor behind the island for the best wind and wake protection in some moderate current. You can leave the anchorage from either side.

At Demopolis, Alabama, the Tombigbee Waterway joins the Black Warrior River. We strongly suggest that you stop at the Demopolis Yacht Basin before going any further. After Demopolis and until you reach Mobile, there are no services and few places to stop for 217 miles. Before starting out, consult your guidebooks for possible anchorages, and speak with the dockmaster about the latest conditions at possible anchorages. We chose to take the 117 mile trip from Demopolis to the Lock 1 Cut Off anchorage at Mile 100.

Due to shoaling, some anchorages that were once excellent places to stop have become impassable. Between Demopolis and the Lock 1 Cut Off anchorage there are two recommended places to stop. The first is Bashi Creek at Mile 145 with room for just a few boats. There is usually 5 feet of water at the entrance and about 6 to 7 feet of water inside the creek. The creek is very narrow, which requires that you put out both a bow and a stern anchor to prevent your boat from swinging. There is good protection from wind and current.

The next place to stop is Bobby's Fish Camp at Mile 118.9. Bobby's has a 100 foot face dock which is available on a "first-come, first-served" basis. Rafting is common, there is limited electrical service, and there is a restaurant on the premises that is open on Thursdays through Saturdays. Call Bobby's at 251 754 9225 for up-to-date information on waterway conditions as well as their services.

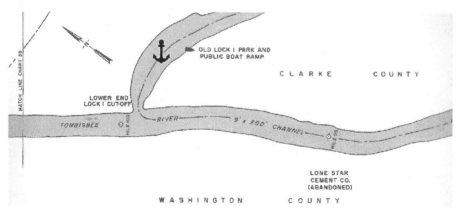

The Lock 1 Cut-Off Anchorage

At Mile 100 is the Lock 1 Cut-Off anchorage. Enter the channel from downstream. Under normal conditions, there is about 5 feet of water at the entrance, and about 6 feet inside the basin near the boat ramp. The holding is fine with good wind and wake protection, and there is room for several boats. At this point you are at sea level. Check your tide charts, and if possible, enter and leave on a favorable tide. The lockmaster at the Coffeeville Lock may also be able to advise you of present conditions at the anchorage entrance.

We have been told by other boaters that there is a good anchorage at Mile 52.8, the Alabama River Cut-Off. There is about 8 feet of water at the entrance and about 10 feet inside. You may want to anchor with a bow and a stern anchor to prevent swinging.

There is another good anchorage a Mile 16.6, Big Bayou Canot. It is reported to be protected and also may require two anchors to prevent swinging.

No matter where you choose to anchor on the Tombigbee Waterways, always consult your guidebooks and try to seek out local knowledge for the latest conditions. Remember that these waterways are in a constant state of change!

Mobile Bay and the Gulf Intracoastal Waterway (Northern Section)

After leaving the Black Warrior-Tombigbee Waterway, you will enter Mobile Bay. The Bay is wide and deep with considerable ship and barge traffic. Red buoys will be on your port side, and, for the first time in many weeks, the buoys will be charted and numbered.

Your route will now head south southeast for about 28 miles to Bon Secour Bay and the Gulf Intracoastal Waterway (GICW) at about Mile Marker 150.

Like the Atlantic and New Jersey Intracoastal Waterways, the red markers will be on the mainland side of the channel, and the green markers will be on the Gulf side. They will also be identified by the small yellow square or triangle on them. See Illustration 3 on page III of the color insert. Depths along the Alabama/Florida Waterway are not a problem, and commercial traffic is light with an occasional tug pushing a barge. There are no drawbridges in this section of the waterway except for a railroad bridge at Mile Marker 347 which is normally open. Be aware that this section of the waterway ends at Mile Marker 375 in Saint George Sound near Carrabelle, Florida.

Anchorages

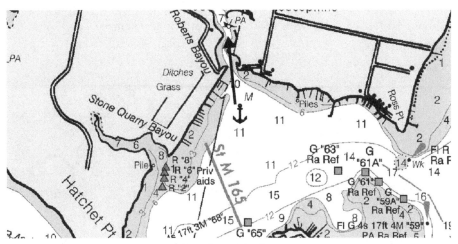

Roberts Bayou Anchorage

We anchored in four places along this section of the GICW. The first was in Roberts Bayou, Alabama, off of Mile Marker 165. Take a north northwest heading from G "65" to the narrow entrance that carries about 9 feet of water into the anchorage. The holding is good, with good wind protection, and there is no current here with room for a few boats.

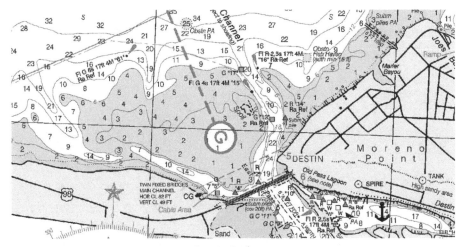

Destin Anchorage

The next anchorage we can recommend is at Destin, Florida, off of Mile Marker 227. From the GICW, follow North Channel to just under the highway bridge.

After passing under the bridge, immediately turn to port and follow the channel along the bridge through the narrow opening into the basin. Holding is good in about 10 feet of water, with good wind protection, no current, and room for numerous boats.

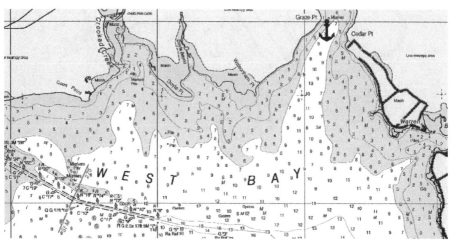

Burnt Mill Anchorage

The third anchorage is Burnt Mill Creek which is located off of Mile Marker 277.5 in West Bay. From G "1", head north northeast for about 3 miles and anchor between Graze Point and Cedar Point in about 7 feet of water. There is good wind protection from all but southerly directions, with good holding, no current, and room for several boats.

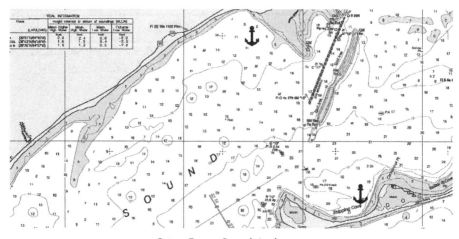

Saint George Sound Anchorages

The last anchorage is in Saint George Sound near Mile Marker 355. If the wind is out of the north, anchor near Carrabelle Beach at 29°49.6' north, 84°41.1' west, in about ten feet of water. If the wind is out of the south, anchor in Shipping Cove off Dog Island at 29°47.1' north, 84°39.3' west, in about 18 feet of water. Both locations have room for many boats with good holding.

The Gulf of Mexico

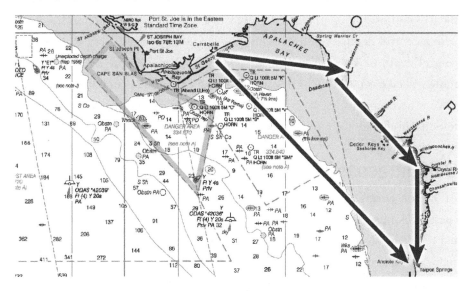

Routes across "The Big Bend"

When this section of the GICW ends, you have two choices, both of which involve heading out into the Gulf of Mexico. You can leave the waterway at Mile 355, and then head south and enter the Gulf of Mexico through Government Cut, or you can leave the waterway at Mile Marker 375, near the Saint George Sound anchorages, and enter the Gulf through East Pass. It is about a 170- to 175-statute mile trip to either Tarpon Springs, Florida, where the waterway begins again at Mile Marker 150, or to Clearwater, Florida, which is farther down the waterway near Mile Marker 135. If you choose to go to Tarpon Springs, be careful because the entrance channel is prone to shoaling. (See "Crossing Open Water" later in the book.)

The Gulf of Mexico is wide and deep with no obstacles in this area. Traffic is nonexistent, except for the occasional shrimp boat. When you are approaching the west coast of Florida, time your arrival for after 10 a.m. There are crab pot floats that can appear as far out as 10 to 20 miles off the coast. With a low morning sun angle, seeing these floats can be difficult, and running over one of them can ruin your whole day.

As described in the section on route planning, you also have the option of making the trip in short jumps around the gulf by first heading to the Steinhatchee River with a control depth of 5-½ feet and then going on to the Crystal River with a control depth of 4-½ feet and finally ending in Tarpon Springs. However, this route will take you three days of good weather on the gulf to complete as opposed to your needing one day of good weather if you take the direct route. Taking this option will also add between 55 and 60 miles to your crossing. This is your choice.

Gulf Intracoastal Waterway (West Coast of Florida)

At Tarpon Springs, the GICW begins again at Mile 150 and follows the west coast of Florida. Again, it follows the Intracoastal Waterway marker rules of having red markers on the mainland side of the channel. There is little commercial traffic on this section of the waterway, and depths are not a problem. There are several draw-bridges along the route with many of them on schedules. (Consult your guidebooks.)

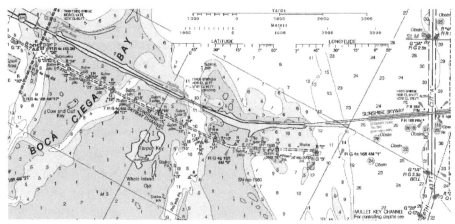

The Sunshine Skyway Channel

At Mile Marker 110.8 in Boca Ciega Bay, if you are not going to Saint Petersburg or Tampa, you can shorten your trip by about 7 miles by leaving the waterway at G "15" and taking the 6 foot deep Sunshine Skyway Channel south along I-275, and then rejoining the waterway near Mile Marker 98 at G "1A".

The GICW ends in San Carlos Bay, just south of Sanibel Island. From here, you have the choice of either taking the Okeechobee Waterway across Florida to Stuart and the AICW, or of going out into the Gulf of Mexico through Matanzas Pass and heading toward the Florida Keys.

Anchorages

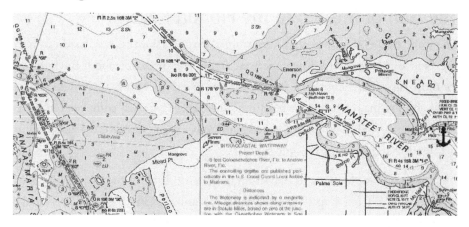

Manatee River Anchorage

In this section of the GICW we only anchored in one place, the Manatee River off of Mile Marker 93. Exit the waterway and enter the marked channel at R "2". Follow it and anchor inside Mc Kay Point in about 9 feet of water. The holding is good, with wind protection from the northwest to northeast, and there is room for many boats. Consult your guidebooks for additional anchorages in this section of the GICW.

The Okeechobee Waterway

The Okeechobee Waterway runs for about one 149 miles from the Gulf Intracoastal Waterway at Mile Marker 0 near Fort Myers Beach to the Atlantic Intracoastal Waterway (ACIW) near Stuart, Florida. Red markers will be on your port side throughout the waterway. The markers display the yellow triangles and squares just like the other intracoastal waterways. The federal project depth of the waterway is 8 feet; if you are taking the direct route across Lake Okeechobee, however, this depth can change due to rainfall amounts. The current minimum depth in the waterway can be checked at: www.saj.usace.army.mil/ by clicking on the Lake Okeechobee link on the right side of the page.

There are five locks along the route and no tolls. For information on the waterway locks, go to www.offshoreblue.com/cruising/okeechobee-locks.php. There are 25 bridges on the waterway; 10 of them require an opening, and some are on schedules. Check your guidebooks for detailed information on the waterway.

The Gulf of Mexico to the Florida Keys

The route to the Florida Keys is very simple. From Matanzas Pass, head out into the Gulf of Mexico and down the west coast of Florida for about 34 miles to Gordon Pass. Then enter the Bay of Naples where there are anchorages and a good city marina, or head down 43 miles to Capri Pass with additional marinas and anchorages. (Do not take the inside route between Naples and Marco Island because the control depth is only 4 feet.)

The trip from Gordon Pass to Marathon in the Florida Keys is a distance of about 105 miles, and from Capri Pass it is about 96 miles. Many boaters like to make the trip over a period of two days by anchoring overnight on the Shark River off Ponce De Leon Bay, 25°21.2' north, 81°07.6', which is about 60 miles south of Capri Pass. From Shark River it is then only about a 46 mile trip to the Keys.

Travel safely, and enjoy these different waterways!

Chapter 13

Crossing Open Water

Many Loopers who have never traveled through large bodies of water such as the Great Lakes, the Gulf of Mexico, or the Atlantic Ocean are naturally concerned about safety and comfort while on the open water. Below are a few suggestions to make your open water passages more enjoyable:

- Travel with other Loopers, as there is often safety in numbers. Knowing that there is at least another boat nearby in case something goes wrong will add to your confidence when making an open water passage. Unless your first few days on the Loop require you to pass through a large body of water by yourself, by the time you are ready to make an open-water crossing, you will have most likely met other Loopers who travel at similar speeds as you, who want to make a crossing at the same time as you do, and who would also like company out on open waters. It is almost impossible not to make friends on the Loop, and you will definitely find other boaters like yourself with whom you will want to travel. These become your "Buddy Boats"!

- Travel when seas are 2 feet or less. For example, when you are ready to make your passage on the Atlantic Ocean along the New Jersey coast, if the weather is not favorable for a couple of days, enjoy that time in Cape May, Atlantic City, or Manasquan. All these seashore resorts have much to offer in the way of beautiful beaches, a variety of restaurants, and numerous historical as well as other unique attractions. Remember that the Great Loop trip is not a race, so make good use of your downtime, be wise, and wait for a more comfortable weather window.

- Seasick medications can be very helpful in adding to a pleasant crossing on open water, however, they are only useful if taken as prescribed before you start out on your daylight/nighttime journey. When we crossed the "Big Bend of Florida" in the Gulf of Mexico, the couple on the boat following us was not used to open water and chose not to use a seasick medication. Soon after getting out into the Gulf they regretted that decision, and by then it was too late.

Wind, Wave, and Weather Information Resources

For wind, wave, and weather information go to: www.nws.noaa.gov/om/marine/zone/usamz.htm, then click on your area of interest on the map, such as, Great Lakes, East (Atlantic Ocean from Main to Georgia), South (Florida Gulf Coast through Georgia on the Atlantic Coast), or Gulf (the Gulf of Mexico from Texas to Florida). Then keep clicking on your area of interest on each succeeding map until the forecast you desire appears.

Another very good website to pinpoint wind and wave conditions is www.weather.gov. On the map that appears, click on the specific body of water in which you are interested. Then click on a more localized area of interest on the next map that appears. Once again, click on the next map to get a pinpoint forecast for wind and wave conditions at a specific location."

Great Lakes Wind and Wave Forecast

For additional wind and wave forecasts on the Great Lakes, go to: www.glerl.noaa. gov/res/glcfs/. Click on the "Winds" or "Waves" for the Great Lake for which you want the forecast. A graphic showing the wind strength or wave height by color and an indication of their direction will appear.

Atlantic Coast Wave Forecast

For a graphic forecast of the wave heights along the Atlantic coast, go to: Storm-surf (Atlantic Ocean) at: www.stormsurfing.com/cgi/display.cgi?a=eus_height. A graphic showing the wave height in feet by color and an indication of their direction will appear.

New Jersey Coast Weather Forecast

To speak to a meteorologist about sea, wind, and weather conditions along the New Jersey coast, call the National Weather Service in Mount Holly, New Jersey at 609 261 6615.

Gulf of Mexico Wave Forecast

For a graphic forecast of the wave heights in the Gulf of Mexico, go to Stormsurf (Gulf of Mexico) at: www.stormsurfing.com/cgi/display.cgi?a=gom_height, and a graphic showing the wave height in feet by color and an indication of their direction will appear.

If you are a member of the America's Great Loop Cruisers' Association, check its Members Forum "Daily Digest" between the months of November and April for sea conditions in the Big Bend area of the Gulf of Mexico.

Gulf of Mexico (Big Bend) Weather Forecast

To speak to a meteorologist about sea, wind, and weather conditions in the Gulf of Mexico, prior to your crossing of the "Big Bend of Florida" call: the National Weather Service in Tallahassee, Florida at 850 942 8833.

Top: Boot Key Harbor – Marathon, Florida
Bottom: The eight step locks between the Ottawa River and the Rideau Canal –
Ottawa, Ontario

Chapter 14

Border Crossings

Entering Canada

Vessels entering Canada are supposed to lower their U. S. courtesy flag, if they are flying one, and raise a "yellow stain" flag on the starboard spreader, bow staff, or masthead of their vessel until they clear customs.

If a boat enters Canada where there is no Customs office (go to www.cbsa-asfc. gc.ca/do-rb/services/drsm-dmsm-eng.html for a list of Direct Reporting Sites for Marine Private Vessels), the captain of the vessel must contact the Canadian Border Services Agency via a land line phone at a Telephone Reporting Site (go to www.cbsa-asfc.gc.ca/do-rb/services/trsm-sdtm-eng.html for a list of Telephone Reporting Sites) at 1-888-226-7277 as soon as he/she lands in Canada. You cannot use your cell phone.

The master is required to follow these steps*:

- give the full name, date of birth, and citizenship for every person on the boat;
- give the destination, purpose of trip, and length of stay in Canada for each passenger who is a nonresident of Canada;
- give the length of absence for each passenger who is a returning resident of Canada;

- give the passport and visa information of passengers, if applicable;

- make sure all passengers have photo identification and proof of citizenship documents;

- declare all goods being imported, including alcoholic beverages (Ships' Stores), firearms, and weapons; (See additional note on Ships' Stores and firearms below)

- report all currency and monetary instruments of a value equal to or greater than CAN$10,000;

- for a returning resident of Canada, declare all repairs or modifications made to goods, including the boat, while outside Canada; and

- give true and complete information.

As proof of presentation, the border services officer will give the master a report number for his records. The master must give this number to a border services officer upon request. Be sure to record this number and keep it with your vessel's papers while in Canada.

For complete information, call: 1-888-226-7277 or visit the Canada Border Services Agency's website at: www.cbsa-asfc.gc.ca/publications/pub/bsf5061-eng.html#s.

Information taken from the CBSA website.

Ships' Stores

The Ships' Stores are goods such as spirits or tobacco products that will be used only *onboard* a vessel while in Canada. Go to the website below, print a copy of Canada Justice Laws Ships' Stores Regulations (SOR/96-40) and carry this information with you. (Your vessel designation is listed under Item 6 – Foreign Yacht):

- http://laws-lois.justice.gc.ca/eng/regulations/sor-96-40/FullText.html

Many Canadian customs agents are not fully acquainted with the details contained in this regulation, so it is a good idea for you to familiarize yourself with the regulations, and have this information available so that you can refer the agent to the regulation and the item number.

The actual details are that if you are a visiting yacht traveling outside (through) Canada, you are allowed to bring into the country these amounts of the following items for the duration of your journey there, duty free:

- Beers and Ales – 1 case (288 ounces) for each adult (over 21) onboard for each week of your voyage – plus

- Wines and Spirits – 1 Imperial quart (40 ounces) for each adult (over 21) onboard for each week of your voyage or 1.5 L (52 fluid ounces) of wine for each person onboard, for each week of a voyage – plus

- Tobacco Products – a reasonable quantity for each person who is 18 years of age or older for each week of your voyage

Please do not over think this regulation it applies to your vessel, many other Loopers and we have used it successfully.

Before starting your Great Loop journey, confirm all the above information with the Canada Border Services Agency, since rules sometimes change.

Note on firearms:

It is illegal to bring any type of hand gun into Canada. If you have one on board your boat when you enter Canada, declare it. It will be confiscated by border officials. If you do not declare the weapon and it is discovered on your boat, not only will the weapon be confiscated, your vessel will also be seized and you will be arrested. For more information on this subject go to the Canadian Border Services Agency website (Importing a Firearm or Weapon Into Canada) at www. cbsa-asfc.gc.ca/publications/pub/bsf5044-eng.html and the Royal Canadian Mounted Police website (Canadian Firearms Program) at www.rcmp-grc.gc.ca/cfp-pcaf/index-eng.htm.

Once you have cleared Canadian customs, lower the "yellow stain" flag. U. S. and other non-Canadian vessels should then raise the Canadian courtesy flag on the starboard spreader, bow staff, or masthead of their vessel.

Travel Documents to Have With You

- Travelers entering Canada must have both proof of identity and proof of citizenship. For U.S. citizens, you must show a valid U.S. passport, but if you do not have one, you can show a government-issued photo ID and proof of U.S. citizenship, such as a U.S. birth certificate. However, if you have to return to the U.S. by air while you are in Canada, you are required to have a valid U.S. passport, and to return by land or by sea, you are required to have a U.S. passport and an Enhanced Drivers' License or other Western Hemisphere Travel Initiative-compliant document.

- Because of the number of cases of international child abduction, children traveling with just one parent or guardian must have either proof of custody or a notarized letter from the other parent, consenting to travel into Canada. Children are also required to have proof of citizenship. Children under age 18 who are traveling alone must have a letter from the parent authorizing travel into Canada.

- Any traveler with a criminal record, including a drunk driving record, may possibly be excluded from entering Canada. To file for a waiver of exclusion, you must contact the Canadian Embassy or Canadian Consulate in the U.S. and pay a fee. This process may take some time.

- A pet cat or dog that is over three months old requires a rabies vaccine certificate signed and dated by a veterinarian. The certificate must also identify the animal by markings, color, sex, breed, weight, and age, as well as give the name of the vaccination and how long it is valid.

Entering the United States

Vessels entering the U. S. are supposed to lower their Canadian courtesy flag, if they are flying one, and then raise a "yellow stain" flag on the starboard spreader, bow staff, or masthead of their vessel until they clear customs.

Enter the U.S. at Drummond Island, Michigan. Call Drummond Island Yacht Haven on your VHF radio and let them know that you will be arriving from Canada. A U.S. Customs agent will come aboard your vessel once you are docked.

- A U.S citizen must have a valid U.S. passport, but if you do not have one, you must show an Enhanced Driver's License or other Western Hemisphere Travel Initiative-compliant document. If a child is under the age of 16, he must present a U.S. birth certificate.

- A Canadian citizen must have a valid Canadian passport to visit the U.S. for business or pleasure. A child under the age of 16 may present a birth certificate. Canadian citizens may stay up to 90 days. An extension for up to 6 months may be obtained by filing form I-539. Proof of the intention to return to Canada at the end of the extended period is also required.

- Canadians and other foreign citizens are allowed to bring certain items into the United States. Visitors may bring in 200 cigarettes, 50 cigars, or up to 2kg (4.4 lbs.) of tobacco without paying customs duties. Individuals over the age of 21 can also bring in up to 1 liter of alcohol. Gifts under $100 can also be brought across the border without paying taxes on those gifts. Personal items that visitors intend to bring with them once they leave the U.S. are also allowable. Customs duties may be assessed on all other items brought across the border.

- To protect United States agriculture, most food items originating from countries other than the U. S. or Canada are prohibited from entering the U.S. from Canada. These foods include meat, plants and plant products (such as fruits and vegetables), dairy products and animal byproducts, in addition to non-food items such as soil. Processed foods are generally exempt from this prohibition. U. S. customs has the right to seize any of these items if they did not originate from the U. S. or Canada. Also, no citrus fruit, goat, or sheep products may be brought into the U.S., no matter what its country of origin.

- Pets – A pet dog that is over three months old requires a rabies vaccine certificate signed and dated by a veterinarian. The certificate must also identify the animal by markings, color, sex, breed, weight, and age; name of the vaccination and how long it is valid must also be included. Review a copy of the U.S. Customs & Border Control booklet, "Pets and Wildlife," regarding cats and other pets.

- U.S. residents leaving Canada are entitled to daily exemptions of U.S. $200 (liquor and tobacco excluded) and to monthly exemptions of U.S. $800 every 30 days following a 48 hour stay in Canada. Families may combine their U.S. $800 per person monthly exemption. (For example, a family of four may combine their exemptions to total U.S. $3,200 for a single purchase.)

- Ships' Stores – All vessels entering the U. S. from Canada are allowed to bring into the U. S. a "reasonable" amount of Ships' Stores of Liquor, Wine, and Beer. All Ships' Stores must be consumed onboard.

- Boat Decal – Vessels 30 feet and over entering the U. S. are required to purchase a private vessel decal from the U. S. Department of Homeland Security. This can be done in advance through: www.cbp.gov/trade/basic-import-export/uftd-info.

Once you have cleared U. S. customs, lower the "yellow stain" flag. Canadian and other non U. S. vessels should then raise the U. S. courtesy flag on the starboard spreader, bow staff, or masthead of their vessel.

For full information regarding U.S. border documentation and procedures see: www.cbp.gov/travel/pleasure-boats-private-flyers.

Canadian "Port of Entry" sign – Confederation Basin Marina – Kingston, Ontario

Chapter 15

Many of the Great Stops on America's Great Loop

St. Louis Gateway Arch

What makes a stop a *Great Stop*? For us, it is a place, ranging in size from one of the world's largest cities to a small country village, which offers a Great Loop visitor at least one outstanding quality from the following list. These locations are well worth a visit!

- Historical Significance
- Local Attractions
- Shopping and Other Services
- Provisioning
- Transportation Hubs
- Unique Local Charm
- Exceptional Fuel Pricing

We will begin our "Great Stops" list in St. Augustine, Florida, travel around the Loop, and end in the Florida Keys.

Great Fuel Stop – Rivers Edge Marina, St. Augustine, FL – 904 827 0520

Location: AICW Mile Marker: 780.0, then turn into the San Sebastian River to Marker 29.

24-hour advanced notice is required for fuel, 50 gal. minimum; fuel deliveries only on weekdays, overnight stay at marina required.

Great Fuel Stop – The Marine Supply and Oil Company, St. Augustine, FL – 904 829 2271 Ex3

Location: AICW Mile Marker: 780.0, then turn into the San Sebastian River to Marker 33.

Fuel is available on weekdays only.

St. Augustine, Florida

The Lightner Museum

Spanish explorer Ponce de Leon, who claimed the region for Spain while reportedly looking for the Fountain of Youth, first explored the area around Saint Augustine in 1513. The city was founded on August 28, 1565, the feast day of Saint Augustine of Hippo, by Spanish explorer Pedro Menéndez de Avilés. It is the oldest city in the continental U.S., and it predates the Jamestown settlement in Virginia by more than 40 years. The French, British, and Spanish battled over who would control Saint Augustine for the next 250 years after its founding, but in 1821 the U.S. took over, and in 1845 the control was finally settled when Florida became a state. Today, the city is a popular tourist attraction and a hub for history buffs wanting to learn more about its Spanish colonial buildings and its 19th century architecture.

Marinas: St. Augustine Municipal Marina – 904 825 1026, Rivers Edge Marina – 904 827 0520

Provisioning: Winn Dixie Supermarket – 1-1/4 miles

Air transport: Jacksonville International Airport – 56 miles

Local Transport: Ace Taxi – 904 824 6888, Yellow Cab – 904 824 2256

Tourist Transport: Old Town Trolley – 888 910 8688

Car Rental: Avis – 904 825 2764, Budget: 904 794 0708

Points of Interest: Castillo de San Marcos, Colonial Spanish Quarter, Mission Nombre de Dios, Lightner Museum, Oldest House Complex, Oldest Wooden Schoolhouse, "Fountain of Youth", Flagler College, St. Augustine Lighthouse, Old Jail

Tourism Website: www.floridahistoriccoast.com

Fernandina Beach, Florida (Amelia Island – Isle of Eight Flags)

Cruise ship traveling the AICW at Fernandina Harbor Marina

Fernandina Beach has the curious distinction of being the only municipality in the U.S. to have flown eight different national flags. The French were the first to plant their flag here when, in 1562, French Huguenot explorer Jean Ribault arrived there and named the island Isle de Mai. Over the next three centuries, it was claimed at various times by Spain, England, insurgents known as the Patriots of Amelia Island who raised a North American Patriot flag, a group of musketeers called "The Brethren of Mexico, Buenos Aires, New Grenada, and Venezuela" who raised the Latin American Green Cross of Florida flag, Mexico, the Confederate States of America, and finally in 1862 by Union forces who raised the flag of the United States of America. Today, Amelia Island and Fernandina Beach are the homes of many upscale resorts, world-class spas, championship golf courses, exclusive restaurants, historic sites, and annual festivals.

Marina: Fernandina Harbor Marina – 904 491 2090, Amelia Island Yacht Basin – 904 277 4615

Provisioning: Winn Dixie & Publix Supermarkets – 3 miles, Atlantic Seafood Market on site – Fernandina Harbor

Air Transport: Jacksonville International Airport – 27 miles

Local Transport: Relax & Ride Taxi – 904 556 2872

Tourist Transport: Old Town Carriage Co. – 904 277 1555, Amelia Island Carriages – 904 556 2662, Amelia Island Trolleys – 904 753 4486

Car Rental: Enterprise – 904 261 1050, Hertz – 800 277 4653

Points of Interest: Palace Saloon, 59 block area of homes and buildings on the National Register of Historic Places, Fort Clinch State Park, and Amelia Island Museum of History

Tourism Website: www.islandchamber.com

Great Fuel Stop – Ocean Petroleum, Brunswick, Georgia – 912 265 2275

Location: 5 miles off of ICW Mile Marker 680.0 on the East River. It is a commercial fuel dock (diesel only) and is open only on weekdays. Call in advance for the latest price, and be sure to ask for the price including all taxes. It consistently has the lowest price for fuel within hundreds of miles of its location – payment by cash or check.

Savannah, Georgia

British General James Oglethorpe overlooks one of the many beautiful squares of Savannah

Founded in 1733 by British General James Oglethorpe, the city of Savannah became the colonial capital of the Province of Georgia and later the first state capital. Although attacked by federal troops during the American Civil War, Savannah was spared the destruction that took place in other southern cities, thus leaving many of its historic homes and buildings intact. Today, Savannah is a mix of modern and historic buildings with an industrial center and an important Atlantic seaport. Each year, millions of visitors come to Savannah to enjoy the city's architecture and historic buildings and its downtown area, which includes the Savannah Victorian Historic District, the Savannah Historic District, with its 22 park-like squares which is one of the largest National Historic Landmark Districts in the U.S.

Marina: Westin-Savannah Harbor Marina – 912 201 2021

Provisioning: Take the complimentary water ferry to River Street – Kroger Supermarket – 1/2 mile

Air Transport: Savannah/Hilton Head International – 9 miles

Rail Transport: Amtrak – 1.3 miles

Local Transport: Miracle Seven Cab Co. – 912 412 3258, Yellow Cab – 912 376 9101

Tourist Transport: Old Town Trolley Tours – 888 910 8687

Car Rental: Enterprise – 912 964 4050

Points of Interest: Cathedral of St. John the Baptist, Historic District, Savannah History Museum, Bonaventure Cemetery, Forsyth Park, Juliette Gordon Low's Birthplace (Girl Scouts), Massie Heritage Center, Ships of the Sea Maritime Museum, Old Fort Jackson, River Street, City Market

Tourism Website: www.savannahvisit.com

Beaufort, South Carolina

One of the many antebellum homes in Beaufort, S. C.

Beaufort was founded in 1711, and it is the second-oldest city in South Carolina after Charleston. The city is recognized for its scenic location and its impressive antebellum architecture. Like Savannah, though occupied by Union forces during the Civil War, it was spared, leaving most of the original structures unharmed.

In spite of new development especially during the 20th Century, Beaufort has managed to retain much of its historic character through its renowned architecture and historic preservation efforts. The city celebrates several festivals during the year including the Water Festival, a two-week extravaganza in Mid July; the Shrimp Festival in October; and The Beaufort International Film Festival held in March which screens independent-made films.

Marinas: Downtown Marina of Beaufort – 843 524 4422, Port Royal Landing Marina – 843 525 6664

Provisioning: Bi-Lo Supermarket – 1.25 miles – Downtown Marina, Publix Supermarket – 2.8 miles – Port Royal

Air Transport: Savannah/Hilton Head International Airport – 48 miles

Local Transport: Port Royal Landing Marina – Courtesy Car, Yellow Cab – 843 522 1121, A Taxi Cab – 843 379 6665, Maude's Cab Co. – 843 524 9096

Tourist Transport: Southern Rose Buggy Tours – 843 524 2900, Carriage Tours of Beaufort – 843 525 1300

Car Rental: Enterprise – 843 524 0494

Points of Interest: Beaufort Movie Tour, Historic Homes Tour, Bay Street Shopping and Restaurants, The Arsenal and Beaufort Museum, St. Helena's Episcopal Church

Tourism Website: www.beaufortsc.org

Charleston, South Carolina

Dock Street Theatre is the oldest theatre in the U. S. – Charleston, S. C.

Charleston, when founded in 1670, was originally named Charles Town and located on the west bank of the Ashley River. In 1680, the city was moved to its present location, and adopted its current name in 1783. It is known as "The Holy City" due to the prominence of its churches and to the fact that it was one of the few cities in the original 13 colonies to provide religious tolerance (as long as you were not Catholic). In 1995, the city was recognized as the "Best-Mannered City" in the U.S. Charleston is steeped in history from the colonial era through the American Revolution, but it is most noted for the firing on its Fort Sumter that started the Civil War.

Marinas: Charleston City Marina – 843 723 5098,
Charleston Maritime Center – 843 853 3625

Provisioning: Harris Teeter Market – 1 mile from the City Marina via courtesy van and .12 mile from the Maritime Center

Air Transport: Charleston International Airport – 16 miles

Local Transport: Green Taxi – 843 762 5705

Tourist Transport: Fort Sumter Tours – 843 722 1691, Old South Carriage Co.- 843 723 9712, Palmetto Carriage – 800 979 3370, Charleston Water Taxi – 843 330 2989, Harbor & Naval Base Tour – 843 722 1691, Charleston Visitor and Transportation Center Free Trolley Ride – 800 774 0006

Car Rental: Budget – 843 577 5195

Points of Interest: The Battery, Fort Sumter, Patriots Point Naval & Maritime Museum, U. S. S. Yorktown, Aiken-Rhett House & Museum, Old City Market, The Citadel, Cathedral of St. John the Baptist, Civil War Museum, The Charleston Museum, The Old Exchange & Provost Dungeon

Tourism Website: Charleston Visitors and Convention Bureau – charlestoncvb.com

Georgetown, South Carolina

The historic district of Georgetown, South Carolina

Some historians claim that American history began in Georgetown in 1526 with the earliest settlement in North America by Europeans with African slaves. It is also believed that the Spanish founded a colony in the area. However, it did not last. The colony failed for a variety of reasons, including disease and a revolt of the slaves. Those who remained failed as farmers and eventually decided that enough was enough and sailed away. Two centuries later, in 1729, Elisha Screven laid the plan for Georgetown and developed the city in a 4-by-8-block grid. Today, the grid is referred to as the Historic District of the city and maintains the original street names and many of the original homes. Georgetown played an important part in the American Revolution with its port supplying General Nathanael Greene's army in the latter part of the conflict; It was also the home territory of General Francis Marion (aka The Swamp Fox), a Revolutionary War hero who famously eluded the British and rescued many American prisoners. Georgetown, like some other towns, was also mostly spared the ravages of the Civil War, thus leaving most of its antebellum structures and outlying plantations intact.

Marina: Harborwalk Marina – 843 546 4250

Provisioning: Kudzu Bakery – .5 mile, Piggly Wiggly Supermarket – 1. 5 miles, Food Lion – 2 miles

Air Transport: Myrtle Beach International Airport – 36 miles

Local Transport: Wragg Tyme Taxi – 843 527 8410, R. A. Bradley Taxi – 843 546 7451.

Tourist Transport: Swamp Fox Tours – 843 527 1112

Car Rental: Hertz Local Edition – 843 520 1535

Points of Interest: Rice Museum, Harborwalk, Williams Ghost Tours – 843 543 1673

Tourism Website: hammockcoastsc.com

Great Fuel Stop – Osprey Marina, Myrtle Beach, South Carolina – 843 215 5353

Location: ICW Mile Marker 373.0. Gives a $.10/gal discount for Boat US members. Consistently has the lowest price for fuel within hundreds of miles of its location.

Great Fuel Stop – Top Rack Marina, Chesapeake, Virginia – 757 227 3041

Location: ICW Mile Marker 8.8 (Elizabeth River, Southern Branch). Consistently has the lowest price for fuel within hundreds of miles of its location.

Norfolk, Virginia

Heading into Norfolk, Virginia on the Elizabeth River

Norfolk was named after Norfolk, England, the birthplace of Adam Thoroughgood, a former indentured servant who became an influential landowner in the area in the mid-1600s. Norfolk grew in the late 17th century when Half Moone Fort (in the shape of a half moon) was constructed, and a 50-acre parcel of land was acquired in exchange for 10,000 pounds of tobacco. Norfolk was incorporated in 1705, and in 1736 George II of England granted Norfolk a royal charter as a borough. By 1775, Norfolk was the most prosperous city in Virginia based on its import and export operations with Great Britain. That tradition continues on today because Norfolk (Port of Virginia) is one of the largest ports in the U.S. handling nearly 50 million tons of cargo each year. It is also the home of the Norfolk Naval Base, the largest naval base in the world!

Marina: Waterside Marina – 757 625 3625

Provisioning: Harris Teeter Market – 2.6 miles (Marina Shuttle)

Air Transport: Norfolk International Airport- 10 miles

Rail Transport: Amtrak (Newport News) – 24 miles

Local Transport: Waterside Taxi 757 531 6430

Tourist Transport: Norfolk Naval Base 804 444 7955, Harbor Cruise – 757 627 7245

Car Rental: Avis 757 625 0040

Points of Interest: Waterside Marketplace, Battleship Wisconsin, Nauticus National Maritime Center, Norfolk Naval Base Tour, Festivals at Town Point Park, Ferry to Portsmouth

Tourism Website: www.visitnorfolktoday.com

Tangier Island, Virginia

This island, which is approximately 12 miles from the mainland in the middle of Chesapeake Bay, can only be reached by boat or airplane. It is often called the "Soft Shelled Crab Capital of the World," and it served as a summer retreat for the Pokomoke Indians prior to the arrival of European explorer John Smith in the 1600s. During the War of 1812, 1,200 British troops lived here along with many escaped slaves who were given their freedom by the British. Today's residents lead quiet lives on the island with no traffic lights and an almost non-existent crime rate. There is a small airport which is only open in daylight hours, and two boats travel daily to Crisfield, Maryland, carrying passengers and mail. The number of boats increases considerably during the summer tourist season. There are several restaurants, bed and breakfasts, and a few gift shops located here, and alcohol is prohibited due to the strong influence of the Methodist Church on the island.

Golf carts, mopeds, and bikes are the only means of transportation on Tangier, and the islanders still retain a Cornish brogue in their speech which is a remnant of the language of their early British ancestors.

Marina: Parks Marina – 757 891 2581/757 891 2567

Provisioning: Daley & Son Grocery – 757 891 2469

Air Transport: Tangier Island Airport (small aircraft only!) – 757 891 2496

Local Transport: Golf Cart and Bike Rentals – 757 891 2999

Tourist Transport: Tangier Island Tours – 757 891 2331
(ask for Glenda or Susan)

Points of Interest: Tangier History Museum and Interpretive Cultural Center, Fisherman's Corner Restaurant, Hilda Crockett's Chesapeake House, Fisherman's Corner Crab Shanty Waterman Visit –
757 891 2269 (ask for Ookire)

Tourism Website: www.tangierisland-va.com

Mount Vernon, Virginia

George Washington's home at Mount Vernon

This 500-acre estate of President George Washington not only includes his mansion as well as his tomb, but also original and re-constructed out-buildings and barns, an operating blacksmith shop, and a pioneer farm. Mt. Vernon's Orientation Center and its Museum and Education Center house 25 theaters and galleries with films, videos, and displays of 18th century artifacts, and its gristmill and distillery are nearby. It is a National Historic Landmark, and it has had more than 80 million visitors since it was first open to the public in 1860.

Marina: Mt. Vernon Estate – 800 429 1520
(Call Wharf Master in advance for permission to pull in)

Points of Interest: Ford Orientation Center, the Mansion and Out-Buildings, Museum and Education Center, Gardens and Grounds, Washington's Tomb, Slave Memorial, Audio Tours, Costumed Interpreters, Walking Tours, Shops, and Food Court

Washington, D. C. (via Alexandria, Virginia)

The Old Town area of Alexandria, Virginia, was originally laid out on the banks of the Potomac River in 1749 and is well-known for its art galleries, antique shops, historic houses, and restaurants. Among its landmarks are General Robert E. Lee's childhood home, Gadsby's Tavern, which was built in the 18th century, and a replica of George Washington's townhouse. The Torpedo Factory Art Studio, which was the site of a U.S. munitions storage area until the end of World War II, is located on the waterfront adjacent to the City Marina, but now houses more than 82 artists' studios as well as various workshops and galleries displaying the work of over 160 artists.

The United States Capitol Building in Washington, D. C.

The U.S. Capital of Washington, D.C., is host to innumerable historic sites and museums, as well as monuments and memorials. All of these, including the White House, the home of the President of the United States, are open for tours. The National Archives houses the Declaration of Independence, the Constitution of the United States, the Bill of Rights, and other documents of importance in America's history. The Smithsonian Institution maintains most of the official museums and galleries, including the Museum of National History, the National Air & Space Museum, the Museum of the American Indian, the National Museum of American History, and various art museums. Washington is also home to the J.F.K. Center for the Performing Arts where the National Symphony Orchestra, the Washington National Opera, and Washington Ballet perform. Allow several days for a visit!

Marina: Alexandria City Marina – 703 746 5487
(Call well ahead for a docking application)

Provisioning: Royal Grocery (Alexandria) – 1.1 miles

Air Transport: Reagan Washington National Airport – 4 miles,
Washington Dulles International Airport – 33 miles

Rail Transport: Amtrak (Alexandria) – 1.4 miles

Local Transport: Alexandria to Washington – take the King Street free trolley to the King Street Metro into the city (In Alexandria – www.dashbus.com/Trolley. In Washington – www.wmata.com)

Tourist Transport: Washington – Old Time Trolley Tours –
888 910 8687 – www.trolleytours.com/washington-dc,
Gray Line Bus Tours – www.graylinedc.com.
Alexandria – Alexandria Tours – 703 329 1122

Car Rental: Thrifty – 703 684 7500, Enterprise 703 461 3520

Points of Interest: Washington – see Old Time Trolley Tours and
Gray Line websites above
Alexandria – Many historic homes & museums – see website below

Tourism Website: Washington – washington.org
Alexandria – www.visitalexandriava.com/things-to-do/tours

Solomons Island, Maryland

Calvert Marine Museum, Solomons, Maryland
(Photo courtesy of Lisa B. Frailey of Sail Solomons)

Back Creek, Solomons, Maryland
(Photo courtesy of Zahniser's Yachting Center)

The community known today as Solomons or Solomons Island was originally called Bourne's Island in the 1600s and then Somervell's Island in the 1700s. Shortly after the Civil War, a businessman from Baltimore, Isaac Solomon, built a cannery here, and his name stuck. Boat building, which supported the work of the local fishermen, became a thriving business in the 19th century. Solomons played an important part in World War II because it was the location for training more than 60,000 troops in mostly amphibious operations. Ironically, many of the servicemen who trained here were sent to fight at the Solomon Islands in the Pacific. Today, Solomons is a boater and tourist destination with marinas, seafood restaurants, gift shops, a boardwalk, a sculpture garden, and the Calvert Marine Museum.

Marina: Zahniser's Yachting Center – 410 326 2166, Spring Cove Marina – 866 539 6039

Provisioning: Marina's ship store or convenience store – 3/4 mile walk – Zahniser's, Marina's ship store or courtesy shuttle to shops – Spring Cove

Air Transport: Reagan Washington National Airport – 48 miles

Local Transport: Courtesy Cab Service – 301 866 9600, E-taxi, LLC – 410 414 3540, Marina's complimentary bicycles – Zahniser's, Marina's courtesy shuttle – Spring Cove

Car Rental: Enterprise – 301 866 9500, National – 301 866 9500, Avis – 301 863 7373

Points of Interest: Calvert Marina and Lighthouse

Tourism Website: www.solomonsmaryland.com

St. Michaels, Maryland

Hooper Strait Lighthouse, St. Michaels, Maryland

The town of St. Michaels was incorporated in 1804 and was given its name for an early Anglican church that pre-dated its development. It became known for its ship-building industry and especially for its fast schooners which were not only able to outwit pirates of the eastern shore area, but also were able to maneuver quickly around blockades made by British ships during the War of 1812. After the defeat of the British, the town's chief industries became oystering and crabbing. Today, it is the location of the Chesapeake Bay Maritime Museum and its premier landmark, the Hooper Strait Lighthouse. The museum contains the world's largest collection of Chesapeake Bay vessels in and around its 35 buildings, and it provides hands-on experiences for its visitors and educates them on the history and culture of the area.

Marinas: St. Michaels Marina – 800 678 8980, St. Michaels Harbor Inn – 410 745 9001, Chesapeake Bay Maritime Museum – 410 745 6088 (call for dockage well ahead!)

Provisioning: Acme Supermarket – .5 mile, Village Shoppe – .5 mile

Air transport: Baltimore/Washington International Airport – 66 miles

Local Transport: Executive Taxi Cab Services – 410 820 8294/ 410 829 0097

Car Rental: Sensible Car Rental – 410 822 8879

Points of Interest: Chesapeake Bay Maritime Museum and Hooper Strait Lighthouse, quaint shopping district with boutiques, antique shops, and art galleries, St. Michaels Winery, Eastern Shore Brewery, and a number of restaurants featuring Chesapeake Bay seafood

Tourism Website: www.stmichaelsmd.org

Rock Hall, Maryland

Rock Hall was incorporated in 1908, and it is said that it was originally named after a mansion in the town that was built out of the white sandstone of the area. In its early days, it was a port that specialized in the shipment of agricultural crops, seafood, and tobacco, but eventually seafood processing, and fishing became its major industries. It continues today to be a working harbor with commercial watermen and charter boat fishermen who continue the Bay maritime heritage of their forefathers.

Marina: Rock Hall Landing Marina – 410 639 2224

Provisioning: Bayside Foods (410 639 2552) –
provides free pick-up and delivery for boaters at marinas

Air Transport: Baltimore/Washington International Airport – 76 miles

Local Transport: Bicycle rentals at the marina, Jab Cab Taxi Service –
410 778 9496

Tourist Transport: Rock Hall Town Trolley (see marina for schedule)

Car Rental: Enterprise – 877 410 7393

Points of Interest: Rock Hall Museum, Tolchester Beach Revisited Museum, The Mainstay Concert Hall, quaint town art galleries and nautical gift shops, boutiques, ice cream parlors, and a variety of restaurants featuring Maryland Eastern Shore Crab-cakes, and Crab feasts

Tourism Website: www.rockhallmd.com

Annapolis, Maryland

Annapolis Harbor

The U.S. Naval Academy in Annapolis, Maryland

The current capital of the state of Maryland, Annapolis was incorporated in 1708 and even served as the capital of the United States from 1783-1784. The town was named after Princess Anne of Denmark and Norway, who became the Queen of Great Britain in 1702. From that time until the American Revolution, it became known as a hub for the wealthy elite whose homes still stand there. Today Annapolis is a sailing "mecca," and it is also the location of the United States Naval Academy, founded in 1845, which is the training institution for future officers in the United States Navy and Marine Corps.

Marinas: Annapolis City Dock – 410 263 7973, Annapolis Yacht Basin – 410 263 3544

Provisioning: Giant Food – 2.6 miles, Whole Foods 4.2 Miles

Air Transport: Baltimore/Washington Airport – 25 miles

Local Transport: Annapolis Taxi – 443 995 1400

Tourist Transport: Annapolis Water Taxi – 410 263 0033/ VHF Channel 68

Car Rental: Enterprise – 410 268 7751

Points of Interest: U. S. Naval Academy, Annapolis Maritime Museum, Maryland State House, Guided Walking Tours

Tourism Website: www.visitannapolis.org

Baltimore, Maryland

The Inner Harbor, Baltimore, Maryland

Baltimore was founded in 1729 and grew quickly as a granary for the sugar producing island colonies of the Carribbean. During the American Revolution, it joined with other American colonies in resisting British taxes and not trading with Great Britain. During a period of three months from December of 1776 to February of 1777, it became the capital of the United States when the second-Continental Congress met here. During the War of 1812, the British attacked the city after previously burning Washington, D.C., but here the U.S. forces were able to successfully defend their harbor from the enemy. It was during this bombardment of Fort McHenry that Francis Scott Key, a Maryland lawyer who was aboard a British ship while trying to negotiate the release of an American prisoner at the time, was inspired to write the words of the "Star-Spangled Banner" which eventually became the national anthem of the United States. Today Baltimore has three distinct areas along its port on the Patapsco River: The Inner Harbor with its National Aquarium, the Maryland Science Center, historic ships, Oriole Park at Camden Yards, hotels, shops, and restaurants, and access to Fort McHenry; Fells Point, long ago a rough area offering "refuge" for sailors, but now re-gentrified;

and Little Italy, the center of the city's Italian-American community with its ethnic restaurants and groceries.

Marina: Inner Harbor East Marina – 410 625 1700

Provisioning: Whole Foods – .25 mile

Air Transport: Baltimore/Washington Airport – 10 miles

Rail Transport: Amtrak – 2 miles

Local Transport: Baltimore Taxi – 410 732 1600

Tourist Transport: Baltimore Trolley Tour – 410 254 8787, Baltimore Water Taxi – 410 563 3900

Car Rental: Budget – 410 276 7266

Points of Interest: National Aquarium, Harborplace, Maryland Science Center, Little Italy, Camden Yards, Baltimore and Ohio Railroad Museum

Tourism Website: www.baltimore.org

Cape May, New Jersey

Victorian Hotels in Cape May

The town of Cape May was named after a Dutch sea captain, Cornelius Jacobsen Mey, who explored and charted the area between 1611 and 1614. Unfortunately, in conferring the honor of naming the town after him, the town fathers incorrectly spelled his last name as "May" instead of "Mey"! By the mid-1700s, Cape May had become a tourist destination for vacationers from Philadelphia, and today the U.S. government recognizes it as the country's oldest seaside resort. Its popularity continued to grow through the 18th century, and it was considered one of the finest resorts in America by the 19th century. In 1876, a massive fire destroyed 30 acres of the town center, thus the homes that were rebuilt were almost all done in the Victorian style of that era. Through preservation efforts, Cape May today is known for its large number of well-maintained Victorian houses which is one of the largest collections of its kind in the U.S. and is second only to that of San Francisco. In 1976, the entire city of Cape May was officially designated as a National Historic Landmark, and it is the only city in the U.S. with such a designation.

Marina: Utsch's Marina – 609 884 2051

Provisioning: Wa Wa Food Market – .7 miles,
Acme Supermarket – 1.4 miles

Air Transport: Atlantic City International Airport – 48 miles

Local Transport: Aart's Cape May Taxi – 609 898 7433

Tourist Transport: Cape May Carriage Co. – 609 884 4466, Great American Trolley Co. – 800 487 6559, Cape May Trolley Tours – 609 884 5404

Car Rental: Hertz Local Edition – 609 889 7722

Points of Interest: The entire city is a National Historic Landmark, Cape May Lighthouse, Emlen Physick Estate, World War II Lookout Tower, Victorian Homes, Historic Cold Spring Village, Cape May Washington Street Mall, Nature Center of Cape May, Cape May Zoo, art galleries, boutiques, and many restaurants offering simple seafood as well as those with fine dining.

Tourism Website: www.capemay.com/visitors-center.html

Atlantic City, New Jersey

Atlantic City, New Jersey.

Because of its location along the New Jersey coast, which is just 60 miles southeast of Philadelphia, Atlantic City became a prime potential resort town for developers, and in 1853 its first commercial hotel, The Belloe House, was opened. During the following year, the Camden and Atlantic Railroad train service began, and Philadelphia tourists started arriving. In 1870, the first boardwalk was constructed to help hotel owners keep sand out of their lobbies, and since then the boardwalk has expanded numerous times. That same year, the first road from the mainland to the city was completed, requiring a 30-cent toll. Within a few years, almost 500,000 passengers a year were coming to Atlantic City by rail, and soon two more rail lines were added to handle the crush of tourists. Soon, larger and larger hotels were constructed, and several entertainment piers, including the famous Steel Pier, were added, and it now became common for guests to visit for weeks at a time. By the 1920s, tourism was at its peak, and during Prohibition, liquor flowed freely with gambling regularly taking place in the back rooms of nightclubs and restaurants. After World War II, however, the city began to decline because with affordable automobiles, tourists came only for weekends instead of weeks. The glory days of Atlantic City seemed all but gone, but in 1976 legalized gambling came to the city. Today it is one of the top 10 casino resort cities in the U.S.

Marina: Historic Gardner's Basin – 609 348 2880 (Ext. 12)

Air Transport: Atlantic City International Airport – 13 miles

Rail Transport: NJ Transit to Philadelphia – 2 miles

Local Transport: Atlantic City Jitney – www.jitneyac.com, Airport Shuttle – 609 344 8642/ 609 576 2776, Mutual Taxi – 609 345 6111

Tourist Transport: Great American Trolley Co. – 800 487 6559

Car Rental: Hertz Local Edition – 609 441 5522, Enterprise – 609 348 2902

Points of Interest: Absecon Lighthouse, Atlantic City Boardwalk, IMAX Theater at Tropicana, Atlantic City Aquarium, Tanger Outlets, Casinos, Aquarium on-site

Tourism Website: www.atlanticcitynj.com

Great Fuel Stop – Beach Haven Yacht Club Marina, Beach Haven, New Jersey – 609 492 9101

Location: NJICW Mile Marker 107.0 (Little Egg Harbor). Consistently has the lowest price for fuel within hundreds of miles of its location

New York City, New York

The New York City Financial District

The Statue of Liberty in New York Harbor

New York is the most populous city in the United States and is located on one of the world's largest natural harbors. It is an international urban power city and the home of the United Nations Headquarters, as well as being a world center of finance, commerce, art, fashion, culture, media, and entertainment. Founded as a Dutch trading post in 1624, it served as the capital of the United States from 1785–1790, and it has been the country's largest city since that time. The city has approximately 55 million visitors a year with 49 million of them tourists! The most popular destinations include: the poignant World Trade Center Memorial, the Statue of Liberty and Ellis Island, the Empire State Building, the Metropolitan Museum of Art, the Museum of Natural History, Times Square, the Broadway Theater district, the Bronx Zoo, Rockefeller Center, the N.Y. Stock Exchange, Central Park, Lincoln Center, the N.Y. Botanical Garden, its Fifth Avenue stores, and famous restaurants that abound.

Marinas: (Jersey City, N. J.) Liberty Harbor Marina – 800 646 2066, Liberty Landing – 201 985 8000

Provisioning: At Liberty Landing Marine Store (convenience goods)

Air Transport: Newark International Airport – 8 miles

Rail Transport: Amtrak – Newark – 8 miles

Local Transport: AAA Taxi – 201 435 1000, A-1 Taxi – 201 432 3333, Jersey City Taxi – 201 798 5556, Exchange Place Taxi – 201 985 1888. From either marina take a taxi to the Journal Square PATH train that will take you to either the World Trade Center site or midtown Manhattan

Tourist Transport:

From Liberty Harbor – take the N. Y. Waterways Ferry to Pier 11 (Wall Street) – 800 533 3779.

From Liberty Landing – take the Liberty Landing Ferry to the World Financial Center.

In New York – take the Gray Line Tours – 800 669 0051 – www.grayline.com/new_york

Car Rental: Thrifty – 201 222 2454

Points of Interest: see Gray Line Tours above for suggested places

Tourism Website: NYC Convention & Visitors Bureau – www.nycgo.com

Another more relaxed way for you to visit New York City is to travel about 25 miles north of the "Big Apple" to Half Moon Bay Marina on the Hudson River in Croton-on-Hudson, New York. From here you can easily take a scenic Metro North train-ride directly into Midtown Manhattan. You can also visit the Culinary Institute of America in Hyde Park, New York, which counts among its famous alumni Chefs Anthony Bourdain, Cat Cora, Rocco Di Spirito, and Sara Moulton. The school offers campus tours as well as dining at its four restaurants. Close by is also the United States Military Academy at West Point which was established on the site of the oldest continuing-operating post in the U.S.in 1802. It is a National Historic Landmark with many monuments and statues, a military cemetery, the oldest military museum in the country, and it covers over 15,000 acres. Among its alumni are two U.S. Presidents, many senators and congressmen, a number of outstanding generals, numerous Medal of Honor winners, and astronauts.

Half Moon Bay Marina at Croton-on-Hudson, New York

Marina: (Croton-on-Hudson, N.Y.) Half Moon Bay Marina 914 271 5400

Provisioning: A gourmet market within walking distance

Air Transport: Westchester County Airport – 18 miles, La Guardia Airport – 40 miles

Rail Transport: An Amtrak and Metro North rail station with direct express service (40 minutes) to New York City – less than 1 mile from the marina

Local Transport: Croton Taxi and Airport Service – 914 774 0621, J and S Taxi and Airport Service – 914 271 4000

Car Rental: Enterprise – 914 271 0100 (across the street from the marina) – offers special "Looper" discounts

Points of Interest: West Point Military Academy – 15 miles, Culinary Institute of America at Hyde Park – 47 miles

Tourism Website: West Point Military Academy – www.usma.edu/Visiting/SitePages/Home.aspx

The United States Military Academy at West Point, New York

Waterford, New York

The Captain and the "Admiral" at the Waterford Harbor Visitors Center near Lock E2 on the Erie Canal

The village of Waterford is the oldest incorporated village in the country. This was done in 1794 even before the town was formed, and it has been host to "Canal Fest" and the "Tugboat Roundup" for years. It is also the eastern gateway to the Erie Canal. Proposed in 1808 and completed in 1825, the Canal links the waters of Lake Erie in the west to the Hudson River in the east. It is an engineering marvel dug by hand to an original depth of 4 feet and a width of 40 feet, and when it was built some called it "The Eighth Wonder of the World." Over the years, it has been improved many times and now contains 36 locks and encompasses a total elevation differential of about 565 feet.

Marina: Waterford Harbor Visitor Center – 518 233 9123 (free dockage)

Provisioning: Hannaford Supermarket & Pharmacy – .5 mile, Price Chopper – .6 mile

Air Transport: Albany International Airport – 13 miles

Local Transport: Acme Taxi – 518 687 2237

Rail Transport: Rensselaer-Albany Station (Amtrak) – 13 miles

Car Rental: Enterprise – 518 383 3444

Points of Interest: Walk to Lock 2 – observe the locking process and meet the lock tender, Tour the tugboat "Urger," Peebles Island State Park, "Don & Paul's Restaurant"– billiards and good food at great prices

Tourism Website: www.town.waterford.ny.us/

Utica, New York

The Tasting Room at the Matt Brewing Company in Utica, New York

Utica was first settled by Europeans in 1773. The town was located there because it was next to the shallowest spot along the Mohawk River making it the best place for fording across to the other side. It was also situated at an Iroquois Indian crossroads, a spot that made trading exceedingly easy for local merchants. Today it is also the location of the Matt Brewing Company which has operated there since 1888 and has earned the reputation of being one of the most respected specialty brewers in the country.

Marina: Utica Historical Marina & Aqua Vino Restaurant – 315 732 0116

Air Transport: Syracuse Hancock International Airport – 56 miles

Provisioning: Hannaford Supermarket & Pharmacy – 2.5 miles

Rail transport: Utica Station (Amtrak) – 1.1 mile

Local Transport: Ace Taxi – 315 735 5055, Elite Taxi – 315 732 0200

Points of Interest: Matt Brewing Company Tour & Trolley – 800 765 6288, Munson-Williams-Proctor Art Institute, Utica Zoo

Tourism Website: www.oneidacountytourism.com

Sylvan Beach, New York

The Captain's brother-in-law, Al, and sister, Pat, at "Bikes on the Beach" night at Sylvan Beach, New York.

Sylvan Beach is a quaint, old lakeshore community on Lake Oneida with four miles of beaches, cottages, restaurants, and even a small amusement park. It is a reminder of how summers in small towns used to be.

Marina: Mariner's Landing Marina – 315 762 0112

Provisioning: Sylvan Beach Deli-Mart – .7 Mile

Air Transport: Syracuse Hancock International Airport – 35 miles

Local Transport: Oneida Taxi – 315 363 3060

Car Rental: Enterprise – 315 363 5753

Points of Interest: "Bikes at the Beach" (Tuesday nights), Sylvan Beach Amusement Park, Erie Canal Village (Rome, NY – 11.5 miles), "Classic Car Cruise Night" (Thursday nights)

Tourism Website: www.sylvanbeachny.com

Great Fuel Stop – Winter Harbor Marina, Central Square, New York – 315 676 9276

> **Location:** Mile Marker 151.0 (Erie Canal, Oneida River). Consistently has the lowest price for fuel within hundreds of miles of its location.

Ottawa, Ontario

Parliament – Ottawa

Ottawa is the capital of Canada and stands on the south bank of the Ottawa River, bordering Gatineau, Quebec. Although it was originally an Irish and French settlement, in 1826 it was eventually given the name, Bytown, in honor of Colonel John By, who was the overseer of the early work on the construction of the Rideau Canal. The canal was built over a period of six years to provide a secure transportation route between Montreal and Kingston which was not only was a means of defense, but would also allow Canadians to by-pass the miles of the St. Lawrence River which border New York State in the U.S. The town was later renamed Ottawa in 1855, and in 1857 was chosen by Britain's Queen Victoria to become the common capital for the Province of Canada because of its location midway between Toronto and Quebec City. As the area continued to grow, some of the world's largest lumber saw-mills were built here, and today the Rideau Canal, which runs through the city and is the oldest continuously-operated canal system in North America, is a registered UNESCO World Heritage site.

Marinas: Rideau Canal – Tie-Up walls are located on the blue line between the Mackenzie King Bridge and the Wellington Street Bridge near the top of Lock 8 – Lockmaster: 613 237 2309, Dows Lake Pavillion – 613 232 1001

Provisioning: ByWard Market area - .6 mile

Air Transport: Ottawa MacDonald-Cartier International Airport – 10 miles

Rail Transport: VIA Rail – 2.5 miles

Local Transport: Capital Taxi – 613 744 3333, Blueline Taxi – 613 238 1111, DJ's Taxi – 613 829 9990, OC Transport (city buses) 613 741 4390

Tourist Transport: Gray Line - 613 562 9090, Paul's Boat Lines – 613 235 8409, Lady Dive – 613 524 2221

Car Rental: Enterprise – 613 236 3366, Hertz - 613 521 3332, Avis – 613 739 3334, Budget – 613 521 4844

Points of Interest: Parliament Hill – Daily Changing of the Guard Ceremony and Tour, Canadian Aviation & Space Museum, Canada, Science & Technology Museum, Canadian War Museum, National Gallery of Canada, Notre Dame Cathedral and Basilica, MOSAIKA – Sound & Light Show on Parliament Hill

Tourism Website: www.ottawatourism.ca

Kingston, Ontario

Flora MacDonald Confederation Basin – Kingston, Ontario

Kingston, Ontario was founded in 1673 as a military base and a fur-trading post by the French, who wanted to establish a presence on Lake Ontario in order to not only be able to control fur trade with the native people of the area, but also to establish a settlement there. Originally called Fort Cataraqui, it eventually was called Fort Frontenac, and was captured by the British during the Seven Year's War in 1758. Later it became a center for British Loyalists who fled north after their loss in the American Revolutionary War. Kingston was the base for the British Naval Fleet during the War of 1812 in its defense against the Americans for the control of Lake Ontario. Because of its prime location at the entrance of the Rideau Canal, after the Canal was completed in 1832, its population grew, and it was chosen as the first capital of the united Canadas. The city is noted for its large number of historic sites, as well as for being at one time the location of the largest locomotive works in the British Empire, and a center for ship-building. Today it is a UNESCO World Heritage Site with seventeen museums, many historic buildings, and the Kingston Public Market which has been in existence since 1801.

Marinas: Flora MacDonald Confederation Basin – 613 546 4291 - ext. 1823, Portsmouth Olympic Harbour – 613 546 4291 - ext. 1700 & 1800, Kingston Marina – 613 549 7747

Provisioning: A&P Food Stores - .7 mile, Kingston Public Market – Market Street and King Street – every Tuesday, Thursday, and Saturday

Air Transport: Ottawa MacDonald- Cartier International Airport – 113 miles, Syracuse Hancock Airport – 127 miles

Rail Transport: VIA Rail from Montreal, Ottawa, and Toronto – 888 VIA-RAIL - Kingston Station – 3.1 miles

Local Transport: Amey's Greenwood Taxi, Ltd. – 613 546 1111, Kingston and Amherst Taxi Co. – 613 384 7000 or 613 542 3333

Tourist Transport: Kingston Trolley Tours – 613 549 5544

Car Rental: Enterprise – 613 545 4044, Avis – 613 531 3311

Points of Interest: City Hall, Royal Military College of Canada, Fort Henry, Marine Museum of the Great Lakes, Penitentiary Museum, Pump House Museum, Queen's University

Tourism Website: www.tourism.kingstoncanada.com

Trenton, Ontario

The National Air Force Museum of Canada – Trenton, Ontario

Europeans first settled the area around the mouth of the Trent River in the 1780s. Assorted settlements and town plots in the area went under a number of names until the Village of Trenton was incorporated in 1853. Trenton grew thanks to its port location and the area's lumber industry, and when the wind is right (or perhaps wrong) you can still smell the pulp mill upriver. During World War I, the town was the location of a large munitions plant, which eventually blew up in an explosion, and an early film production studio. It is also the eastern gateway to the Trent-Severn Waterway. The Trent-Severn Waterway had been formerly used for commercial purposes, but is now used exclusively for pleasure boats and connects Lake Ontario at Trenton to the Georgian Bay area of Lake Huron at Port Severn.

Marina: Trent Port Marina – 613 392 2841 x7100

Provisioning: Metro Market – 0.1 Miles, LCBO (liquor) – .3 mile

Air Transport: Billy Bishop Toronto City Airport – 108 miles, Toronto Pearson International Airport – 115 Miles

Rail Transport: Trenton Junction (VIA-RAIL) – 2.2 miles

Local Transport: ABC Taxi 613 392 8505 or 613 392 3525, Quinte Access – 613 392 9640

Car Rental: Enterprise – 613 394 0160, Discount – 613 394 3676, National – 613 392 3300

Points of Interest: The National Air Force Museum of Canada, Farmers' Market (Tuesdays, Thursdays, Saturdays (April to November – 6 a.m. to 2 p.m.)

Tourism Website: www.quintewesttourism.ca, www.downtowntrenton.ca

Peterborough, Ontario

Peterborough, Ontario – Farmers' Market

Peterborough has a population of about 75,000 and is known as the gateway to the Kawartha Lakes, otherwise known as "cottage country," a large recreational region in that part of Ontario. Named after Peter Robinson, a Canadian politician who oversaw the first major immigration to the area, the city has been the seat of Peterborough County since 1983. Located here is Artspace, one of Canada's oldest art centers run by artists, and the Peterborough Museum & Archives which is home to a diverse collection of local artifacts. Several large companies, including General Electric and Quaker Oats, also maintain large operations in the area.

Marina: Peterborough Marina – 705 745 8787

Provisioning: The Pasta Shop – .6 mile, Freshco – .9 mile, Sobey's – 1.2 miles

Air Transport: Billy Bishop Toronto City Airport – 86 miles, Toronto Pearson International Airport – 89 miles

Local Transport: City Cab – 705 743 9090, Village Taxi – 705 748 8294,

Car Rental: Enterprise – 705 748 2707/705 745 7275

Points of Interest: Farmers' Market (every Saturday and Sunday morning – May to November – parking lot of Municipal Centre), Downtown Farmers' Market (daily- May to November- Charlotte St. between Water and George Sts.), Artspace, Riverview Park & Zoo, Canadian Canoe Museum, Peterborough Museum and Archives, downtown shopping and restaurants

Tourism Website: www.peterborough.ca, www.thekawarthas.com

Orillia, Ontario

Orillia, Ontario – Opera House

No one seems to know how the city as well as its port got its name, but the first recorded use of the name to describe the region was in 1820. Known as the "Sunshine City", Orillia's large waterfront attracts hundreds of boaters traveling the Trent-Severn Waterway every year, as do annual festivals and other cultural attractions that are held here.

Marina: Port of Orillia Marina – 705 326 6314

Air Transport: Toronto Pearson International Airport – 79 miles

Provisioning: Two A&P Food Stores/Super Fresh stores – .11 miles and .28 miles

Local Transport: Able Taxi – 705 325 0632

Car Rental: Enterprise – 705 325 1212

Points of Interest: Farmers' Market (City Hall Centre – Andrew St. South – every Saturday 7:30 a.m. to 12:30 p.m.), Casino Rama Hotel and Casino, Orillia Opera House, Orillia Museum of Art and History

Tourism Website: www.simcoemuskoka.com.

Midland, Ontario

Discovery Harbor – Penetanguishene, Ontario

Midland was founded in 1871 when the Midland Railway of Canada selected it as the new terminus of the railway. The once-small village thrived on the shipping, lumber, and grain trade and was incorporated as a town in 1890. Today, Midland is the economic center of the region and is the main town in the southern Georgian Bay area with a summer population of more than 100,000. Overlooking the main harbor, painted on silos, observe a massive mural painted by artist Fred Lenz.

Marina: Bay Port Yachting Centre – 705 527 7678

Provisioning: IGA Midland – 2.3 miles, Valu-Mart – 1.3 miles

Air Transport: Toronto Pearson International Airport – 87 miles

Local Transport: Waterside Taxi 757 531 6430

Tourist Transport: Possibly by marina staff – if available, Central Taxi – 705 527 4444, Busy Bee Taxi – 705 526 2424, Mercury Taxi (Penetanguishene) – 705 549 8877

Car Rental: Enterprise – 705 526 3100

Points of Interest: Ste. Marie Among the Hurons (historic site), Martyrs' Shrine, Huronia Museum & Quendat Village, Discovery Harbor – Penetanguishene

Tourism Website: www.town.midland.on.ca

Killarney, Ontario

Above is the old "Mr. Perch" Fish & Chips it has been replaced with a modern restaurant, still with great food – Killarney, Ontario

For many years, Killarney was known as Shebahonaning, an Ojibwe name meaning "canoe passage." There seems to be no exact date when the community was established and when and why the name was changed to Killarney (maybe because it is easier to say) is also unknown. Fur trading, logging, commercial fishing, mining, and tourism have all played a major role in Killarney's economy, yet before 1962 there was no road access to it. However, steamships that carried passengers and freight to locations around the area were able to service the community.

Marina: Killarney Mountain Lodge – 800 461 1117

Provisioning: Pitfield's Killarney General Store & Laundromat – .4 mile, Herbert Fisheries – .3 mile, Liquor Control Board of Ontario (LCBO) – .3 mile

Points of Interest: "Mr. Perch" Fish & Chips, General Store, Farquhar's Ice Cream, Killarney Mountain Lodge's Carousel Bar

Tourism Website: www.municipality.killarney.on.ca

Little Current, Ontario

The harbor at Little Current, Ontario

The town of Little Current on Manitoulin Island was created in 1998 as an amalgamation of several communities of which Little Current was the largest. It was so named for the strong and swift-moving water currents that run between the narrow passage connecting Georgian Bay and the North Channel, and its economy today is based on tourism, farming, and lumbering. It is also the home each July and August morning of the "Little Current Cruisers' Net," a daily radio show broadcast on VHF Channel 71 to boaters within a 50-mile North Channel radius of Little Current, via a tower and antenna atop the hotel roof of the Anchor Inn. The announcer is Roy Eaton, a retired school principal and past commodore of the Little Current Yacht Club. He begins each day's broadcast by first asking if there are any emergencies. If there are none, he will then report North Channel and Georgian Bay weather, international, national, and local news as well as Island events and sports. Roy then invites all boaters to give their boat's name and current location as well as their future plans and/or messages. Many boaters, when docked at Little Current, join Roy at his studio at the Anchor Inn Bar and Grill and volunteer to assist him in writing down and logging in all his boat call-ins, which have reached well over 6,000 in a single season. His work has proven to be not only a vital support system to boaters, but also to the Thunder Bay Coast Guard and the Trenton Air, Search, and Rescue Team in locating and helping mariners in the area.

Marina: Port of Little Current Downtown Docks – 705 368 1725

Air Transport: Sudbury Airport – 96 miles with connections to Toronto

Provisioning: Valumart – .6 mile, GG' s Food Land – .6 mile, The Beer Store – .6 mile, LCBO (Liquor Control Board of Ontario) – .6 mile

Points of Interest: Anchor Inn – radio show – "The Little Current Cruisers' Network" (9 a.m. every day in July and August – VHF Channel 71), Farmers' Market (Saturday mornings in the summer – downtown), The Centennial Museum & Park

Tourism Website: www.manitoulintourism.com

St. Ignace /Mackinac Island, Michigan

The Grand Hotel, Mackinac Island, Michigan

Saint Ignace is one of the oldest cities founded by the Europeans in Michigan. French explorer and priest Jacques Marquette built the Saint Ignace Mission which he named for Saint Ignatius of Loyola, the superior of the Jesuit religious order, in 1671. In 1763, the British took over the territory after their victory over the French in the Seven Years War, and it became part of the U.S. in 1783 after the "pesky" American revolutionaries won their fight with the English. After being kicked back and forth from country to country, it was finally incorporated as a Michigan city in 1833. Today, Saint Ignace is the location of one of the ferry crossings to Mackinac Island, and it stands on the northern side of the vast Mackinac Island Bridge over the Straits.

Mackinac Island was explored by Europeans during the 17th century, and native peoples lived there about 700 years prior to that. It was a strategic location for the Great Lakes fur trade which led to the establishment of Fort Mackinac by the British during the American Revolutionary War. It was in the late 19th century that Mackinac Island became a popular tourist attraction, and much of the island has undergone such extensive historical preservation and restoration that the entire island has been put on the National Historic Landmarks register. It is well known for its cultural events, the famous Grand Hotel, its fudge, and its ban on all motor vehicles except those for fire and police. Not to arouse suspicion by any wrongdoers, the single (and only) police car on the island is unmarked!

Marinas: St. Ignace Municipal Marina – 906 643 8131, Mackinac Island State Dock – 906 847 3561,or access either marina via the Michigan Harbor Reservation System – 800 447 2757

Provisioning: St. Ignace – Doud's Market – .5 mile

Air Transport: St. Ignace and Mackinac Island – Boyne Mountain Airport (Boyne Mountain, MI) – 72 miles"

Local Transport: Shepler's Mackinac Island Ferry – 800 828 6157/ 231 436 5023, Star-Line Ferry – 800 638 9892/ 906 643 7635

Tourist Transport: Mackinac Island Carriage Tours – 906 847 3307

Points of Interest:

St. Ignace: Museum of Ojibwa Culture & Marquette Mission Park, Fort de Baude

Mackinac Island: Fort Mackinac, The Grand Hotel, Carriage Tours, Shopping

Tourism Website: St. Ignace: www.stignace.com

Mackinac Island: www.mackinacisland.org

Ludington, Michigan

*The **Badger** – the last coal fired steam ship on Lake Michigan*

European explorers first arrived in the Ludington area as early as the late 1600s, and the first permanent residents didn't appear until 1847. The town was originally named Pere Marquette, but was later renamed after industrialist James Ludington who ran the logging operation there. It was incorporated as a city in 1873, and today Ludington has more than 8,000 residents and is a center of tourism for boating, hunting, fishing, and camping interests. The downtown shopping area has several clothing stores, art galleries, jewelry stores, an ice cream parlor, and restaurants. It is also the home port for The *S.S. Badger* steamship that went into service in 1953. This imposing 410 foot vessel carries 620 passengers and 180 vehicles of all types including RVs, buses, cars, trucks, and motorcycles on a four-hour crossing of Lake Michigan. She was originally designed to carry railroad cars, automobiles, and passengers and was built with a reinforced hull for ice breaking for year-round service. As the last of her kind, she now makes the journey only between May and October and is truly a sight to behold!

Marina: Ludington Municipal Marina – 231 843 9611

Provisioning: K&L Foods – .2 miles, Roundys Supermarket – 3 miles, Northside Market – 2 miles

Air transport: Gerald R. Ford International Airport (Grand Rapids, MI) – 109 miles

Local Transport: Town and Country Taxi – 231 425 3134

Points of Interest: S. S. Badger (Lake Michigan Car Ferry Service), Port of Ludington Maritime Museum, Big Sable, Little Sable, and North Breakwater Lighthouses, Pere Marquette Memorial, White Pine Village

Tourism Website: www.pureludington.com

Grand Haven, Michigan

The Marina at Grand Haven, Michigan

Grand Haven originally was a fur trading post called Gabagouache, a Pottawattamie Indian name for the area. The city was first called Grand Haven in 1835 and was incorporated as a city in 1867. In the mid-to-late 19th century, Grand Haven's economy was centered on logging and shipbuilding, and by the early 20th century, the area was producing automobiles, furniture, lighting, and pianos. Today, Grand Haven is an active resort as well as a boating and fishing community with more than 100 miles of bike trails, a state beach, a boardwalk, and a large charter fishing fleet. It is also well-known for its famous "Musical Fountain" performance, an impressive synchronized program with water, music, and a multi-colored light show held each evening during the summer.

Marina: Grand Haven Municipal Marina – 616 847 3478 (see Great Fuel Stop info below)

Provisioning: Fortino's Gourmet Grocery – .2 miles, D&W Food Center – 2.5 miles

Air Transport: Grand Rapids, Michigan – Gerald R. Ford International Airport – 46 miles

Local Transport: Harbor Transit Buses – 616 842 3200, Rosebud Taxi – 616 935 1291, Blue Dog Taxi – 616 844 9292

Tourist Transport: Harbor Trolley (historic trolley rides) – harbortransit.org/trolley

Car Rental: Enterprise – 616 846 2100, Gage Rent-a-Car – 616 842 7680

Points of Interest: Grand Haven Lighthouse and Pier, Grand Haven Boardwalk, Grand Haven Musical Fountain, Odd Side Ales (micro-brewery), Lemon Creek Winery Tasting Room, Santo Stefano del Logo (wine tastings), Farmers' Market at Chinook Pier, Tri-Cities Historical Museum

Tourism Website: www.visitgrandhaven.com

Great Fuel Stop – Grand Haven Municipal Marina, Grand Haven, Michigan – 616 842 2550

Location: Lake Michigan. One night stay at the marina required. Ask for a slip on the western end of the marina. Call Crystal Flash Energy @ (800) 875-4851 – 24 hour advanced notice required for fuel – 200 gal. minimum – deliveries only on weekdays. Its fuel prices were the lowest we found in Michigan.

Chicago, Illinois

Michigan Avenue, Chicago, Illinois

Chicago was incorporated in 1837 and is the third most populous city in the United States. It is located at the water gap which connects the navigable waterways of the Great Lakes with those of the Mississippi River, and is also the nation's railroad center which links its east and west coasts. Not only known as an international center for commerce, industry, and transportation, the city has made many contributions to the arts in the fields of improvisational comedy, jazz, and sculpture. The Chicago Park District operates the nation's largest harbor system, providing berthing availability for over 6,000 boats in this city which is known for its 552 parks. Chicago's most popular tourist destinations include: Millennium Park with its reflective Cloud Gate sculpture; the Art Institute of Chicago; the Navy Pier with its stores, restaurants, and Ferris wheel; the Adler Planetarium; the Field Museum of Natural History; the Shedd Aquarium; its architectural boat tours on the Chicago River; as well as its skyscrapers, shopping, and restaurants.

Marina: Du Sable Harbor – 312 742 3577

Provisioning: Lake Shore Grocers – 1.2 miles

Air Transport: Chicago O'Hare International Airport -19 miles, Chicago Midway Airport – 9 miles

Rail Transport: Chicago Union Station – 2.5 miles

Local Transport: Yellow Cab – 312 829 4222, Checker Taxi – 312 243 2537

Tourist Transport: Architectural Tours by Boat, Chicago Trolley Tours, Walking Tours, Mini Bus Tours – www.chicagotours.us (888 881 3284)

Points of Interest: Art Institute of Chicago, Millennium Park, Chicago Museum of Science and Industry, Wrigley Field, Shops on Michigan Ave., John Hancock Center/Observatory, Lincoln Park Zoo, The Field Museum, Buckingham Fountain, Holy Name Cathedral

Tourism Website & Phone Nos.: Chicago Office of Tourism – 312 774 2400, Chicago Convention & Visitors Bureau – 312 567 8500 – www.chicagotraveller.com

Hardin, Illinois

Mel's Riverdock Restaurant – Harden, Illinois (Very good food at reasonable prices)

The village of Hardin has a population of about 960 and was named in 1847 in honor of Colonel John J. Hardin of the first Illinois volunteers, who, at the beginning of the Mexican Indian War, was killed while leading a charge. The largest of five incorporated towns often referred to as the "Kingdom," it is located in sparsely populated Calhoun County, which is almost surrounded on three sides by the Illinois and Mississippi Rivers. Hardin is a haven for bald eagle watchers in the fall and winter months, and the area with its rural charm is accessed by four ferries and the Joe Page Bridge.

Marina: Mel's Riverdock Restaurant – 618 576 2362

Provisioning: Northside Family Foods – .2 miles, C. R. Bakery – .2 miles

Points of Interest: Dinner at Mel's Riverdock Restaurant, Calhoun County Historical Society Museum – 618 576 2660

Tourism Website: www.greatriverroad.com/cities/hardin/hardincover.htm

Alton, Illinois/St. Louis, Missouri

The St. Louis Gateway Arch – St. Louis, Missouri

Alton, Illinois, has had its impact on American history. It originally was developed as a river town in 1818 and eventually grew into an industrial and trading center. Within a few years, it also became an important location for abolitionists because Illinois was a free state located immediately across the river from the slave state of Missouri. Escaped slaves would cross the Mississippi to seek refuge in Alton and then would proceed to safe houses through stations of the Underground Railroad. Noting also its pre-Civil War's importance, there is a memorial site in downtown Alton commemorating the seventh Lincoln-Douglas debate, which took place there on October 15, 1858. Alton is also the most convenient spot to get a car rental in order to visit St. Louis and its magnificent Gateway Arch.

The Gateway Arch in St. Louis, Missouri, was built as a monument to the westward expansion of the U.S., and it is the centerpiece of the Jefferson National Expansion Memorial. At 630 feet, it is the tallest man-made monument in the U.S. Although the Arch was originally designed in 1947, its construction did not begin until 1963, and it finally opened to the public on July 10, 1967. Adjacent to the

Arch is the Museum of Westward Expansion, which follows the lives of American explorers such as Lewis and Clark, and notes their impact on the exploration of the American West.

Marina: Alton Marina – 618 462 9860 (See Great Fuel Stop info below)

Provisioning: Pearl Market – 1.1 miles, Stop 'n Save – 3.8 miles

Air Transport: Lambert – St. Louis International Airport – 13 miles

Local Transport: Comfort Cab – 618 465 2010, Liberty Cab – 618 462 6437

Car Rental: Enterprise – 618 245 0638/ 618 258 4402

Points of Interest:

Alton: Alton Museum of History and Art, Confederate Prison, Fast Eddie's Bon Air (a unique bar and eatery and "a must stop"), Argosy Casino, The National Great Rivers Museum.

St. Louis: St. Louis Gateway Arch, Jefferson National Expansion Memorial Park, Museum of Westward Expansion, Cathedral Basilica of St. Louis, St Louis Botanical Gardens, St. Louis Zoo

Tourism Website:

Alton: Alton Visitors Bureau – www.visitalton.com

St. Louis: St. Louis Convention & Visitors Commission – www.explorestlouis.com

Great Fuel Stop – Alton Marina, Alton, Illinois – 618 462 9860

Location: Mississippi River. Fuel prices here were the lowest we found since leaving Michigan.

Important Fuel Stop – Hoppie's Marine Service, Kimmswick, Missouri – 636 467 6154

Location: Mississippi River. Last reliable chance for fuel and the only marina for the next 249 miles! Meet with owner, Fern Hopkins, a well-known expert on the rivers, to review your charts, suggest good anchorages, and to point out potential trouble spots.

Grand Rivers, Kentucky

Green Turtle Marina – Grand Rivers, Kentucky
(Photo courtesy of the Grand Rivers Tourist Commission)

Grand Rivers is a city with a population of about 400 residents. It originally was named Nickelville; however, because of the nearby iron ore deposits, it was renamed Grand Rivers in expectation of its establishment as a major steel-producing city. Unfortunately, the steel-producing enterprise died within a few years, but the lovely name remained. Today, Grand Rivers is a small tourist village with antique shops, clothing stores, a playhouse, several restaurants, and a grocery store. Because the village is located in a dry county, there are no liquor stores or bars in the area.

Marina: Green Turtle Bay Resort & Marina – 270 362 8364

Provisioning: IGA Grocery Store – 1 mile

Air Transport: Paducah, Kentucky – Barkley Regional Airport – 36 miles, Nashville International Airport – 122 miles

Local Transport: Marina courtesy van, golf cart rentals, airport shuttle service (for a fee) – during business hours with advance notification

Car Rental: Avis – 270 744 8411, Enterprise – 270 444 5223, Thrifty – 800 367 2277, Hertz – 270-744-6000

Points of Interest: The Badgett Playhouse, Patti's 1880's Settlement, Kentucky Opry

Tourism Website: www.grandrivers.org

Counce, Tennessee

Grand Harbor Marina – Counce, Tennessee

Counce is a small unincorporated community in Hardin County adjacent to the Tennessee River near the Tenn-Tombigbee Waterway. Located on Pickwick Lake, it provides easy access to the Shiloh National Military Park which includes: The Shiloh Battlefield where, during the Civil War, 65,000 Union and 44,000 Confederate troops engaged in a two-day battle resulting in 24,000 men killed, wounded, and missing, and was a decisive defeat of the Confederate forces; the Corinth Battlefield which consists of 14 historic sites associated with the Siege and Battle of Corinth; The Shiloh National Cemetery where, within its twenty acres, both Union and Confederate soldiers are buried, most of them unknown having been re-interred there after the Civil War; and the Shiloh Indian Mounds Site where earthen mounds which pre-dated the Egyptian pyramids by 1,000 years were built by the indigenous native peoples of the Mississippian area of North America.

Marina: Grand Harbor Marina – 662 667 5551

Provisioning: Pickwick Supermarket – 4.9 miles

Air Transport: Muscle Shoals, Alabama – Northwest Alabama Regional Airport – 61 miles, Memphis International Airport – 108 miles

Local Transport: Marina courtesy van

Points of Interest: Shiloh National Military Park, including: Shiloh Battlefield, Shiloh National Cemetery, Shiloh Indian Mounds, and Corinth Battlefield

Tourism Website: www.nps.gov/shil

Mobile, Alabama

The Battle Ship "Alabama" – Mobile, Alabama

Mobile is the largest municipality on the Gulf Coast between New Orleans, Louisiana, and Saint Petersburg, Florida. It began as the first capital of colonial French Louisiana in 1702, and for the first 100 years of its existence, it was a colony of France, Britain, and then finally Spain. Mobile first became a part of the U.S. in 1810 with the annexation of West Florida. In 1861, it left the Union when

Alabama joined the Confederate States of America, but it came back in again in 1865 after the end of the Civil War. Mobile is the only seaport in Alabama and the ninth largest port in the U.S. The port has always played a major role in the economic health of the city since its beginning as a key trading center between the French and Native Americans. The city has several art museums, a symphony orchestra, a professional opera, a ballet company, and a large concentration of historic architecture. It is also known for having the oldest organized carnival celebrations in the U.S., which began in the 18th century and pre-date the New Orleans Mardi Gras.

Marina: Dog River Marina – 251 471 4517 or 251 471 5449 or 251 476 4546

Provisioning: Food World – 3.1 miles

Air Transport: Mobile Regional Airport- 17 miles

Local Transport: Marina courtesy car, K & K Shuttle Service (Taxi) – 251 450 0670

Car Rental: See marina for info.

Points of Interest: Dauphin Island Sea Lab, Bellingrath Gardens and Home, Battleship Memorial Park, Mobile Carnival Museum, Oakleigh House, Museum of Mobile

Tourism Website: Mobile Convention & Visitors Corp – www.mobile.org, Fort Conde Welcome Center – www.museumofmobile.com

Great Fuel Stop – Dog River Marina, Mobile, Alabama – 251 471 4517

Location: Dog River. Fuel prices here were the lowest we found within hundreds of miles of its location.

Fairhope, Alabama

Sunset in Fairhope, Alabama

The Fairhope Industrial Association, a group of 28 followers of economist Henry George, founded Fairhope in 1894 as a utopian single-tax colony. They combined their funds to purchase land and then divided it into leaseholds. The corporation paid all taxes from rents paid by the lessees, thus replicating a single tax. It might have been a single tax, but, in reality, lessees still paid taxes. The purpose of the single tax colony was to encourage productive use of land which would thereby retain the value of the land for all. The Fairhope Single Tax Corporation still operates with 1,800 leaseholds covering several thousand acres in the area. Today, Fairhope is a resort community and a suburb of Mobile, and although it might not exactly be a tax-free Utopia, it is a lovely place to visit.

Marina: Eastern Shore Marine – 251 928 1283 or 800 458 7245

Provisioning: Winn Dixie, Food World, and many specialty shops (Deli, Bakery, Wine & Cheese) – 1 mile (approx.)

Air Transport: Mobile Regional Airport – 37 miles, Pensacola Gulf Coast Regional Airport – 58 miles

Local Transport: Marina courtesy car

Car Rental: See marina for info.

Points of Interest: Great shopping and browsing opportunities in boutiques, bookstores, gift shops, and art galleries, as well as many great places to dine

Tourism Website: www.fairhopemerchants.com

Panama City, Florida

Panama City Marina
(Photo provided courtesy of Bay County Chamber of Commerce)

Panama City was incorporated in 1909, and the developer of the town, George W. West, came up with its name because it was on a direct line between Chicago and Panama City, Panama. It claims that its nearby beach is one of the best-known and most beloved resorts in the world with white, sandy beaches and every imaginable water sport, including scuba diving and fishing.

Marina: Panama City Marina – 850 872 7272

Provisioning: Wal-Mart via Bay Town Trolley – 20 minutes

Air Transport: Northwest Florida Beaches International Airport (northwest of Panama City) – 22 miles

Local Transport: Bay Town Trolley (stops at the marina with many routes around town), Yellow Cab – 850 763 4691, Checker Cab – 850 785 4448, Bay Taxi & Limo – 850 265 8294

Car Rental: Enterprise – 850 769 2383, Budget- 850 763 0108, National – 769 2383

Points of Interest: Bear Creek Feline Center, St. Andrews State Park, Museum of Man in the Sea

Tourism Website: www.go-florida.com/Panama-City/Tourism-Information

Port St. Joe, Florida

Once a bustling port, Port St. Joe is now a tourist destination with a soft, white sand dune beach, snorkeling, fishing, and a variety of dining options.

Marina: Port St. Joe Marina – 850 227 9393

Provisioning: Duren's Piggly Wiggly Supermarket – .5 mile, Farmers' Market – 1st and 3rd Saturdays

Air Transport: Northwest Florida Beaches International Airport (Panama City) – 57 miles

Local Transport: Complimentary bicycles are available at the marina, Dixson and Sons Taxi Service – 850 227 1303

Car Rental: Enterprise – 877 410 7393

Points of Interest: Many restaurants and boutique shopping within a downtown area 4 blocks from the marina, St. Joseph Peninsula State Park, Constitutional Convention State Park

Tourism Website: www.visitgulf.com

Great Fuel Stop – Ballard Oil Company, Fort Myers Beach, Florida – 239 463 7677

Location: Matanzas Pass. Fuel prices here were the lowest we found on Florida's west coast.

Naples, Florida

Naples was founded during the late 1880s. Throughout the 1870's and 80's, stories in various magazines and newspapers described the area's mild climate and excellent fishing, often likening it to the sunny Italian peninsula. When promoters described its bay as "surpassing the bay in Naples, Italy," the name stuck. Today, Naples is a shopper's and diner's dream with numerous upscale shops and restaurants along its Fifth Avenue and Third Street shopping districts, and its close access to lovely Marco Island.

Marina: Naples City Dock – 239 213 3070

Provisioning: Publix – 3.7 miles

Air Transport: Southwest Florida International Airport (Fort Myers) – 36 miles

Local Transport: Taxi Time – 239 200 0000

Car Rental: Thrifty – 239 213 1671, Enterprise – 239 643 5308

Points of Interest: Naples Pier, Delnor-Wiggins Pass State Park, Naples Botanical Garden, Corkscrew Swamp Sanctuary, Barefoot Beach, Third Street South Shops & Boutiques, Naples Zoo at Caribbean Gardens, Naples Museum of Art, Collier County Museum, The Waterside Shops, Tin City, Fifth Avenue South

Tourism Website: Naples Visitors Information Center – www.napleschamber.org

Marathon/Key West, Florida

Boot Key Harbor – Marathon, Florida

Marathon's city limits encompass 13 islands in the Florida Keys. Among them are: Knight's Key, Boot Key, Key Vaca, Fat Deer Key, Long Point Key, Crawl Key, and Grassy Key. Although the Weather Channel often incorrectly refers to Marathon as Marathon Key, there is no Marathon Key. The name of Marathon dates back to the building of the Florida East Coast Railroad through the Keys. The name got its origins from the railroad workers who worked night and day to complete the railway. When many of them complained that the work had become a real "marathon", the name stuck. Today, Marathon is a vacation destination well known for its sports fishing on the Gulf of Mexico and Atlantic Ocean sides, plus its nearby bountiful reefs make it a popular diving, snorkeling, spear fishing, and lobster tickling area. It also has of one of the last untouched tropical hardwood hammocks in the Keys located at the Crane Point Museum, and, as we can attest, it is a wonderful place to spend the winter!

Key West is the southernmost city in the continental U.S., and, at its closest point, is 94 miles from the island of Cuba. Besides being a tourist destination, it is also the home of Naval Station Key West which is an important naval aviation training site. In the 1800s its major industries were salt production, fishing, and wreck salvage, and by 1860, wrecking made Key West not only the largest and richest city in Florida, but also the wealthiest town per capita in the U.S. It remained isolated until 1912, when the city was finally connected to the mainland by Henry Flagler's Florida East Coast Railway. In the 20th century writers Ernest Hemingway and Tennessee Williams wrote various literary works while living here and today's Key West Historic district includes the tourist destinations of Duval Street, Mallory Square, Fort Zachary Taylor, and the Truman Annex. The city is a "go-to" location for artists of all genres from the serious to the "bizarre," and its "Fantasy Fest" at the end of October attracts around 80,000 attendees each year who come to see the "sights"!

Marinas: City of Marathon Marina – 305 289 8877, Marathon Marina & Boat Yard – 305 743 6575, Banana Bay Resort and Marina – 305 289 1009

Provisioning: Publix & Winn Dixie Supermarkets – .5 mile to 2.7 miles depending on the marina

Air Transport: Key West International – 47 miles, Miami International – 115 miles

Bus Transport: Lower Keys Shuttle Bus (Marathon to Key West) – 305 809 3910, Greyhound Bus – 305 296 9073, Keys Shuttle to Miami and Fort Lauderdale airports – 888 765 9997/305 289 9997

Local Transport: Island Taxi – 305 731 9022, On Time Taxi – 305 289 5656

Car Rental: Enterprise – 305 289 7601, Avis – 305 743 5428, Budget – 305 743 3398

Points of Interest:

Marathon: The Turtle Hospital, Dolphin Research Center, Pigeon Key Preservation, Crane Point Museum and Nature Center, San Pablo Church Prayer Garden, Sombrero Beach.

Key West: Mel Fisher Maritime Heritage Museum, Key West Butterfly and Nature Conservancy, Harry S. Truman Little White House, U. S. Coast Guard Cutter Ingham Maritime Museum, Ernest Hemingway Home and Museum, Mallory Square at Sunset, Duval Street Shopping and Bars, Fort Zackary Taylor State Park, Conch Tour Train

Tourism Website:

Marathon: Greater Marathon Chamber of Commerce – www.floridakeysmarathon.com

Key West: Key West Visitors Center – www.keywest123.com

Chapter 16

Final Thoughts

The Oxford Dictionary defines the word "adventure" as "an unusual and exciting or daring experience", and your own America's Great Loop experience will certainly live up to that definition. It is often considered *unusual* because in reality only a small number of boaters out of an enormous boating population are able to experience it for a variety of reasons. Completing this trip successfully most often requires an appropriate vessel, enough time to do the trip, some financial means, necessary boating skills and education, and the desire to do so. It is *exciting* because you will expand your normal cruising area enormously, and you will have the opportunity to meet wonderful new people and to visit a wide variety of fascinating locations beyond your current norm. It is *daring* because it causes you to leave your "comfort zone", to live in the moment, and to exercise new skills. Ultimately, you will also gain a wealth of knowledge about yourself, your spouse or partner, and others by taking a chance on doing something new.

In the course of this book, we hope that we have been able to answer some of your most-asked questions about America's Great Loop and have also managed to ease many of your possible concerns about "traveling into the unknown". Our biggest goals, however, have been to give you the information you will need to make educated decisions about your own particular adventure, to assist you in planning and preparing for it, and to finally get you underway so that can enjoy this fabulous "journey of a lifetime" both comfortably and safely.

We have been in your place and would like to offer you some thoughts from our perspective today as boaters who have already made this journey and will do so again:

To those of you who are in the "Planning Stage":

- As Captain George likes to assure his audiences – If you can pull your boat away from the dock safely, travel to an anchorage, get your boat anchored for the night, find your boat in the same place where you anchored the next morning, pull up your anchor, and then get back to the dock safely without hurting the dock, the boat, you, or anyone else on the boat or the dock – you can make this trip!

- If possible, plan to make the trip sooner rather than later, because we all know that in some cases "someday" never comes. The timing may not be exactly perfect, but you will find a way to make it work if you so desire. We don't so much regret in life what we've done, but what we haven't done!

To those of you who already are "Making Preparations":

- Make sure that you have educated yourself so that you are able to exercise good judgment and make good decisions on your journey. Also, remember that the diligent efforts that you make to get you, your home, and your boat ready will serve you well on your trip and make it an enjoyable and safe one.

- Listen to positive people, and avoid "nay-sayers", "doubters", or those who try to make you second-guess yourself, most times because of their own personal insecurities. Trust yourself, and have confidence in your own capabilities. Also, don't give in to those in your life who may try to make you feel guilty for leaving. Remember that you can always get back somehow in the case of a real emergency.

To those of you who are ready to "Get Underway":

- Though you may be about to follow a path that others have taken, your journey will truly be unique to you alone because of the choices you have already made, the decisions you have yet to make, and the particular circumstances and people that you will encounter along the way.

- The moments just prior to your leaving the dock can offer up a mixture of emotions as you are about to embark on this journey. As you say sentimental "good-byes" to those on the shore, you will also find yourself incredibly anxious to leave, because this is when you realize that your long-held dream is about to become a reality! Finally, the moment that you have been waiting for arrives, and your own "Great Loop" adventure is about to begin! We are excited for you, and we wish you "Godspeed"! It's time to cast off your lines!

Glossary

Terms Often Used On the Great Loop

Admiral — The wife of the Captain. She is sometimes known as the First Mate, but is actually the one in charge of the boat. There is truth to the saying, "If the Admiral isn't happy, no one aboard is happy!"

Aground — Description of a boat sitting with its keel on the bottom of a body of water, an unplanned event that could ruin a boater's day or a longer period of time, depending on the amount of damage done.

Automatic Identification System (AIS) — Provides information such as identification, position, course, and speed of nearby vessels equipped with an AIS transmitter. It is extremely useful in identifying commercial vessels that cannot be seen around bends in rivers and waterways. All commercial vessels are required to transmit AIS; however, some of them do not, so stay alert.

America's Great Loop Cruisers' Association — An association for boaters who share navigational and cruising information specifically about the eastern North American waterway connection route and for those who dream about one day making the journey. Members are quickly identified by their burgee, which has a map of the Great Loop journey embellished on it.

Anchor — (1) A metal object attached to the boat by a line or chain that is cast overboard to keep the vessel in place by attaching itself to the bottom (and hopefully staying attached to the bottom) until the captain decides to bring it back onboard. (2) To hold fast to the bottom preferably without slipping, so the captain can get a good night's rest.

Anchor Crown — Located at the opposite end of the anchor shank from where the chain is normally attached. The anchor crown usually has an opening where the trip line can be secured. (It is not a royal headdress made from an anchor, although the Admiral has often said under certain circumstances that she would like to "crown" the Captain.)

Anchor Light — A white light used after dark in the rigging of a boat, usually at its highest point, to signify that the boat is riding at anchor. Unfortunately, some boaters like to live life dangerously and choose not to show such a light, thus risking a collision at night with another passing vessel.

Anchorage — A safe place out of boat traffic to stay overnight at anchor; however, the word "safe" is a relative term.

Autopilot — An electromechanical device that can steer a boat in many situations more effectively than a human. It is almost like having another crew member onboard who does not eat, drink, sleep, or complain. It is especially valuable on open water, and should not be used on narrow channels.

Beam — Describes the breadth of a vessel (and sometimes a person) at its widest point.

Bilge — The lowest interior compartment of a boat or ship. It often contains stagnant water and other slimy stuff and is one of the Captain's "favorite" places to make a repair.

Bollard — A thick, short post made of steel on a ship, wharf, or in a lock that is used for securing lines (some folks resemble bollards).

Bow — The "pointy" end of the boat.

Bow Thruster — A small propulsion device located in the bow of the vessel to assist in maneuvering in confined spaces. Ideally, it helps you cause less damage when docking than you would have without it.

Buoy — A floating navigational aid. It can become a navigational hazard, however, on flooded rivers when it becomes submerged.

Burgee — A small flag mounted on a boat which displays the colors of the yacht club or nautical "gang" to which you belong.

Captain — The husband of the Admiral and the one who thinks he is in charge of the boat.

Channel — The deepest section of a waterway. Straying out of it could cause a number of problems (See "Aground").

Chart — a nautical paper map. That is especially useful when your electronic charting devices decide to quit working.

Cleat — An anvil-shaped piece of hardware on a vessel or a dock to which a line can be fastened and will hopefully stay fastened.

Crew — A group of friends or relatives who come along for a boat ride. If you are lucky, they might help out.

Depth Sounder — An electronic device that displays the depth of the water and warns you that you are about to go aground.

Dinghy — (1) A small open boat carried by a larger boat as a tender. (2) A term to describe a person who is not playing with a "full deck."

Docking — Maneuvering a boat to a structure (dock, seawall, etc.). It can sometimes be an act of sheer terror.

Docktails — These "bring your own" adult beverages are enjoyed with your fellow "Loopers" on the dock, and are not to be confused with cocktails which are consumed aboard your boat, possibility in the cockpit.

Draft — The amount of water depth required to float a vessel and an important number to know (see "Aground").

Engine Room — An area below deck where the propulsion machinery is housed. It is a bit damp, cramped, and an excellent place to bloody your knuckles with a low overhead (ceiling) at just the right height to cause minor brain damage when the Captain tries to stand up. Lots of "colorful" words can often be heard coming from this area.

Fender — An inflatable device hung off the side of a boat to protect the hull from damage, often referred to as a "bumper" by the nautically-challenged among us.

Floating Dock — A dock that is attached to piles in such a way that it can move up and down with the rise and fall of the water level. This is the Captain and the Admiral's favorite kind of dock.

Forward — (1) The direction toward the front of the boat. (2) The usual direction in which you might want to proceed.

Galley — The boat's small kitchen from which many amazingly delicious large meals appear.

GPS Chartplotter — An electronic device that displays the boat's position on a nautical map, but which can also get you into trouble if you focus too much on the device and not what is in plain sight (see "Aground").

Happy Hour — A pre-dinner gathering of the Captain, the Admiral, the Crew, and other like-minded people to discuss the day's events, and perhaps tomorrow's plans. Snacks and an adult beverage accompany it, and depending on the happenings of the day, there might be the need for several adult beverages.

Head — A marine toilet or the compartment where the toilet is located. The origin of the term is somewhat clouded, but here is one explanation: Sailors returning from shore leave who had too much to drink frequently found themselves with their head in the bowl as they held the "porcelain goddess" in order

to purge. Fortunately, this Captain has not found it necessary to hold the "goddess" in many years.

Helm — The steering station on a boat or ship. The person, whether male or female, who is at the helm and steering the vessel is called the helmsman, not the helmsperson. (So much for political correctness!)

Holding Tank — A storage container on a boat for toilet water. Depending on who is aboard, some boats might need larger tanks to hold more than others because they can fill up quickly.

Ice Maker — The most important mechanical device onboard the boat, because having no ice equals no cold drinks, and no cold drinks equals no happy hour, and no happy hour equals an unhappy captain.

Intracoastal Waterway — An inland water route that follows much of the Gulf and Atlantic coasts. It is often winding and shallow.

Keel — A structure that runs along the centerline of the bottom of the boat that adds stability. It is the first thing that finds the bottom of a waterway when going aground.

Line — Another term for rope. However, in boating, if you call a line a rope, everyone will know you are a rookie.

Loopers — Boaters who are "on the Loop" or who have completed the Great Loop journey. They can often be found traveling together as buddy boats, and are known for giving strong assistance and support to one another, as well as for having terrific dock parties and happy hours.

National Oceanic andAtmospheric Administration (NOAA) — A federal government agency. Among its many responsibilities are weather, sea conditions, and tide and current forecasts. Unfortunately NOAA does not always know, and when their predictions are off a bit, it can make for a very interesting day on the water.

Personal Flotation Device (PFD) — Another term for what is commonly known as a life vest or a life jacket. You are required to carry one for each bunk or person onboard (whichever is greater) and each must be Coast Guard-approved for the size of your boat. (Swim Floaties don't count!).

Piling — A pole-like structure made of wood, steel, or concrete, often used with a line in the securing of a boat to a dock. It is also something else a boat can hit while docking.

Port — (1) The left side of the boat when looking forward. (2) A safe place where ships or boats can dock. (3) A sweet red wine that might be consumed in big quantities depending on how the docking procedure went.

Radar — An electronic object-detection system that uses radio waves to determine the range, direction, or speed of objects. It is very useful in limited visibility situations, especially on open water. However, it is somewhat limited in its use on narrow waterways.

Radar Arch — A sometimes-hinged, arch-shaped structure near the boat's highest point, which supports the vessel's radar and other antennas. It often requires bridge openings for it to clear without damage.

Rudder — A vertically-hinged plate mounted at the stern of the boat for the purpose of steering, ideally, in a straight line.

Security (pronounced "say-cure-ee-tay" for clarity on the radio) Call — Made on VHF Channels 13 and 16 to announce a warning of navigational hazards, or impending treacherous conditions. Example:

"Security, Security, Security! This is the vessel, *Reflection,* heading north-bound entering the Rock Pile; all south-bound commercial traffic please come back." Not making this call before entering a narrow channel could have some unpleasant consequences.

Skinny Water – A shallow depth of water through which a boat can barely pass, and usually not a good place for "Skinny Dipping".

Starboard — The right side of the boat when looking forward.

Stern — (1) The wide end of the boat. (2) The expression on the faces of the Coast Guard or the Marine Police if they have to stop and board your vessel for an infraction.

Trip Line — (1) A length of line that you attach at one end to the back end of the anchor (the opposite end of where the anchor chain is attached), and then attach the other end to a float. When anchoring in areas where the bottom is foul, deploying the anchor with a trip line and float will allow the anchor to be brought up backwards, thus freeing it from snags. (2) One of the many lines that you can trip over on your boat.

VHF (Very High Frequency) Radio — A device for boaters to communicate with the Coast Guard in an emergency and with each other. Unfortunately, it is also sometimes used for mindless chatter.

Wake — Waves created by a boat moving through the water. The faster the boat travels, the larger the wake. The larger the wake, the more nearby boats rock, sometimes violently. This often results in the waked captains wanting to attend the offending captain's "wake" (memorial before a funeral).

Biographies

About the Authors

George Hospodar began his nautical life by purchasing a 14-foot sailboat, *Rum Dum*, in 1970. His wife, Pat, joined him in 1971, and together they have cruised more than 45,000 miles aboard their two sailboats, *Adventuress* and *Temptress*, and on their motor yacht, *Reflection*. As boaters for over 40 years, they have extensively explored the coastal waters from Nantucket to Norfolk, including Chesapeake Bay. Since 2008, they have traveled up and down the Atlantic Intracoastal Waterway numerous times and have completed the America's Great Loop waterway trip through the U.S. and Canada twice: in 2009 – 2010 and again in 2015. In addition, they have been cruising editors for "Waterway Guide" for the Atlantic ICW, Northern, and Great Lakes/Great Loop editions.

George graduated from the New Jersey Institute of Technology with a Bachelor of Science degree in Computer Science and spent a majority of his career as a consultant in the design, programming, and installation of financial systems for the banking industry. He is a Past Commodore of the Bristol Sailing Club of Bay Head, New Jersey, was the owner of a marine canvas business, served on the Board of Directors of the New Jersey Marine Trades Association, and is a Past President of the Chesapeake Marine Canvas Fabricators Association. George has been a 100-ton U.S. Coast Guard-licensed captain for almost 25 years.

Patricia Hospodar holds a Bachelor of Arts degree in Music Education from Rutgers University, a Master of Arts in Education from Seton Hall University, and has done additional post-graduate study at Rider University's Westminster Choir College. She retired after 36 years of service as a music educator in the Irvington (New Jersey) public school system, where she was the community and Essex County Teacher of the Year and an award-winning middle school choral director whose choirs performed at a wide variety of venues and in numerous choral festivals and competitions in Canada and the U.S.

George and Pat are members of the Marathon Yacht Club and are lifetime members of the America's Great Loop Cruisers' Association. Together they have also authored *"Reflection* on America's Great Loop" and are featured speakers at numerous boat shows, trawler fests, and other nautical events. They currently divide their time between their home on Barnegat Bay in Brick, New Jersey, and their "adopted" home aboard *Reflection* in Banana Bay Marina in Marathon, Florida.

Index

Cruising Essentials
(beach chair optional)

When you have *Waterway Guide* on board, you get much more than pretty pictures and directions to anchorages. You get the knowledge and experience of on-the-water cruising editors and in-house staff who provide detailed mile-by-mile coverage to the best destinations. You also get access to our real-time updates on our user-friendly web site, which provides the most current navigational news and alerts. And when you join our cruising club, you get the added benefit of member-only discounts and privileges. So take advantage of cruising essentials from *Waterway Guide*. Everything else is optional.

WATERWAY GUIDE
THE CRUISING AUTHORITY

WaterwayGuide.com
1-800-233-3359

PassageMaker presents
Trawler~Fest ®

BOAT SHOW. EDUCATION. RENDEZVOUS.

THE NATION'S PREMIER CRUISING EVENT

ANACORTES | BALTIMORE | LAKE PARK, FL

trawlerfest@passagemaker.com | TrawlerFest.com | 954-761-8843

Made in the USA
Monee, IL
26 August 2021